833

W9-ADP-880

WITHDRAWN

THE PHENOMENOLOGY OF
HENRY JAMES

THE PHENOMENOLOGY OF
HENRY JAMES

BY PAUL B. ARMSTRONG

THE UNIVERSITY OF NORTH CAROLINA PRESS

CHAPEL HILL AND LONDON

For Tina

© 1983 The University of North Carolina Press

All rights reserved

Manufactured in the United States of America

Library of Congress Cataloging in Publication Data

Armstrong, Paul B., 1949–
The phenomenology of Henry James.

Includes index.
1. James, Henry, 1843–1916—Criticism and interpretation.   2. Phenomenology and literature.   I. Title.
PS2124.A67 1983   813'.4   82-24713
ISBN 0-8078-1556-X

CONTENTS

Preface
vii

CHAPTER 1
Consciousness and Moral Vision in
What Maisie Knew
3

CHAPTER 2
Knowing in James: The Impression and the Art of Fiction
37

CHAPTER 3
Imagination and Existence:
Extravagance in *Roderick Hudson*
69

CHAPTER 4
Freedom and Necessity: The Servile Will and
The Portrait of a Lady
99

CHAPTER 5
Self and Other: Conflict versus Care in
The Golden Bowl
136

CHAPTER 6
Society and History: The Politics of
Experience and *The Spoils of Poynton*
187

Contents

Epilogue:
The Modernity of Henry James
206

Notes
215

Index
239

PREFACE

This book offers an interpretation of Henry James from a phenomenological perspective. But this interpretation suggests in turn that James's own perspective is essentially phenomenological—that his understanding of the process of knowing, the art of fiction, and experience as a whole coincides in important ways with the standpoint of phenomenology. This convergence between art and philosophy indicates that phenomenological thought is less foreign to our country's cultural and intellectual heritage than most critics and literary historians realize. As we shall see, both William and Henry James rank as important American participants in the phenomenological tradition.

The main purpose of my study is to shed new light on an issue with a long and distinguished history in James criticism—the relation between his fascination with consciousness and what is commonly called his "moral vision." An important justification for invoking phenomenology to interpret James is that it provides a conceptual framework that can illuminate the connections between these two dimensions of his fiction. Guided by phenomenology's theories about the workings of consciousness and the structure of existence, I have identified and analyzed five major aspects of experience that, together, map James's understanding of human being—the "impression" as a way of knowing, the imagination, freedom, personal relations, and the politics of the social world. The network of connections between these various categories helps to explain the interdependence of the epistemological and moral explorations that James's art undertakes. From the early *Roderick Hudson* to his final masterpiece *The Golden Bowl*, these five aspects of experience are the underlying bases on which his house of fiction rests.

One of my secondary goals is to provide an introduction to phenomenology for the humanist who may know James but who is less well acquainted with contemporary philosophy.[1] Certain kinds of phenomenological criticism have enjoyed wide currency in the United States—particularly Georges Poulet's "Geneva School" and, more recently, some of the reader-response theories. But at least in this country, the philosophical tradition behind them is hardly known and rarely understood. Many of its major names appear with considerable

regularity in discussions of literary theory. But even theorists all too
frequently have at most a passing familiarity with phenomenology's
main concepts and are little more than vaguely acquainted with its
complicated, diverse philosophical backgrounds. These backgrounds
are important for understanding phenomenology's thinking about aesthetics. They are also, as I hope to show, a useful source of concepts
to aid practical interpretation. My exposition of the basic elements of
the phenomenological tradition may be of benefit to both the literary
theorist and the practical critic.[2]

The question "What is phenomenology?" is difficult to answer
in part because no single credo contains *the* phenomenological perspective. My book offers *a* phenomenological perspective on James's
achievement, but this many-faceted school could sanction other approaches as well. Phenomenology is less a monolithic entity than a
lively family with substantial differences between its members. I point
out their disagreements in the course of my interpretation—for example, the dispute between Sartre and Heidegger about the basic nature
of personal relations that I describe in Chapter 5—and I try to make
use of them in delineating the precise shade of James's phenomenological significance. But I also hope to develop a coherent picture of
the underlying assumptions that the members of the phenomenological tradition share as participants in a recognizable style of thought.

Generally speaking, the philosophical assumptions of phenomenology lead to two different kinds of theories about literature. On the one
hand, theorists like Ingarden, Sartre, Poulet, and Iser approach the
literary work by studying its relation to consciousness. Although the
work is not reducible to the motives of its author, it nevertheless depends for its existence on the acts of consciousness that constitute it.
These acts lie dormant in the work, hibernating and waiting for the
reader to bring them to life by lending them his or her subjectivity.
Poulet seeks to unite himself with the subjectivity present in the work
by "going back, within the sphere of the work, from the objective elements systematically arranged, to a certain power of organization inherent in the work itself, as if the latter showed itself to be an intentional consciousness determining its arrangements and solving its
problems."[3] Sartre's method of "existential psychoanalysis" looks for
the "original choice" that an author expresses in his creations.[4] Turning from the author to the reader, Iser attempts to identify the kinds of
tasks that a work sets for its audience and to characterize the discov-

eries that a reader makes in the very process of activating the text.[5] On the other hand, ontological theorists stress the work's relation not to consciousness but to Being. Heidegger regards man as that being whose being is an issue for itself and who, consequently, asks about the meaning of Being. In Heidegger's view, poetry is the original naming that discloses beings and brings Being into the open.[6] Bachelard's interest in the imagination might seem to make him a theorist of consciousness. But Bachelard understands poetic creation and the aesthetic experience as ways of enabling the presence of Being to shine forth.[7]

Although I refer to many of these theorists, my approach to James is not identical with any one of their methods. My study belongs first of all to the grand old tradition of cultural criticism. By employing the central concepts of phenomenology to clarify the relation between consciousness and moral vision in James, I have undertaken a comparative study of philosophy and literature in the spirit of the many previous investigations of his work that have placed him in the context of such intellectual figures as his brother William, the British empiricists, Swedenborg, and Nietzsche. The goal of such comparative analysis is twofold. Concepts borrowed from a nonliterary context can sometimes make possible a more penetrating interpretation of a literary issue than purely intrinsic study might allow—in the case of James and phenomenology, a deeper understanding of his epistemology and its relation to his ethics. Comparative studies also further the work of cultural history; identifying Henry James as a literary ally of the phenomenological tradition illuminates an important, hitherto insufficiently recognized connection between modern thought and literature.

The specifically phenomenological components of my method have to do with both consciousness and Being. Because of their importance to the shape and structure of his world as a novelist, the five aspects of experience that I have identified qualify as the "intentional foundations" of his authorial consciousness—a term I explain in Chapter 1. It refers, briefly, to the characteristic tendencies, assumptions, and rules of operation that govern the creation of meaning in a writer's fictional universe. The "impression," the imagination, freedom, personal relations, and the politics of daily life—these are the defining preoccupations of James's consciousness as a creator. But they are also demarcations of man's being. In reading James's novels as testi-

mony to his understanding of the structure of experience, I follow
Ricoeur's suggestion that "texts speak of possible worlds and of possible ways of orienting oneself in those worlds"—worlds that disclose
"possible modes of being, . . . symbolic dimensions of our being-in-
the-world."[8] The worlds projected in James's works are occasions for
explorations of the essential constituents of man's experience. James
is not a poet of Being in Heidegger's almost spiritual sense; more secular in orientation, and with more immediate relevance to everyday
life, he is a novelist of experience. His approach to man is ontic
rather than ontological, existential rather than metaphysical.

I have chosen to read a few texts closely instead of sketching interpretations for all or most of James's works. This decision reflects in
part a desire to respect the integrity of the world of each novel and to
follow carefully its process of disclosure. Close reading of selected
works also minimizes the risk of fitting the text to the context, a danger that comparative approaches must always try to avoid. Nevertheless, I have chosen my texts and themes so that they might suggest
how a reading of his entire canon would follow from the view of James
that this book outlines. For example, I have attempted to make diachronic inclusiveness one of my principles of selection by dealing
with texts from each decade of James's mature artistic life (*Roderick
Hudson* from the 1870s, *The Portrait of a Lady* and "The Art of Fiction" from the 1880s, *What Maisie Knew* and *The Spoils of Poynton*
from the 1890s, and *The Golden Bowl* from the 1900s). The global
reading of *What Maisie Knew* in Chapter 1 surveys all of the major
aspects of experience that preoccupy James's imagination as they
come together in a single work. Each later chapter then focuses in
more detail on one dimension of his exploration of experience.

This selective approach to James could support further individual
readings that would demonstrate not only how different works give
special prominence to various aspects of man's being but also how
each displays all of them in their fundamental unity. For example,
among James's later works, Lambert Strether's adventure in *The Ambassadors* primarily invokes the contradiction between the exhilarating call of freedom and the limiting claims of necessity, where *The
Wings of the Dove* (in this respect like *The Golden Bowl*) explores the
complexities of conflict and care through the entanglements in which
Milly Theale, Merton Densher, and Kate Croy are enmeshed. More
than either of these novels, *The Sacred Fount* depicts the values and

risks of extravagant imagination as well as the perceptual possibilities and liabilities of the impression as a way of knowing. All of these works explore the politics of social life because all portray struggles over power. Inasmuch as all of the aspects of experience of concern to James are inextricably related, however, Strether's adventure is also a story of how his imagination responds to the wonderful yet dangerous inspiration of Europe and how he struggles with his impressions to achieve a revealing but reliable understanding of his world. And, of course, his involvements with Chad, Madame de Vionnet, and Maria Gostrey show all of the complications that the opposing possibilities of antagonism and communion can lead to in personal relations. Although my treatment of James's works is selective, each reading has more extensive implications for interpreting his canon.

During my interpretations I quote widely from the major figures in the phenomenological tradition. This strategy is a deliberate departure from the standard critical practice of making one's argument exclusively in one's own words, with methodological and theoretical sources acknowledged in the notes. The following pages contain many names—some of them domestic, like William James and Charles Sanders Peirce, and others foreign, like Husserl, Heidegger, Sartre, and Merleau-Ponty. I have invoked these names and their words in part for the purpose of acquainting the reader with phenomenology's leading theorists, their thought, and their major works. My reading of James provides, then, a kind of running annotated bibliography on phenomenology. I also hope to domesticate the many foreign theorists I invoke by setting their names and words next to the name and words of Henry James. Placing these Continental thinkers with James in the same world of discourse is a way of emphasizing that the phenomenological tradition belongs both to America and to Europe. My strategy of quotation is an attempt to dramatize rhetorically the convergence of perspectives that joins Henry James and phenomenology.

There will be different audiences for this book as there are for all interdisciplinary studies. I have already described what I hope the book offers to its primary audience—practical critics and students of literature with at most a general acquaintance with modern philosophy. Literary theorists and philosophers already well versed in the phenomenological canon will probably be most interested in my argument about the relations between James and intellectual history. They may also be interested in the use this book makes of philosophical concepts in order to advance our understanding of certain literary texts. My main focus, however, is on Henry James. Technical controversies that have consumed the attention of many philosophers are discussed in the body of the argument only when they help to elucidate James's artistic world and his phenomenological significance. Otherwise they are referred to in the notes.

A phenomenological reading is obviously not the last word on Henry James, but it does have a place in the ongoing critical activity of interpreting and assessing his artistic achievement. As far back as 1931, William Troy observed that James "has come to mean something different to each of the successive literary generations that have taken up his work."[9] Like all interpretation, a reading of James that reaches back to his past achievement from the standpoint of phenomenology in the present contributes to the constant process of appropriating anew the meaning of his work—the process that enables his voice to speak across the span of generations. Such acts of interpretation are part of the work of making sense of ourselves by engaging in dialogue with the past, and this work in turn is one of the crucial forces that give momentum to cultural history. If a phenomenological reading seeks to appropriate James anew for the present, my study also hopes to shed light on his place within the past itself by helping to clarify one aspect of America's intellectual and literary history. Phenomenology is widely regarded as a European movement that comes to us as a transatlantic import. With his brother William, though, Henry James places phenomenology firmly on native ground as part of America's cultural heritage. James was always fascinated, of course, with relations between America and Europe. It is only fitting and proper, then, that James should contribute another chapter to the "international theme" as he does when we recognize his phenomenological perspective.

It is a pleasure to acknowledge the many debts I have acquired in writing this book. I alone, of course, am responsible for its failings. David Halliburton gave sound advice when I began the project, and he made important criticisms of the first draft. Thomas C. Moser has been an unfailing source of wise counsel and generous encouragement. Jonathan Arac read the entire manuscript at a crucial stage and offered invaluable suggestions for revisions. I am grateful to Austin E. Quigley for his tireless interest in my ideas, his shrewd criticisms of their weak points, and his persistent belief in the worthiness of this work. I also wish to give special thanks to a number of friends and colleagues who made helpful criticisms of parts or all of the book: George Dekker, Darryl J. Gless, Harry Hellenbrand, David Langston, and David Levin. The press's anonymous readers offered much good advice that I was glad to take advantage of and that I wish to acknowledge even if I cannot thank them by name.

The Committee on Research at the University of Virginia generously awarded a grant that freed me to complete and revise the book. The same source provided funds for typing. The finishing touches were applied while I held a research fellowship from the Alexander von Humboldt Foundation. In preparing the manuscript, I had intelligent, diligent help from Nancy Prothro, Sue Ellen Campbell, Pam Fitzgerald, and Anita Wiseman. Parts of Chapters 1 and 2 appeared in somewhat different form in *Texas Studies in Literature and Language* 20 (1978): 517–37 and *Novel: A Forum on Fiction* 12 (1978): 5–20. I am grateful to the editors for permission to reprint them here.

My greatest debt, however, is to my wife, Christina Buck, who was with me from the start of this project to its end.

THE PHENOMENOLOGY OF
HENRY JAMES

CONSCIOUSNESS
AND MORAL VISION IN
WHAT MAISIE KNEW

ONE

Joseph Conrad calls Henry James "the historian of fine consciences."[1]
As many have noticed, Conrad's description is particularly apt because it plays on the French "*conscience*"—a word that refers to both
consciousness and morality as does the double focus of James's art.
The vicissitudes of consciousness fascinate James. To know and how
to know, that is the question for James the epistemological novelist.
But James is also a moral dramatist. His novels and tales dramatize
the explorations of a deeply probing moral vision. These two aspects
of James's achievement raise a question that many of his readers and
critics have pondered: What is the relation between James the epistemological novelist and James the moral dramatist? Namely, what
connections join his interest in consciousness and his concern with
moral themes?

A phenomenological approach to describing and explaining these
connections suggests itself because of the close relation between
James's art and his brother William's philosophy. Many critics have
been intrigued by Henry's surprised discovery that he had "uncon-
sciously pragmatised" in much of his life and work. They have shown
the extent to which he was right when, politely ignoring their marked
differences in temperament and taste, he told William that "philo-
sophically, in short, I am 'with' you, almost completely."[2] But William
James's pragmatic, pluralistic radical empiricism itself anticipates the
concerns of phenomenology and its scion, existentialism. Husserl
read James's *Principles of Psychology* early in his career and later acknowledged its influence on his thought. Moreover, along with his

friend and colleague Charles Sanders Peirce, William James has come to be regarded as a founder of an American phenomenology. The growing awareness in philosophical circles of William's significance as a pioneering precursor of Husserl, Heidegger, Merleau-Ponty, and Sartre should lead us to inquire whether Henry's achievement has affinities with the phenomenological tradition.[3] I will attempt to explain the phenomenological implications of William's philosophy as I use his thought in my interpretations of his brother's art. It seems obvious, though, that if Henry and William share similar concerns and, further, if William and phenomenology share similar concerns, then (almost by syllogism) we can reasonably expect Henry's work to have phenomenological significance.

Guided by this expectation, we can pose the following questions about consciousness and morality in James: What is the relation between James's understanding of consciousness and phenomenological theories of knowing? Does James's moral vision converge with existential theory in such areas as freedom, responsibility, and the dilemmas of personal relations? Can the links between phenomenology and existentialism help to illuminate the connections between James's epistemological and moral concerns?

James often acknowledges in his critical writings that for him the epistemological and the moral are a single concern, not separate issues. In his preface to *The Portrait of a Lady*, for example, James claims that "the 'moral' sense of a work of art . . . is but another name for the more or less close connexion of the subject with some mark made on the intelligence, with some sincere experience." According to James, the artist decides "the projected morality" of his work at the same moment he chooses which of the innumerable "possible windows" in "the house of fiction" to look through at the world and how to do this looking.[4]

At least two major implications about the relationship between the epistemological and the moral can be drawn from these deceptively simple but remarkably rich remarks. First, with a radical empiricism similar to his brother's insistence on the primacy of experience, Henry James suggests here that we cannot go behind or beyond our lived engagement with the world. Specifically, an artist cannot claim foundations in some ideal or universal realm for his moral values or, by extension, for any other aspect of his vision. An artist's moral vision rests on his experience as a knowing being, and experience provides a foundation that rests on nothing but itself. Second, James suggests that the epistemological and the moral are unified because they are systematically related to each other. They are correlated in such a way that an artist's way of knowing—his way of looking at the world through his own particular "window"—necessarily implies and agrees with the "projected morality" of his work.

Just as James argues that the morality and truth of a novel depend at bottom on how the artist knows the world, so phenomenology finds that morality and truth in general can claim no other foundation than lived experience. This discovery throws conventional certainties about knowledge and human activity into a crisis both for James and for phenomenology. Since we cannot directly grasp the thing-itself, Husserl explains, but have only the phenomenon directed toward it, "knowledge, which in ordinary prephilosophical thought is the most natural thing in the world, suddenly emerges as a mystery."[5] When the myth of absolute knowledge falls, the dream of moral certainty collapses as well. As Merleau-Ponty argues, "morality is not something given but something to be created." And so, "morality cannot consist in the private adherence to a system of values. Principles are mystifications unless they are put into practice" and "animate our relations with others." Since morality depends solely on what we make of our experience, Merleau-Ponty concludes, "nothing guarantees us that morality is possible"—although "even less is there any fatal assurance that morality is impossible."[6] This perilous struggle to achieve morality on foundations no more certain than experience itself is a privileged subject for James's dramatic art.

Because ethics depends on experience for James, he defines the moral realm broadly. His moral vision addresses more than criteria of judgment or standards for conduct. Rather, it surveys the whole field of human activity. It thereby cuts beneath the claim of inherited conventions to provide indubitable criteria for guiding and evaluating behavior. James is fascinated with social conventions, but he does not consider them fundamental as arbiters of right and wrong. This perceptive student of manners recognizes that conventions are socially codified ways of interpreting the world and relating to others—culturally contingent customs that organize experience along particular lines and that owe their existence to the agreement of the community to practice them. For James, then, morality cannot find its ultimate justification in conventions; derivative rather than fundamental, conventions are structures of experience.

James is intrigued by the endless complications and ambiguities that arise in trying to differentiate between right and wrong. But he is less interested in where the line between them lies than in how one draws it, and with what legitimation. For James, questions of morality can only be decided—to the extent they are answerable at all— by consulting the structure of experience and studying the basic constituents of human activity. Descending beneath the contingency of conventions and the abstractions of ethical debate, his moral vision probes the concrete immediacy of human experience: the risks and values of the imagination, the dialectic between possibilities and their limits, the shifting balance between conflict and care in personal relations, and the struggles over power that give a political dimension to daily life. These matters are more fundamental to James than the right and wrong of conduct because they provide the ultimate basis upon which any distinction between these ethical poles must rest. Where James the epistemological novelist explores the vicissitudes of knowing, the moral dramatist takes as his domain human doing in all its many aspects. Consciousness and moral vision are consequently unified for James just as knowing and doing are; knowing is a kind of activity, and modes of doing grasp the world according to a particular understanding of it.

This description of James's moral vision leads us back to the second major implication of the remarks I quoted earlier about the relation for him between an artist's way of knowing and the "projected morality" of his work. If James assumes that the epistemological and the moral realms form parts of a systematically unified whole—a whole where each part implies and agrees with all the others—then this unity depends on the unity of knowing and doing I have just described. Our worlds do not naturally divide themselves into independent parts like mind and body, consciousness and behavior, knowing and doing. Phenomenology regards such divisions as artificial categories that we construct after the fact in order to understand various aspects of existence that actually resist such compartmentalization because they belong to a seamless totality. In refuting the subject-object split, for example, William James argues that experience is all a unity and that we divide it up into subject and object only by looking at it retrospectively in particular ways that serve particular purposes.[7] With Henry James, this holistic unity of our worlds is what supports the unity between matters of knowing and doing, consciousness and activity, epistemology and morality.

The relation between knowing and doing in James finds an instructive parallel, I think, in the historical connections between Husserl's first phenomenological investigations on the foundations of knowledge and later existential researches on the activity of being-in-the-world. Like James, only as a philosopher rather than an artist, Husserl devoted much of his life and work to reflecting on the activity of knowing. He found that "objects exist for me, and are for me what they are, only as objects of actual and possible consciousness." Equally and oppositely, he declared, all consciousness is "consciousness *of* something."[8] For Husserl, consciousness is not a passive receptacle for contents from the outside world but, instead, directs itself actively and even creatively toward its objects to posit, constitute, and give meaning to them. For example, when we are presented with three sides of what seems like a cube, he argues, we assume the existence of the other three hidden sides as we construct the "intentional object" that our "intentional acts" presume to deal with. If we discover later that these sides do not exist, our surprise only shows that we had been intentionally active in assuming them earlier.[9] We know the world through phenomena that endow objects with meaning through this process of "intentionality." The basic structure of consciousness is the relation between intentional acts and intentional objects. When Husserl describes consciousness as "intentional," however, he does not mean to portray it as self-consciously purposive in the colloquial sense of the term. Rather, for him, "intentionality" refers more broadly to the entire activity of engaging ourselves with the objects in our world.

This theory of knowing invites an existential turn, as first Heidegger but then many others after him realized, including Husserl himself. Existentialists are phenomenologists who have taken Husserl's theory of intentionality as a guide for studying a wider range of phenomena than he at first considered. Existential phenomenologists contend that "it is not only the mind of man which is intentionally related to the world . . . it is man himself, as a concrete, living, experiencing, thinking, perceiving, imagining, willing, loving, hating, communicating being who is intentional of the world."[10] This reformulation of intentionality builds on Husserl's assertion that knowing is an activity by pointing out that all human activity is a way of knowing the world. As Sartre points out, "knowledge and action are only two abstract aspects of an original, concrete relation" between man and the world.[11] Heidegger calls this relation "being-in-the-world"— a concept that describes how man comes to know himself, his objects, and other people in his world by the activity of projecting himself in the present toward his possibilities in the future. Working from Husserl's theory of intentionality, existential phenomenologists have studied such aspects of being-in-the-world as the imagination, freedom, our relations with others, and our relation to social history. Although different from each other in many respects, these aspects of experience are not only unified as parts of a coherent whole but also have homologous structures to the extent that they share the characteristics of intentionality that Husserl first posited for consciousness.

Henry James's achievement has phenomenological significance because of the similarities between the ways in which he and Husserl's compatriots understand the various aspects of experience. Through interpretations of James's works in the chapters that follow, I will attempt to describe these aspects of experience and to explain further how and why they combine to form a systematically unified whole for him and phenomenology. Obviously, only concrete interpretation can hope to demonstrate the usefulness of a phenomenological approach to James both in the particular task of explicating his writings and in the general work of clarifying the relation between his epistemology and his moral themes. Let me therefore single out one work for detailed analysis to provide a vehicle for introducing my overall argument. *What Maisie Knew* offers a kind of paradigm of the relation between consciousness and moral vision in James's fictional universe. By showing the underlying unity of Maisie's epistemological and moral crises, I hope to clarify further the unity between knowing and doing that both James and phenomenology assert. My interpretation will also introduce the conceptual framework that will guide the rest of my study.

Readers of *What Maisie Knew* customarily ask what she knows and whether she develops a "moral sense." They are divided, though, over whether she triumphs morally or ends up utterly depraved. One side argues that she transcends her vulgar surroundings by learning to penetrate the evil ways of her parents and stepparents. For example, in a classic statement of this side's claim, Pelham Edgar insists that Maisie acquires "a sense of the distinction between the right and the wrong of conduct." [12] Those on the other side agree with Oscar Cargill, however, that Maisie remains to the last "the refuse-catching vortex about whom a current of dissolute life pulses and whirls." [13] We may be able to cut beneath this controversy if we rephrase the central issues under dispute. Instead of asking "What did Maisie know? And was she moral?," we should turn to the more fundamental problems that make these questions possible. That is, we should ask: "How can Maisie know? And how does her initiation into the activity of knowing involve her in struggles where the stakes are her freedom and her relations with others?" We shall address these questions one at a time from a phenomenological perspective that, in exploring the relation between Maisie's epistemological and existential dilemmas, may clarify further the relation between James's fascination with knowing and his "moral vision."

T W O

Maisie's dilemma begins as a distressing epistemological situation. James observes in his preface that, in general, "small children have many more perceptions than they have terms to translate them; their vision is at any moment much richer, their apprehension even constantly stronger, than their prompt, their at all producible, vocabulary." [14] But in Maisie's situation, this general condition has taken on extreme proportions. "It was to be the fate of this patient little girl to see much more than she at first understood, but also even at first to understand much more than any little girl, however patient, had perhaps ever understood before." [15] No matter how valiantly Maisie translates what she sees into something she can understand, she seems ever unable—at least until the end—to eliminate the obscurity caused by the excess of her seeing over her understanding. It is her burden to carry "in her mind a collection of images and echoes to which meanings were attachable—images and echoes kept for her in the childish dusk, the dim closet, the high drawers, like games she wasn't yet big enough to play" (p. 12). She can only grow "big enough" to manage her dilemma by learning to attach meanings to these ambiguous, bewildering "images and echoes." The excess of seeing over understanding that imprisons Maisie in a world of ambiguity is the surplus of her unreflective experience over what she can appropriate in reflection. Maisie's dilemma presents an extreme instance of a general condition Merleau-Ponty has described. Once we begin to reflect, he argues, all of us find that we—like Maisie—have already been thrown into unreflective engagement with the world. Some obscurity will always haunt us because our efforts to achieve self-conscious clarity can never completely catch up with our original experience.[16] Maisie's challenge is to make the unreflected less obscure so that she can gain knowledge and freedom in a situation that threatens her with ambiguity and bondage. Maisie's "moral sense" and her overall development depend on her struggle to achieve epistemological competence.

Many obstacles impede Maisie's work of transforming her confusion into clarity. For example: "To be 'involved' was of the essence of everybody's affairs, and also at every particular moment to be more involved than usual" (p. 137). Consequently, it is that much more "involved" a job for her to make sense of her situation. It is difficult, for example, to achieve a coherent understanding of your world's interpersonal structure when that structure refuses to hold together coherently. Maisie's trouble here begins with "the opposed principles" in which her parents try to "educate" her—each insisting on the other's irremediable evil. Instead of helping her develop confidence in herself and her world, they confront her with contradictory perceptions and then abandon her "to fit them together as she might" (p. 6). Maisie's entanglement in everyone's conflicting affairs only gets more incoherent, unstable, and contradictory as her story unfolds. Maisie is not just thrown into a situation; she finds herself thrown from situation to situation with unsettling unpredictability. The rude shocks, the sudden stops and starts in Maisie's world frustrate any historical genesis of meaning. Husserl points out that the creation of meaning develops temporally—that children and adults build and change their worlds by adding to acquired habits of intentional activity.[17] But Maisie cannot trust her life to develop steadily from one minute to the next so that she might increase her competence as a knower by modifying and refining past practices of understanding. Such habits might even be more a liability for her than an asset, since they would limit the flexibility she needs to react quickly to unexpected temporal jolts. She cannot build much meaning without the foundations that confidence in the reliability of past experience would provide. And the construction of meaning seems futile without assurances about continuity with the future.

Still, despite the odds against her, Maisie does try again and again to wrest meaning from her confusion and thus to liberate herself from the prison of obscurity. One of the earliest of these efforts is the play she undertakes with her doll Lisette. She uses her doll to counter the bewildering shock of being laughed at unexpectedly by adults when she displays her naiveté. Maisie may try quite seriously to ask a question that would clarify an ambiguity—only to find that she has set off a round of guffaws among the people she had trusted to assist her. This laughter "seemed always, like some trick in a frightening game, to leap forth and make her jump" (p. 31). Jolts like these upset the genesis of meaning she seeks. But Maisie's failures to find consistent meaning in real situations induce her to experiment in play. And with her doll's help,

> Little by little . . . she understood more, for it befell that she was enlightened by Lisette's questions, which reproduced the effect of her own upon those for whom she sat in the very darkness of Lisette. Was she not herself convulsed by such innocence? . . . There were at any rate things she really couldn't tell even a French doll. She could only pass on her lessons and study to produce on Lisette the impression of having great mysteries in her life. (p. 34)

Maisie reverses roles, of course, by projecting ambiguity and bondage onto her doll in order to appropriate clarity and freedom for herself. Even more, though, Maisie uses Lisette to help her reflect on the unreflected; she finds that she can explore in the safety of fantasy what overwhelms her in the immediacy of experience. She takes advantage of the way in which play enables children to master through absence what they find baffling in presence by constructing meanings which themselves are absent from presence; signs have the power to mean, after all, by virtue of the distance between them and what they signify. [18] Maisie's dilemma is that the usual resources that children employ to create meaning do not suffice for her situation.

Outside of her nursery, Maisie pursues meaning and mastery by using her imagination. As James explains in his preface, Maisie "has simply to wonder" and objects "begin to have meanings, aspects, solidarities, connexions" that help to reduce the fund of obscurity in her world.[19] In order to understand what she sees, Maisie calls on her imagination to spin out hypotheses about the hidden sides that lie beyond her immediate, limited view of a situation. And her imagination works hardest when she has to rise to meet a sudden crisis.

Consider, for example, her idyllic outing with Sir Claude to Kensington Gardens that comes to an all too abrupt halt when they run into her mother strolling with her latest boyfriend. Suddenly and without warning, Maisie must deal with the shock of a rare pleasure interrupted, the nuisance of Ida's appearance, the mystery of her mother's presence contradicting Sir Claude's understanding that she is in Brussels, the anxiety of her stepfather's annoyance and then anger, the violence of being embraced by her mother "as if she had suddenly been thrust, with a smash of glass, into a jeweller's shopfront, but only to be as suddenly ejected with a push" (p. 145), and—as if all this were not already enough—the confusion of the new boyfriend's identity. Most immediately, Maisie needs to penetrate the opacities surrounding her—to clarify what she sees and to understand it. As always, though, she is poorly positioned for the task. Exiled with the Captain while Sir Claude and Ida quarrel, Maisie finds herself in her accustomed position of "hanging over banisters" (p. 55) and wondering about what's happening downstairs. Her standpoint as an observer grants her an extremely limited perspective on the situation at hand, with more sides of what she sees hidden than disclosed. But she can only understand what she sees by questioning what her perspective reveals in order to guess what lies beyond it. She must develop hypotheses about the hidden sides implied by the side she perceives, just as anyone presented with three sides of what seems like a cube— to recall the example I gave earlier—must posit the existence of three other hidden sides in order to construct the intentional object that his or her intentional acts presume to deal with.

Husserl's theory of intentionality suggests that to know is to believe. Indeed, Peirce argues that our "truths" are simply hypotheses on which we act in the faith that they will bear themselves out.[20] Hence William James's contention that "'the true,' to put it very briefly, is only the expedient in the way of our thinking. . . . The 'absolutely' true, meaning what no farther experience will ever alter, is that ideal vanishing-point towards which we imagine that all our temporary truths will some day converge."[21] To dispel her confusion,

Maisie desperately needs some hypothesis on which to act with full faith in its truth. She consequently makes a guess about hidden sides in her extravagant, imaginative interpretation of the Captain as her mother's knight in shining armor. By romantically believing him the only one to appreciate Ida justly, to love her truly, and to offer her the hope of salvation, Maisie secures herself a hypothesis on which to act according to an understanding of her situation; that is, she can play the part of "the young lady at the ball" (p. 148) with her noble escort. In constructing this fantasy, she assumes an attitude of good faith toward her surroundings—an attitude that normally underlies everyone's dealings with objects, but one that is usually denied her. She also asserts her freedom by discovering invigorating possibilities in a deadly dilemma. She does so by adeptly creating meaning out of mystery.

Sudden shocks may require Maisie to respond with considerable imaginative agility. But many of the surprises that spring on her show how unexpected hidden sides can emerge and shatter her hypotheses about what lies beyond her grasp. William James warns: "Woe to him whose beliefs play fast and loose with the order which realities follow in his experience: they will lead him nowhere or else make false connexions." [22] "Reality" can be distinguished from "illusion" because our beliefs have consequences. If Maisie plays "fast and loose" in her fantasies at Kensington Gardens, the consequences of her "false connexions" follow at Folkestone when Ida reappears. Maisie's fantasies give her a set of expectations about how her experience will unfold and disclose the sides hidden from her but implied (she assumes) in her perspective. She expects that their emergence will confirm her hypotheses about her mother's love life. But Ida's reappearance robs Maisie of the validation she anticipates for her imaginative interpretation of the Captain.

Fittingly enough, Ida's unexpected entrance interrupts yet another of Maisie's performances in the art of imaginative world-construction; at first, Maisie regards her mother as a threat to the glamorous adventure on which Sir Claude has whisked her away. Once again poorly positioned to discover what's happening behind the scenes, Maisie "wondered intensely, . . . was mystified and charmed, puzzled" (p. 211) about Ida's motives and the state of her relations with Sir Claude. Then, after Ida's charm and sweetness dispel Maisie's sense of imminent danger, the child gets a wonderful inspiration. She decides to exploit her apparent safety by constructing a bridge between her world with Sir Claude and her world with the Captain. Conjecturing that the Captain is saving Ida just as Sir Claude is rescuing her, Maisie allows herself to enjoy two fantasies instead of just one. Also, she thus wins a clue to her mother's motives that can serve as a cue for her own actions. Furthermore, Maisie's inspired connection of one situation in her history with another later is an attempt to unify and strengthen her world by relating meanings across time and building on acquired habits of understanding. She is only trying to sustain the situation—as she understands it—when she invokes the Captain as a witness in support of Ida's plea that no one has done her justice. But "her mother gave her one of the looks that slammed the door in her face; never in a career of unsuccessful experiments had Maisie had to take such a stare" (p. 223). Maisie has unfortunately extensive experience with surprise in her "career of unsuccessful experiments." She errs more than rarely in the hypotheses that she tests, and she most often finds that those errors compound her mystification instead of improving her acquaintance with her world.

James's experiments with point of view in the novel call on the reader to understand Maisie and her world better than she does. James explains in his preface that he adheres to her perspective because her "wonder" transforms the "vulgar and empty" into "the stuff of poetry and tragedy and art."[23] He thereby runs the risk of misleading the reader, however; Maisie's imagination is epistemologically unreliable precisely because it is so nobly persistent in dressing out the worst circumstances in romantic finery. James avoids this trap by the juxtaposition he establishes between her perspective and his own narrative voice. His preface claims that his "own commentary constantly attends and amplifies" Maisie's adventures by going "'behind' the facts of her spectacle" to point out hidden sides so that we can "take advantage of these things better than she herself."[24] For the most part, however, James's narrator is too subtle and self-effacing to offer explicit evaluations of his heroine; his most revealing and pervasive form of commentary is the complex ironic attitude he maintains toward her interpretations—an amused detachment that exposes her foibles with a mild touch of comic demystification, balanced against sympathetic involvement with her trials that invokes our pity for her and encourages us to participate in her struggles. Iser claims that all reading requires both immersion and observation as we alternate between inhabiting a fictional world and criticizing the perspectives within it.[25] With James's novel, however, this dialectic reduplicates in the experience of reading the dialectic between belief and doubt in knowing which the story itself explores. The narrator's irony calls upon the reader to join Maisie in the hypotheses she projects but at the same time to criticize them and to learn the necessity of suspicion even while appreciating the reasons for her faith. This dialectic inducts the reader into the double motion of belief and doubt that all understanding entails.

It also prompts us to counter Maisie's hypotheses with guesses of our own about the hidden sides she misconstrues and the patterns she misapprehends. Iser argues that we read by filling in gaps and joining elements together in consistent arrangements—completing indeterminacies and discovering modes of coherence that join the parts of a text into a whole.[26] Once again, however, James orchestrates these processes into a commentary on the activities of knowing which his novel takes as a major theme. Just as Maisie's guesses try to fill in blanks that lie beyond her horizons and to build a consistent image of her contradictory, topsy-turvy world, so the reader of her story must do the same—but projecting different hidden sides and a different pattern of meanings than she does, at least until her awakening at the end. Because aspects we misconstrue often contain hints that could lead to a more appropriate understanding of the object, the reader of Maisie's history can (and must) study her perspective on the events she misconstrues to disclose other interpretations it might allow. The narrator's irony encourages and guides the reader in this endeavor. The ironic distance between our own interpretations and Maisie's theories calls for us to reflect about the hazardous but inescapable role that hypotheses play in understanding, whether in reading a text or making sense of an ambiguous situation. In *Maisie* as in many of his other novels, James manipulates point of view and narrative authority to draw attention to the vicissitudes of consciousness as a process of projecting hidden sides and seeking consistency. This is one hallmark of James's modernity if, as Iser claims, modern fiction asks the reader "to become aware" of "the functioning of [his] own faculties of perception, . . . of his own tendency to link things together in consistent patterns, and indeed of the whole thought process that constitutes his relations with the world outside himself."[27]

Maisie could hardly avoid much of the ambiguity and many of the surprises she suffers, though, because the hidden sides of other minds are particularly elusive. We have access to the Other's world through our understanding of his expressions—not only his speech but also his bodily gestures—and through a usually dim awareness that the horizons of our world shade off into more or less distant possibilities that can belong to him if not to us. But as Merleau-Ponty contends, "I am necessarily destined never to experience the presence of another person to himself."[28] We can never know the Other's world as he or she knows it, inasmuch as we can never understand the Other's experience except from the position of our own experience. Husserl was too sanguine, then, in supposing intersubjectivity guaranteed by our ability to project ourselves into the Other's position by empathy or analogy so as to understand him as experiencing aspects "like those I should have if I should go over there and be where he is."[29] Maisie is not a solipsist. Others matter to her a great deal. She is continually involved with others whom she understands at least enough to talk with and whom she often wants to understand better. But when others laugh at her naive questions or remarks, for example, Maisie learns that meanings in her world can have different and inaccessible meanings in other worlds. Her misunderstanding of the Captain's status and of Ida's situation at Folkestone are failed experiments in intersubjectivity which show that reading the Other's speeches and gestures correctly can be extremely difficult. She can only understand others through their Self-for-Others, which may or may not provide a reliable guide to their Self-for-Themselves. Her story dramatizes the difficulty of achieving intersubjective clarity since the Other must always remain somewhat opaque.

Intersubjective opacity makes the lie possible, as Maisie discovers—or, too often, gullibly fails to discover—in her dealings with her parents and stepparents. Maisie inhabits a world of disingenuous appearances where intrigues and deceptions take unfortunate advantage of the necessary element of mystery in the Other. Maisie knows from Mrs. Beale, for example, that she had kept things "perfectly proper" while the former governess was winning Mr. Farange's affections and that she later helped her stepmother and Sir Claude by "bringing them together" and "doing them good" in myriad unspecified ways (pp. 39, 64, 133). But Maisie's comforting sense of the family joys made possible by this talent of hers for facilitating relationships hardly corresponds to her stepmother's calculating understanding of the possibilities for sexual intrigue in the same situations. Many critics have noted with Dupee that Maisie "never knows where she stands with her elders"—that "her life is poor chiefly in affection and serenity; it is poor in candor, in transparency."[30] Her elders' lies exploit her inevitable blindness to the Other's innermost feelings and motives by manipulating the signs that Maisie takes in good faith as representative of their worlds. Her understanding of others cannot readily increase if they refuse to cooperate. But Maisie's parents and stepparents are too intent for their own purposes on making themselves ambiguous to care much about helping her clear up the opacity of the Other.

Maisie often helps her elders more than they help her, in fact, since she often seems not to want to expose the lies that confound her understanding. Quite the contrary, she frequently seems to prefer that the hidden sides of her interpersonal world stay hidden, if only because it is more pleasant to dwell in fantasies than to face disillusionment. Turning a blind eye to deceptions with the help of her imagination acts to cover up the jolting discontinuities in Maisie's world and to establish the security of apparent clarity where confusion threatens. Mrs. Beale may have darker designs on Sir Claude than she will admit; but uncovering them might hurt Maisie more than help her, since the appearance of caring with him for the child that her stepmother cultivates for her plot "really gave Maisie a happier sense than she had yet had of being very dear at least to two persons" (p. 163). More innocent, perhaps, than her other manipulators because less resolute and more deceived himself, Sir Claude has even less trouble deceiving Maisie than anyone else does because she trusts and depends on him more. Consequently, "to shuffle away her sense of being duped he had only, from under his lovely mustache, to breathe upon it" (p. 137). Since he promises to guarantee continuity and security in her world by promising that he will "never, never forsake her" (p. 107), Maisie works to protect his guarantee by ignoring signs of its weakness. Mrs. Wix may be the only adult who tries not to lie to Maisie. But her own romantic notions about Sir Claude's possible role as their savior feed Maisie's fantasies when more clear-headed guidance might have helped the child pierce the veil of deception around her.

What Maisie knows, then, is insecure and unreliable—as insecure and unreliable as her precarious moral and existential situation.

When Mrs. Wix attacks Maisie for lacking "the moral sense," she tells the child her righteous indignation started when she saw "how it was that without your seeming to condemn—for you didn't, you remember!—you yet did seem to *know*." Maisie responds with a question: "If I did know—?" But Mrs. Wix admonishes her: "If you do condemn" (pp. 283–84). Yet Maisie's question is the right one. To condemn is itself nothing more than to know in a particular way by taking an attitude toward a situation that reveals it in a particular light. Examining her moral dilemma in light of her epistemological confusion, we could defend the child by arguing that Maisie did not know what she was saying when she asked, "Why shouldn't we be four?" (p. 271)—the governess, the child, and her amorous stepparents all one big happy family in adultery. This episode ranks as one among many where Maisie fails to understand the moves in the games played by manipulators like Mrs. Beale and Sir Claude. She acquiesced to her stepmother's lie of caring nobly for her stepfather because both cared for her. Her imagination filled out the pretended meaning of this lie romantically and reassuringly, and she misconstrued the hidden side behind its facade. Once again, then, as so often before, Maisie's unreflected experience has outstripped her ability to assimilate it. Maisie's "moral sense" is no more certain than what she can know from her experience, and that is none too certain.

But if Mrs. Wix errs in assuming that Maisie knows with such certainty that she can and should know a situation by condemning it, she errs equally in assuming that only a sense of right and wrong is at stake in the drama of the child's development. From Maisie's play in her nursery to her struggles with understanding at Folkestone and Kensington Gardens, her epistemological difficulties are never separate from more encompassing trials. For Maisie to resolve her epistemological dilemmas would mean not simply to develop an ethics but, more fundamentally, to transform her situation by changing the possibilities disclosed to her choice. Wresting clarity from ambiguity might mean, then, wresting freedom from bondage. Unmasking lies and making transparent the opacity of others would reveal to Maisie what her prospects for caring personal relations really are. So far we have concentrated on the epistemological aspects of Maisie's situation. But now, moving toward the existential dynamics of James's "moral vision," we must examine the problems of freedom, limitation, and personal relations in which her trials with knowing play a part, although an undeniably critical part.

THREE

Maisie faces crises in freedom and care. When Maisie struggles with perception, reflection, and meaning-creation to interpret her situation and even to construct a world for herself imaginatively, she is trying to disclose the limits and range of the choices available to her. Kierkegaard defines freedom as the "possibility for possibility."[31] But freedom is never unconditional. We can have our possibilities only from a position that excludes us from other alternatives. As Heidegger explains, we can project ourselves into our possibilities only by accepting the limits of the "ground" onto which we have been "thrown" as the starting point for our freedom.[32] This "ground" includes every contingency of our existence that we must accept because we cannot disavow it, such as our place in geography and history, or our body, our past, and our relations with others insofar as they have already been established for us. We cannot choose the ground of our existence, but we can choose what to make of it by the way we open the possibilities it offers and the way we select from them to construct the world we will inhabit. Maisie's epistemological struggles are an attempt to understand the ground of her freedom and, if possible, to reveal it in an enhancing light. We have seen, though, that she misleads herself about her possibilities when she fails to recognize the dismal limits imposed on them. The givenness that she must accept gives her little possibility for possibility. The prospects look grim, then, that Maisie could ever secure a meaningful freedom given such unpromising conditions.

Maisie could afford a larger faith in her possibilities if anyone cared about her freedom and ground other than herself. But she inhabits a world of rampant carelessness. According to Heidegger, care (or *Sorge*) is the founding structure of existence. The decision how to care for Being is, in his view, the fundamental choice at the heart of existence. We show care toward our possibilities and have various relations of care with our environment (*Umwelt*) and our world of others (*Mitwelt*).[33] Maisie is thrown into conditions where such symbols of care as marriage and the family have lost significance and where divorce and separation reign, declaring that care has gone wrong. "With two fathers, two mothers, and two homes, six protections in all," Maisie enjoys little actual protection; she even faces the prospect that someday "she shouldn't know 'wherever' to go" (p. 99) since fewer and fewer people really care what becomes of her. Elsewhere James laments "the exposure indeed, the helpless plasticity of childhood that isn't dear or sacred to *some*body!"[34] Childhood is an area where care's fate is decided from generation to generation, since it is a time when a liberating solicitude should prepare the young to make choices, explore possibilities, and accept the responsibilities of existence. But no one carefully nourishes the ground of Maisie's possibilities or encourages her freedom through care, and too many do just the opposite in disregard of anyone's possibilities except their own.

The crisis in care that Maisie faces is an indictment of her social world. James does not write often or even particularly well on explicitly political themes. But the topics an author chooses do not tell much in themselves about the relation of his work to historical and social concerns. At deeper levels, regardless of an author's themes, the patterns that govern the world of his art reflect and respond to his historical situation in a politically meaningful way.[35] In James's case, the private dramas he portrays nonetheless have wider social significance because they suggest much about the world on their horizons— the social circumstances that provide their setting, the general conditions of which they offer a particularly illuminating instance. Maisie's situation may be unusual, but her dilemma is not simply her own. Her misfortunes cannot be written off to bad luck in the parents she has; the rampant carelessness with which she is treated, for example, is typical in its very uniqueness as a sign of breakdowns in the Victorian family. Unlike Dickens in *Great Expectations* or Tolstoy in *Anna Karenina*, James does not regard the family as a moral institution that is potentially a carrier of transcendent, ideal values. He views it as a setting for existential development and a way of organizing experience. Reversing the negative image that Maisie's story presents, a positive family structure would provide a child with security and continuity in its early steps toward epistemological competence, a facilitative arena for testing possibilities, and a basis for trust and reciprocity in personal relations. As a social institution, the family is for James a conventional manner of arranging the various dimensions of experience—a structure that serves the basic conditions of existence either well or poorly. Maisie's family relations do not serve her well, and her trials condemn the institutional structure in which they unfold.

The lies practiced on Maisie that we examined earlier as epistemological dilemmas reveal the bankruptcy of care in her world. The most fundamental lie—and the one aimed at Maisie most often—takes the form of a contradiction in care. "We care about you and want to care for you," her parents and stepparents all claim on one occasion or another. But their behavior declares: "We don't care one bit, or at least not enough to outweigh our other concerns." Consider, for example, the elaborate subterfuge that Beale Farange tries to perpetrate on his daughter at the Countess's apartment after his embarrassing run-in with Mrs. Beale at the Exhibition. With "foolishly tender" gestures intended to carry off the "awkwardness" (p. 180) of having showed so little interest in his daughter for so long, Beale pretends to exhibit solicitude for her welfare by offering to take her to America. But he seems more concerned even to Maisie with securing the convenience to himself that her refusal of this overture would bring. She feels "that this was their parting, their parting forever, and that he had brought her there for so many caresses only because it was important such an occasion should look better for him than any other" (p. 186). He claims to be enabling Maisie to decide her future by picking freely from the options he magnanimously presents her. But instead of broadening the ground of her possibilities with a liberating solicitude, he narrows them in a manipulative deception to the single possibility he wants her to choose.

However much accustomed to "rebounding from racquet to racquet" in the games of others "like a tennis-ball or shuttlecock,"[36] Maisie tenaciously persists in caring about care. Finding herself "deficient in something that would meet the general desire" (p. 10), she desperately wants to discover means that might supply her the love she has never sufficiently received. "She was ready, in this interest, for an immense surrender" if such a strategy would establish care: "To give something, to give here on the spot, was all her own desire" (p. 182). She is willing to give her father anything he wants, since her diplomacy in playing along with his manipulation allows her to show that she at least loves him. Furthermore, by meeting his desire, she might even inspire him to care for her too out of appreciation for her self-sacrificing pliability. But her strategy is undermined by a fateful contradiction. Showing care by pretending indifference if he abandons her, Maisie can win his care in return only on the condition she forfeit it. By meeting the contradiction of his lie with a deception of her own to carry it on, she creates a volatile, contradictory situation bound to collapse—or to explode, as it does, when she breaks down and gives up her strategy, shortly to undertake a disordered, frantic retreat. Nothing Maisie can do on her own can get past the fundamental collapse of care that Beale betrays by failing to answer her plea: "I can't give you up" (p. 192).[37]

Maisie's quest for a care that has eluded her is part of her attempt to convert this episode in her history into an occasion for the freedom and possibility she has seldom enjoyed because the ground of her existence is so barren. Her compassion for Beale gives her "an extemporised, expensive treat" (p. 176) with "such possibilities of vibration, of response, that it needed nothing more than this to make up to her in fact for omissions" (p. 180) that had deprived her so in the past. These omissions might deprive her in her current situation if she did not convert the awkwardness of their position together into an occasion for her own romantic pleasure. She discloses more congenial possibilities for herself by taking a storybook attitude toward her situation—"the Arabian Nights had quite closed round her" (p. 175)—than she might if she regarded her encounter with her father in a starker light. The same imaginative activity that we saw functioning before as a way of interpreting ambiguous signs also serves to assert her freedom. With the help of her imagination, Maisie can at least play at being a loving, dutiful daughter even if circumstances will not let her be one—although just those circumstances undermine her role as insecure and self-deceptive.

Because freedom can only strive from its grounded position, Maisie's struggles for possibility and care have dire consequences whenever they ignore the limits of her situation. The hidden sides that we saw her imagination misconstrue earlier are, to move from the epistemological to the existential, part of her thrownness that Maisie's projects either deny or do not comprehend adequately. The shocks that follow the breakdown of her diplomacy with Beale show that mere wishing for freedom and care ultimately closes off possibilities more than it discloses them.[38] Maisie's imagination paints her into a corner that she can only get out of by fleeing—by jumping into a cab and pretending that the "cluster of sovereigns" given her for the fare means "it was still at any rate the Arabian Nights" (p. 197). When she all too generously overlooks Beale's selfishness and romantically exaggerates her own competence, Maisie constructs a narrow, extravagant castle in the air for herself that denies her the openness to change that a better grounded freedom would provide. According to Binswanger, people who live in such "ethereal worlds" only increase their risk of disastrous disillusionment because the ground they deny does not vanish but lingers on as a "tomb world" ever ready to rise up unexpectedly with haunting specters.[39] The Countess's hideous, even terrifying appearance has metaphoric value as an ugly specter insisting on Beale's vulgar avarice and on the sordidness attached to any dealings with him, no matter what romantic yarns to the contrary Maisie might like to spin.

We should now be better able to see what I meant earlier by characterizing Mrs. Wix's vision of Maisie's dilemma as not only epistemologically naive but also existentially narrow. The young girl's only reliable—perhaps too insistently reliable—caretaker, Mrs. Wix shows a solicitude for Maisie's welfare that does not liberate the child's potentiality-for-Being.[40] Rather, despite her well-meaning motives, she dominates the girl with much the same stifling effect as the manipulations practiced by others with less righteous aims. Mrs. Wix is "a mother," which is "something Miss Overmore was not, something (strangely, confusingly) that mamma was even less" (p. 24). But she answers Maisie's needs just as little by smothering her with an allegiance that is likened to Mrs. Micawber's as Ida does by "impatiently giving the child a push" to get rid of her (p. 23). When she grills Maisie about her "moral sense," Mrs. Wix construes the "moral" not in an invigorating way that would facilitate freedom, responsibility, and care. On the contrary, she gives it a narrow, tyrannical definition that denies any possibility except the option of condemning or any freedom except the choice of a course of action that would advance her scheme of setting up an establishment with Sir Claude. Maisie's moral dilemma in the broadest sense is an existential dilemma that Mrs. Wix hurts more than helps. A victim of her own weakness for the "great garden of romance" (p. 27), she cannot help Maisie confront her situation openly and suspiciously, without imaginative extravagance. Understandably anxious to flee from her own unfed, unhoused, and unloved situation, Mrs. Wix is hardly the one to encourage Maisie to face her ground squarely and pursue freedom resolutely in a world where fleeing and covering up prevail everywhere.

Maisie can trust no one but herself to rescue her from her plight. But she makes an inauspicious beginning in the way she starts toward the climactic scene that opens her eyes and sets her feet back firmly on the ground of her situation. Although she leaves France enlightened at the end, she originally arrives there in a heady mist of imaginative extravagance. As our reading so far should have led us to expect, Maisie's commitment to a wish-world based on romantic interpretations reaches its most extreme in response to the most unsettling series of shocks and jolts. Maisie suffers the shock of confronting the Countess and fleeing in disarray, the upset of Susan Ash threatening a "revolution" in Mrs. Beale's household, and the jolt of Sir Claude unexpectedly and without explanation whisking the maid and the child away. She responds by inferring wishfully that Sir Claude has finally decided to disentangle himself from his affairs with her mother and stepmother. She imagines him bravely undertaking a noble "sacrifice" for "the real good of the little unfortunate" girl that would fulfill "Mrs. Wix's dream" that he care for both of them with "his errors renounced and his delinquencies redeemed" (p. 203). "Maisie's light little brain . . . hummed away hour after hour and caused the first outlook" on her situation "to swim in a softness of colour and sound" that revived "the spirit of their old happy times" and foretold "a promise of safety" in "the far-off white cliffs" across the Channel (pp. 204–7). On reaching Boulogne, Maisie loses herself "in the great ecstasy of a larger impression of life" (p. 231)—with the new horizons opened to her by the Continent's possibilities reaffirming her trust in the possibilities for her existence opened by her flights of interpretation. Maisie little suspects the fragility of her revelations about what France and Sir Claude hold in store for her. Sir Claude's silence about his motives forces Maisie to guess the meaning of the events overtaking her. But it also allows her to indulge in the wishful interpretations she loves to construct.

When Sir Claude declares "I'm free—I'm free" (p. 229), he mirrors Maisie's state of mind and shows himself equally engaged in an extravagant denial of limits. His "freedom," like hers, is not a consent to the necessity imposed by the conditions of his possibilities but a dream more wished for than secured. He may know more than Maisie about the reasons for their journey and the state of his affairs in London. But then he should know that his "freedom" is an escape—a flight from his involvements with Ida, Mrs. Wix, and Mrs. Beale, all women he was "simply afraid of" and "before whom he had undeniably quailed" (pp. 249–50). And indeed, "the agitation of his soul" (p. 230) when he insists he is "free" does hint at the weaknesses undermining his wishful declaration. He has good reason to feel worried because all of the dangers he is fleeing return to plague him. Ida asserts her still undiminished power by packing Mrs. Wix off to intimidate him, and Mrs. Beale then turns up to insist he has not seen the last of her either. These three women are all part of his thrownness because they represent past involvements that bear on his present situation. Together, they offer dramatic proof that our ground follows after us if we try to flee it. Maisie resorts to imaginative extravagance in a pitiably naive attempt to know her situation and embrace its possibilities, where Sir Claude resorts to flight in a better informed and more deliberate attempt to escape what he knows and to avoid possibilities eager to embrace him. Still, both make appropriate companions for each other because both are reaching for more freedom than their ground enables them to hold onto.

How do those so precariously overextended rescue themselves and then begin to establish a more grounded freedom? One starting point is the experience that existential theorists call "*Angst*" or "dread"—an anguish that confronts us with our thrownness by making us feel guilty for neglecting the claims of care and the responsibilities of freedom.[41] Maisie experiences an ultimately saving anguish when her dreams about Sir Claude and the Continent collapse. When Sir Claude puts it upon her to decide her fate—"*Can* you choose?"—she finds in "the coldness of her terror" that "she was afraid of herself" just as he was "afraid of himself" (pp. 338, 326). Maisie's "terror" is not "fear" in the strict sense of the word. According to Sartre, "fear is fear of beings in the world whereas anguish is anguish before myself."[42] Fear is directed toward an external object, and we may quite appropriately decide to flee the object of our fear in defense. Maisie's "terror" is "anguish" because she herself is the object of her own anxiety. "Afraid of herself," Maisie feels anguish about her ability to exercise her freedom by choosing how to care for herself and others. Unlike fear, if we respond to anguish by fleeing, we are only deceiving ourselves because the object of our anxiety necessarily comes right along with us. In their anguish, Maisie and Sir Claude face a crisis that calls upon them to confront the responsibilities for deciding their existence with a new seriousness.

Sir Claude, of course, wants to flee his anguish by letting Maisie decide for him between the claims of Mrs. Beale and Mrs. Wix. He seems to hope that she will agree to abandon the governess and go along with her stepparents. But such a scheme would hardly fulfill Maisie's dreams of living happily ever after under the safety of his care, undisturbed by the manipulations directed at her or him. The choice Sir Claude presents her with would rob her once again of her freedom to choose. By accepting either of its alternatives—staying with Mrs. Wix or joining her stepparents—she would continue to allow others to decide her future for her while retaining for herself only the freedom to accommodate herself to what they have chosen. She would retain little more than her by now much discredited freedom of imagination. Still, what can Maisie choose that would fulfill her demands for freedom, possibility, and care without extravagantly exceeding what her situation offers? She had decided earlier that she would settle for "him alone or nobody" (p. 309). But how can she expect Sir Claude and Mrs. Beale to react to this stipulation, and can she trust herself to bear the consequences of making this demand?

With no clearly adequate choice before her, Maisie understandably prefers to avoid forcing a crisis that might permanently dash her hopes—a crisis that would confront her with the unpromising conditions that her wish-world had tried to evade. "If they were afraid of themselves it was themselves they would find at the inn" (p. 342) where the potential crisis revealed by their (but particularly her) anguish awaits them in the persons of Mrs. Beale and Mrs. Wix. But as Maisie and Sir Claude roam restlessly about town, postponing the dreaded confrontation, their anguish is brought back to them at the railroad station when the child says "I wish we could go" on the Paris train; then, realizing that this wish might offer an escape route for following her dreams, Maisie urges Sir Claude to take her away: "*Prenny, prenny. Oh prenny!*" (pp. 344–45). "You *have* chosen then?" Sir Claude asks, thinking she had agreed to Mrs. Beale's terms. But Maisie wishes to be swept off to Paris on the original terms she imagined herself under. She wants, without being forced to choose, to be carried along by events in a flight that would avoid the crisis she feels unable to meet. Still, unlike Sir Claude, she comes to realize the futility of such escapes as an answer to her anguish about herself and her situation. After the train leaves without them, Maisie understands that "she had had a real fright but had fallen back to earth. The odd thing was that in her fall her fear too had been dashed down and broken. It was gone," although Sir Claude's was not (p. 345). After a final flight of wishful thinking, Maisie understands the hopelessness of dreaming away troubles instead of confronting her situation with the resoluteness her anguish demands.

Maisie meets her crisis by embracing it as a turning point for her existence. With "fine appreciation" for a courage he lacks, Sir Claude exclaims over how Maisie "made her condition—with such a sense of what it should be! She made the only right one" (p. 356). Her "condition," of course, is that she will give up Mrs. Wix as he asks if he will give up Mrs. Beale. Instead of allowing herself to be chosen for by accepting the alternatives he had presented, Maisie asserts her freedom to choose for herself by proposing her own alternative—one that transcends the limits of his original proposition and thus comments on its inadequacy. Moreover, instead of dreaming idly about reaching some safe haven of care and freedom with Sir Claude, she shows by disclosing her "condition" that she is willing to struggle to see whether such a goal is a possibility within the limits of her situation, since pretending it is has not made it so. Eschewing the extravagance of imaginative interpretations, she presents her "condition" as a test of what she would like to believe possible for Sir Claude, whose weaknesses she is learning to recognize but also seems willing to accept if he will stop fleeing from situations and commit himself seriously to her. Maisie does not seek to dominate him; rather, she proposes a liberating, mutually reciprocal relation when she offers to choose him if he will choose her and to care for him if he will care for her. Maisie's offer would put an end to Mrs. Beale's and Mrs. Wix's practice of manipulating her choices for her and his choices for him. Her "condition" asserts the freedom of each to choose for herself and himself.

Although not equal to such existential heroics himself, Sir Claude does show care for Maisie by protecting her from the vengeance of the two women her "condition" defies—that is, by "facing the loud adversaries" and insisting that "she's free—she's free" (pp. 358–59). Perhaps secure in the realization that Maisie's choice, since it cannot bind him, allows him to continue fleeing his own anguish, Sir Claude nonetheless recognizes as no one else does that "something still deeper than a moral sense" was showing itself in the child's heroics:

"I don't know what to call it—I haven't even known how decently to deal with it, to approach it; but, whatever it is, it's the most beautiful thing I've ever met—it's exquisite, it's sacred" (p. 354). His insistence on the beautiful sacredness of Maisie's freedom differs from his own feeble declaration of freedom earlier; she, unlike him, takes freedom as a task that demands struggling with adversity. Although she fails to win the terms her "condition" had desired, she succeeds in clarifying her situation by forcing everyone to declare the degree of their willingness to accommodate themselves to a choice of hers and by forcing herself to consent to the necessity imposed by these declarations. She thus overcomes, at least for the moment, the mystifying opacity of the Other that we saw at work before. She loses Sir Claude, but her hope for him was simply "the last flare of her dream" (p. 352). Without dreams and without illusions, "she was afraid of nothing" and found that "bewilderment had simply gone or at any rate was going fast" (pp. 352, 357). Maisie can feel self-confident and no longer anguished because she has freely chosen to decide her own future by seriously questioning the limits to her possibilities and by resolutely resigning herself to what that questioning discloses.

Now admittedly, Maisie's horizons do not look particularly bright when she crosses back over the Channel with Mrs. Wix at the end. Mrs. Beale cannot be completely denied when she questions the meaning of the freedom Sir Claude claims Maisie has won: "Free to starve with this pauper lunatic?" (p. 359). Sir Claude cannot be trusted to carry out his promise to keep a watchful, caring eye on Maisie. Still, in a world where care has lapsed, consenting to the necessity that hardly anyone cares may be a necessary condition for confronting one's own responsibilities for taking care of one's own potentiality-for-Being. By leaving Maisie *en l'air* at the finish, with the question unresolved of what the child will make for the future of the crisis she has experienced, James shows that no one can determine in advance what will become of us since the task of deciding our existence is one we are never finished with. Maisie certainly will not let Mrs. Wix appropriate any more of her decisions for her. By demonstrating the courage Mrs. Wix lacks to "look back" at the balcony for Sir Claude and to accept that he has deserted her because "he wasn't there" (p. 363), Maisie has firmly established the ascendancy of her resolve and her understanding over that woman's timidity and blindness. "What Maisie knew" is that she holds her existence in her own hands and that she must not follow Sir Claude in trying to avoid that burden. Having taken a critical stance toward her ground and having learned to brave the worst it could impose on her, she goes back to London more open to her real possibilities than she was when she came to France dreaming of unreal possibilities. For Maisie, knowing the worst with certainty is the epistemological triumph that gives her existence a firmer foundation than it has ever had before.

The open ending of the novel also calls for reflection about Maisie's social world. By returning his heroine to England and casting her adrift there to fend for herself, James encourages his readers to imagine for themselves the conditions that lie beyond Maisie's horizons—conditions that extend indeterminately but ominously beyond what his ending specifies. Maisie's bleak prospects remind us that such aspects of experience as knowing, freedom, and care, although universal in structure, are always situated in particular social and historical circumstances. The child's isolation, attenuated only by the cold comfort of companionship with Mrs. Wix, emphasizes what the novel has suggested from the beginning—that the conventions and institutions in her social world do not perform well in their fundamental function as mediators designed to hold people together despite their differences and their mutual opacity. The conventions of marriage provide a way of structuring the relation between Self and Other, institutionalizing a collectively sanctioned mode of care. Even the laws and procedures of divorce are an exercise in mediation—an attempt to regulate the conflict between selves and to restrain its potential violence. In Maisie's world, however, mediation seems to fail as often as it succeeds. Although not the total anarchy that the absence of all mediation could bring, her world is constantly threatened by battles for power and self-interest; these battles use the conventions governing marriage and divorce as occasions for conflict and weapons in their strategies and not as means for preserving the community. Maisie herself has often served as a mediator between her parents and stepparents. As a "shuttlecock" accustomed to bounding back and forth between contesting parties, however, Maisie is usually a negative rather than a positive mediator, helpless to create the conditions of care she longs for because she is employed as a means in the selfish schemes of others. Although she has finally extricated herself at the end from the battles that have devastated her childhood, her liberation gives her not harmony and love but loneliness and isolation. As the novel closes, the question remains whether the world beyond her horizons will allow her to find the care she has sought for so long.

FOUR

James the epistemological novelist and James the moral dramatist complement and complete each other because, as Maisie's story shows from beginning to end, dilemmas with knowing and existential trials are inseparable. Again and again, epistemological dilemmas that we first explored from the perspective of phenomenology reappeared in existential form when we turned our attention to the crises she faces in freedom and care. This recurrence demonstrated the inextricable unity of knowing in James and his "moral" concerns—concerns that reflect a deep awareness of the dilemmas involved in such areas of existence as freedom, limitation, and our relations with others.

A moral vision deeper than Mrs. Wix's moral sense emerges in Maisie at the end. As we saw, Mrs. Wix understands ethical responsibility as the duty to condemn whatever violates certain principles of good and evil. But as we also saw, Maisie's difficulties are not confined to the challenge of learning to make ethical judgments. Her "moral" trials include the dilemmas of discovering how to find a meaningful freedom within the limits that bind her and how to establish caring relations with others in a world where care has lapsed. Maisie's epistemological struggles also have a moral dimension, inasmuch as learning how to know her bewildering world adequately is an integral part of discovering how to conduct herself properly. These are still ethical dilemmas where normative standards can be applied—where right and wrong can still be judged if only because, as Maisie gradually finds out, some ways of approaching her difficulties with knowing, freedom, and care are more appropriate than others to the problems and possibilities inherent in those areas of existence. Mrs. Wix invokes an extrinsic set of norms that prescribe rigid criteria for proper conduct. But the normative standards that apply to Maisie's epistemological and existential trials are intrinsic rather than extrinsic because they derive not from a fixed set of principles but from the conditions that the structure of experience sets for adequate knowing, responsible freedom, and genuine care. These standards are flexible rather than rigid, inasmuch as they will vary with the circumstances of every individual's project of being-in-the-world. This variability is the source, indeed, of much of the moral complexity and ambiguity for which James's novels are so well known.

Amplifying and refining the view of James suggested by my reading of *Maisie*, the chapters that follow will chart in greater detail the relations that join his epistemological and moral concerns. Carrying further my inquiry into James's understanding of consciousness, Chapter 2 will focus on "The Art of Fiction" in order to examine the "impression" as a way of knowing and to consider its implications for his theory of the novel. The analysis of *Roderick Hudson* in Chapter 3 will explore further James's awareness of the wonders and dangers of the imaginative extravagance that Maisie often succumbs to. My study of her difficulties in establishing a well-grounded freedom gave a preview of the more extensive examination in Chapter 4 of the relation between possibility and limitation in *The Portrait of a Lady*. The theme of the analysis of *The Golden Bowl* in Chapter 5 will be the epistemological dilemma of intersubjectivity and the existential crisis of care. Power, mediation, and the relation of individual experience to its social context will be the main topics in my reading of *The Spoils of Poynton* in Chapter 6.

The organization of my study reflects what I consider the five major aspects of experience for both James and phenomenology—again: consciousness, the imagination, freedom, personal relations, and our relation to social history. We could, however, draw different lines across the field of experience. Existence does not divide itself naturally into separate compartments. I have therefore marked out categories deliberately with an eye toward James's major concerns. These divisions identify issues and themes that his many readers agree, often with the support of James's own testimony, figure prominently in the way his work organizes itself. Moving from the private realm of consciousness outward toward the public stage of politics and society, the categories I have chosen describe the range of James's vision as an epistemological novelist and a moral dramatist. But these five aspects of experience also represent major concerns of phenomenology that might suggest themselves independently. They are areas of inquiry that assert their importance for phenomenology by the frequency of their recurrence in its meditations on our experience as knowing and doing beings.

For both James and phenomenology, all of these aspects of experience are unified because they participate in the dynamics of transcendence that underlie existence as a whole. Heidegger calls existence fundamentally transcendent because we are always beyond ourselves—always "*sich vorweg*" in his terms, always outside and ahead of ourselves as we project ourselves toward our worlds and anticipate our future in the process of becoming ourselves.[43] Following Heidegger, Sartre identifies this process of "going beyond" as the factor that distinguishes the "for itself" of human existence from the rest of Being—from what he calls the "in itself" because it cannot transcend itself.[44] Husserl's dictum that all consciousness is consciousness of something means that acts of knowing always direct themselves toward an object. Because the thing-itself eludes the grasp of our intentional acts, we can have an object only in a certain "aspect"—that is, from a single position at one moment which reveals that object in a particular, partial perspective. Knowing involves transcendence not only spatially but also temporally, then, since consciousness points beyond itself toward its objects and ahead of itself to future acts that will confirm or deny our expectations about their hidden sides. Perception may be "*sich vorweg*," but then the imagination is so even more. We are never further ahead of and beyond ourselves than when we leave our real, everyday worlds to enter the unreal world of the imagination where we can exercise freely our powers to create meanings and project possibilities, unconstrained by the resistances of actuality.

Like consciousness and the imagination, freedom is essentially transcendent. Although our possibilities are limited by the situation we find ourselves in, they are what they are—potential rather than actual—because they lie beyond it. We have possibilities because we enjoy the ability to transcend our current conditions and project ourselves into the future, if always on the basis of constraints inherited from the past. Transcendence and its limits similarly contribute to the vicissitudes of personal relations. The Other is somewhat opaque to me because his world lies beyond my horizons. I know him from the outside, according to his Self-for-Others, but not from the inside, within his Self-for-Himself. We can still move out of ourselves toward others, though, through acts of understanding and sympathy that can reduce the gap between us even if they cannot eliminate it. Finally, our relation to social history is defined by transcendence as well. We are social beings because our engagement with the world involves us with groups beyond our individual existence. As we study the various aspects of experience in James and phenomenology, we shall be examining various forms that transcendence can take in human existence.

The aspects of experience that are particularly significant for James and phenomenology can also be regarded as James's "intentional foundations" because of their importance in the way his artistic world organizes itself. This term does not refer to what James had in mind self-consciously when he wrote his fiction and criticism. As I pointed out earlier, the phenomenological notion of intentionality does not coincide with the customary understanding of "intention" as someone's deliberate purpose. A work of art bears witness to the subjectivity that originated it, but it does not offer direct, unmediated access to the consciousness of its author. James's works do not necessarily tell us about his biography. Rather, the worlds of his works testify to and form part of the world he inhabits as an artist—that world of his art as a whole whose consistent pattern of meanings and values enables us to recognize different works as part of the same overall project, at one with itself even over changes that mark the evolution of his career.

"Intentional foundations" are the assumptions and rules of operation that govern the creation of meaning in an artist's world. The intentional activity of consciousness, although inherently free, does not occur haphazardly but instead follows certain patterns that we can identify after the fact. We develop certain habits of thinking and acting as we generate meaning in our worlds. These "intentional foundations" form the "intentional arc," to borrow Merleau-Ponty's phrase, which supports and unifies our worlds.[45] We have unified worlds to the extent that the assumptions and rules of operation in one area of our existence imply and agree with the assumptions and rules of operation in other areas. This further explains the unity of knowing and doing that we have already demonstrated on other grounds. James has a unified view of the aspects of experience not only because he understands experience as a unified field but also because he himself has a unified world—because, that is, his epistemological assumptions imply and agree with his assumptions about the imagination, freedom, personal relations, and the politics of our experience as social beings.[46]

The conceptual framework that guides my study of James repre-

sents a departure from traditional approaches to his canon. But the
issues that this framework hopes to clarify—the unity of knowing and
doing in James, the relation between his fascination with consciousness and his moral vision—belong to the mainstream of the critical
heritage. A list of critics of consciousness in James reads like a history of great moments in the appreciation of his achievement: J. W.
Beach on the relation between James's concern with the inward life
and his ethical considerations, Percy Lubbock on "point of view,"
F. O. Matthiessen on "the art of reflection" and "the religion of consciousness," and Leon Edel on psychological realism.[47] Equally eminent moral critics like F. W. Dupee and Dorothea Krook have acknowledged the epistemological foundations of Jamesian ethics.[48] If
this is an obvious and well-trodden area of inquiry, that is only because it is so important. These and other critics who will be acknowledged as we proceed have helped set the tasks this book undertakes.
It seeks less to blaze new trails for James criticism than to help us
move a bit further down paths already charted. What will matter is
whether a phenomenological perspective can help illuminate concerns already well established as important by the critical tradition
built up around James—by describing his understanding of consciousness more fully, for example, or by establishing more systematically the relationship between knowing and doing in James's
world.

    Precedent already exists for taking a philosophical approach to
James. It is a mixed precedent, though, which shows the dangers as
well as the justification of such an approach. J. H. Raleigh, for example, goes so far as to contend that James is more a "metaphysician"
than a psychologist, that "his characters are not human beings but
meaning-functions" in a "system" based on "certain theoretical assumptions."[49] Raleigh then claims to show that the philosophical assumptions of John Locke and the British empiricists provide the key
that unlocks the elaborate metaphysical metaphor that constitutes
James's achievement. There is also Quentin Anderson who has pic-
tured James as the poet of his father's theology and has discovered
a unified Swedenborgian allegory in the three great novels of the
master's major phase.[50] Raleigh is guilty of the reductionism that
threatens all interdisciplinary approaches if they fail to restrain their
method with a respect for the aesthetic integrity of their subject. Although the characters in a novel are not incarnate, ontologically au-

tonomous human beings, they have nonetheless been endowed with a kind of quasi-subjectivity that we as readers bring to life by animating their worlds with our own powers of consciousness. Anderson is too sensitive a reader to commit Raleigh's error, but he shows the danger of a similar one-sidedness in the exaggerated claims he makes for his reading.

Both of these critics do show, however, that a philosophical approach can illuminate an artist's place in his cultural, literary, and intellectual history. We can, no doubt, better understand James's overall significance if we understand his relation to British empiricism and to his father's theology, with its connections in turn to New England transcendentalism and other intellectual movements of the period. By the same token, understanding James's relation to the phenomenological tradition should contribute to defining his place in cultural history.[51] The relations between texts are as legitimate an area of inquiry as the texts themselves. Furthermore, because understanding is inherently diacritical—a process of determining what something is by defining what it is not—intertextual study can often help to illuminate the specific identity of the work in its own right. The belief that extrinsic approaches necessarily detract from intrinsic considerations is an unwarranted prejudice.

Unfortunately, asking philosophical questions of Henry James strikes some as suspect. Their doubts would seem to draw support from James himself, who found his own mind "as receptive . . . of any scrap of enacted story or evoked picture as it was closed to the dry or the abstract proposition."[52] Krook rejects the value of a philosophical approach to James, for example, because she denies that his "view of reality and its essential logic" derive

> from anywhere, or anybody, in particular: neither from Hegel, nor F. H. Bradley, nor from his brother William's Pragmatism, nor (least of all) from his father's Swedenborgian system. I have supposed he took it from the ambient air of nineteenth-century speculation, whose main current was the preoccupation with the phenomenon of self-consciousness.[53]

Krook seems justifiably concerned with the dangers of reductionism and exaggeration that threaten interdisciplinary approaches. She seems concerned too, and rightly so, that James's intellectual debts and relationships not obscure his unique identity and achievement.

These are reasons for proceeding with caution, of course, but not for abandoning philosophy altogether. James himself noted that "imaginative writers of the first order always give us an impression that they have a kind of philosophy." And he claimed that "the great question as to a poet or a novelist is, How does he feel about life? what, in the last analysis, is his philosophy?"[54] Existential phenomenology can help us answer that question about Henry James.

• 2 •

KNOWING IN JAMES:

THE IMPRESSION AND

THE ART OF FICTION

O N E

Consciousness in James is the first of his "intentional foundations" and the first aspect of experience that we must consider. To ask about James's understanding of consciousness is to inquire into what the "impression" means for him as a way of knowing. For him, this word carries a multitude of meanings and references. In "The Art of Fiction," James calls the novel "a personal, a direct impression of life."[1] In the creative process, according to James, a work of fiction begins with the author's impressions. Then, in the reading process, it achieves the ends of representation by evoking impressions in its audience. In the work itself, when he pleads for economy of construction, James asks above all that a novel adhere to "unity of impression"[2] as its principle of composition. Further, in his own fictions, James's heroes and heroines have dramas because they have impressions; indeed, their dramas are their impressions. And he tells their stories by relating the impressions of observers, registers, or reflectors who constitute a work's aesthetic center by acting as its center of consciousness. If James is an epistemological novelist, tireless in his wonder at the workings of consciousness, then this abiding concern with the process of knowing shows itself in the importance he assigns to the "impression" as a broadly significant category, applicable in a wide variety of contexts. James's understanding of the "impression" is the key to his understanding of experience as a whole. Its way of knowing leads him to develop a phenomenological theory of representation as well as an existential aesthetic of value.

We do not transform James from an artist into a philosopher, however, when we study the "impression" in light of phenomenology. James always engages troublesome issues of epistemology and aesthetics with an artistic intuition that leads him to frame his responses in polyvalent expressions rather than in the straightforward, univocal propositions of most philosophy. This practice has misled some into faulting the novelist for a lack of rigor, as Hazard Adams does when he discounts "the theoretical value of the pronouncements" in "The Art of Fiction" because James "is not very precise about the meaning of his terms."[3] More like art than philosophy, though, James's observations about knowing in literature and life hold multiple levels of meaning that require active interpretation to disclose their controlling presuppositions and underlying unity.

We shall begin with a prolonged meditation on consciousness in James that aims to bring this kind of interpretation to his many descriptions of what the "impression" means as a way of knowing. Then, more briefly, we shall take up two implications of James's epistemology for his understanding of the art of fiction—namely, his theory of representation and his position on the aesthetic value of the novel. These two implications of the Jamesian "impression" will point the way toward the other aspects of experience that we shall consider, in due course, in light of his understanding of consciousness.

T W O

An artist even when an epistemologist, James reveals most about his theory of the impression when he tells it as a story. Let us listen, then, to his story in "The Art of Fiction" about how Anne Thackeray Ritchie came to know French Protestant youth through an impression that inspired her first novel, *The Story of Elizabeth*:[4]

> I remember an English novelist, a woman of genius, telling me
> that she was much commended for the impression she had man-
> aged to give in one of her tales of the nature and way of life of
> the French Protestant youth. She had been asked where she
> learned so much about this recondite being, she had been con-
> gratulated on her peculiar opportunities. These opportunities
> consisted in her having once, in Paris, as she ascended a stair-
> case, passed an open door where, in the household of a *pas-*

teur, some of the young Protestants were seated at a table round a finished meal. The glimpse made a picture; it lasted only a moment, but that moment was experience. She had got her direct personal impression, and she turned out her type. She knew what youth was, and what Protestantism; she also had the advantage of having seen what it was to be French, so that she converted these ideas into a concrete image and produced a reality. Above all, however, she was blessed with the faculty which when you give it an inch takes an ell, and which for the artist is a much greater source of strength than any accident of residence or of place in the social scale. The power to guess the unseen from the seen, to trace the implication of things, to judge the whole piece by the pattern, the condition of feeling life in general so completely that you are well on your way to knowing any particular corner of it—this cluster of gifts may almost be said to constitute experience. . . . If experience consists of impressions, it may be said that impressions *are* experience, just as (have we not seen it?) they are the very air we breathe. (*PP*, pp. 388–89)

Once again insisting on a broad use for his term, James describes how the "impression" Ritchie gives in representation depends on the "direct personal impression" she receives in her chance glimpse of a pastor's household. Our first question must be: How does Ritchie's "impression" on the staircase enable her to know French Protestant youth?

Her example shows that, in James's view, the impression has almost miraculous revelatory power. He tells Ritchie's story to emphasize how her one fleeting impression of a French Protestant group reveals to her so much insight about her subject that everyone at once attributes it to fortunate research and not to a single, almost accidental perception. Ritchie may already have known "what youth was, and what Protestantism" as well as "what it was to be French." But in one act of perception she goes far beyond what she knew before and even what the scene itself would seem to contain. Nevertheless, her transcendent powers of revelation are simply an extreme instance of the general workings of consciousness as both James and phenomenology understand them. The extremity of her case highlights characteristics of consciousness that usually go unnoticed in ordinary acts of know-

ing. According to Heidegger, understanding is always "ahead of itself" (*sich vorweg*) in a revelatory manner. Understanding clears the
way for interpretation by disclosing possibilities that explication then
lays out thematically.[5] Ritchie's impression projects her ahead of herself, then, to disclose possibilities about the pastor's household that
she extrapolates from the scene before her with the help of her prior
stores of knowledge. Her rendition of her impression is an explication
of those possibilities—making explicit what she assumes to be implicit on the horizons of what she observes.

Similarly, in acts of knowing described in James's fictions, Isabel
Archer and Lambert Strether are ahead of themselves when their early
impressions of Europe promise an enthralling enlargement of experience. We have already seen how Maisie gets ahead of herself with her
many guesses about hidden sides. Everyone's impressions have the
potential for revelation that Ritchie exploits, but an artist makes the
most of what the ordinary structure of perception offers. According to
James, "a man of genius" differs from the norm because his mind
"takes to itself the faintest hints of life, it converts the very pulses of
the air into revelations" (*PP*, p. 388). The impression is teleological
and futural. The teleology of the impression reflects what I have described as the fundamental transcendence of existence—that process
of "going beyond" thanks to which we are always outside and ahead of
ourselves as we project ourselves toward our worlds and anticipate our
future. The impression's revelatory power comes from its teleological
impulse.

We must still clarify, though, precisely how the impression's teleological impulse triumphs over the many handicaps that would seem
to prevent Ritchie from knowing much, if anything, about the group
she observes. Although she acquires an intimate acquaintance with
French Protestant youth, her knowledge derives from an impression
achieved as an outside observer at a distance (physical as well as social, economic, and psychological) from the scene she perceives. She
begins with a limited and not panoramic view. She sees a dinner gathering that can serve at most as a sample of her subject, and she only
sees that sample in one pose, from one side, at one angle, in one moment. Ritchie's attempt "to guess the unseen from the seen, to trace
the implication of things, to judge the whole piece by the pattern"
might seem to run the risk of solipsistic delusion. As we shall see,
though, James does nothing more here than accept certain necessary

limits to perception that phenomenology's theory of consciousness can help to explain.

Ritchie's distance from the group expresses symbolically the epistemological dilemma posed by the transcendence of any object to any perceiver. She glances at the gathering from the staircase and never even enters the room where the diners sit. She does not come into contact with them except through her impression. In Kant's terms, she knows them phenomenally, as given to her in an impression, but not noumenally, as things-in-themselves. When we direct our attention toward an object—like the group Ritchie sees around a finished meal—we know that object only as an intentional object correlated to the intentional acts that evoke it. Just as Ritchie's impression points toward the group at the table but never reaches them, so the intentional activity of consciousness creates nothing but "empty intentions" that aim at objects without possessing them. The "real" may be, as Peirce argues, "that whose characters are independent of what anybody may think them to be."[6] But, he adds, since we can know the "real" only through some mediation like the impression or the phenomenon, we cannot claim to know it with absolute certainty but must instead regard it as an ultimate limit to strive toward. Consequently, according to William James, all observations about reality, truth, and meaning should frame themselves within the limits of the "hypothetic words *may be*."[7] Ritchie seems to concede the gulf between herself and her transcendent object at the same time as she tries to bridge it, then, when she accepts the aegis of the "may be" in order to spin out hypotheses about the reality of French Protestant youth—hypotheses that follow from the teleological impulse of her original impression.

Because of the object's transcendence, all perception is a leap of faith. Ritchie's impression of French Protestant youth may have led her into illusion, but she is entitled to act as if it has not until her trust proves misplaced. Again, Isabel Archer, Lambert Strether, and Maisie all take similar epistemological leaps of faith by trusting what their impressions seem to reveal, although in each case with less fortunate consequences than Ritchie. Indeed, as we shall see, the faith required by phenomenal knowing is a theme of central, never-ending interest for James. Ritchie could find justification for her faith in William James's insistence that "we have the right to believe at our own risk any hypothesis that is live enough to tempt our will." Always aware that the challenge of epistemological faith requires "courage weighted with responsibility," he warns against "the opposite dangers of believing too little or of believing too much" and admonishes that "with 'real' objects . . . consequences always accrue."[8] But he also insists that if nothing is risked, then nothing is gained. In his story about Ritchie, Henry James shows he agrees with his brother about the value of risks. Undaunted by the transcendence of her object, Ritchie converts an apparently debilitating limit of perception into an enabling, even invigorating, possibility by demonstrating that the impression's power depends on the faith of the observer.

Faith thrives on stumbling blocks. But faith in the impression's power to reveal must still account for Ritchie's ability to gain such encompassing knowledge from such a limited perspective on the scene she observes. Because the thing-itself is ultimately unattainable, no act of perception can deliver more than incomplete access to anything. Since "the ipseity" (or ultimate being) of the thing is "never reached," Merleau-Ponty argues, "each aspect of the thing which falls to our perception is still only an invitation to perceive beyond it, still only a momentary halt in the perceptual process."[9] The cultural object constituted by "French Protestant youth" has, of course, a more complex "ipseity" than more mundane objects like the furnishings in the room where the pastor and his friends sit. But no single impression could give Ritchie a view of even their table except in one pose, from one side, at one angle, in one moment. Analyzed phenomenologically,

> each act of perception seizes the perceived object only in a
> certain respect. Expressed in a correlated way, any perceptible
> thing is always perceived from a determined standpoint, a well-
> defined viewpoint. . . . The perceived gives itself in and
> through the act of perception only by means of profiles (*Ab-
> schattungen*) which are correlated to a determined attitude and
> standpoint of the perceiver.[10]

Ritchie's impression gives the group she perceives in just such a "profile." Or, to apply another word often used to translate Husserl's term "*Abschattung*" but one that also belongs to James's vocabulary, her impression is an "aspect" constituted by her standpoint as the perceiver, the position of the object thus open to her gaze, and the creative attention she brings to this occasion. The open doorway in front of her frames the scene in a way that emphasizes the perspectival quality of her impression and highlights the structure of an "aspect." Positioned on the staircase, she sees a figure against a background whose horizons recede beyond her grasp. What lies behind this after-dinner gathering, and what lies ahead of it? Her view gives her what James calls elsewhere a "foreshortened image"[11] of her subject. The "marked inveteracy of a certain indirect and oblique view"[12] of people, places, and things in his fiction derives from James's fascination with this perspectival relation between the knower and the known and shows his respect for the inevitable incompleteness of perception by aspects.

Ritchie fills out her knowledge of French Protestant youth by taking advantage of the way in which an aspect points beyond itself toward the fulfillment in more complete knowledge that further aspects would provide. What Merleau-Ponty calls the aspect's "invitation to perceive beyond it" is the dynamic that impels the teleology of the impression and that lends it the power to reveal more than it contains. Heidegger's analysis of the relation between understanding and interpretation develops out of Husserl's argument that, in perception, "every actuality involves its potentialities." Every aspect displays "the 'genuinely perceived' sides of the object of perception," he explains, but these in turn refer "to the sides 'also meant'—not yet perceived, but only anticipated" on the "horizon" that delimits that perspective. "We can ask any horizon what 'lies in it,' we can explicate or unfold it, and 'uncover' the potentialities" it holds that other aspects could actualize to fulfill our knowledge.[13] Briefly stated, then, every aspect implies "a quasi-infinite series" of "different but harmonious aspects" that would "confirm, complement, and perfect one another."[14]

All of this helps to explain the miracle of Ritchie's epistemological faith—to justify how she can know so much about something she knows so little. When she spins out her hypotheses about French Protestant youth, she is simply following up the possibilities suggested by the perspectival structure of her impression. She imaginatively envisions all the other aspects implied by the aspect she has as its continuation and, in this way, explicates the horizons of her impression to uncover what lies behind this dinner gathering and what lies ahead. Her general knowledge about youth, Protestants, and the French comes into play here to help her explicate this particular aspect's horizons because we base our assumptions about an object's unknown hidden sides on our knowledge about the sides of similar objects we are better acquainted with—because, that is, our acquaintance with objects in the present and our expectations about them in the future grow out of our experiences with them in the past as part of the ongoing temporal process of their unfolding in aspects.

To the extent that Ritchie's impression explicates her prior stores of experience, it is not only an act of perception; it is also, at the same time, an act of self-examination. By drawing on her own resources to complete the scene before her, she thematizes and brings into the open aspects of herself that may have hitherto been unformulated and unrecognized. Imaginative acts of seeing are thus for James one way of transforming unreflective experience into conscious awareness. Ritchie's story implies that the challenge of understanding others can lead to growth in self-understanding. As we shall see with Isabel Archer and Maggie Verver, for whom unexpected impressions of their spouses give rise to more explicit and extensive self-recognition than Ritchie achieves, the act of knowing becomes an occasion for self-knowledge when indeterminacies and anomalies compel the perceiver to turn inward to examine his or her own consciousness and memory. Consciousness is never far from self-consciousness for James.

Of course, Ritchie might stand on surer ground if she could undertake further acts of perception to test the hypothetical aspects she generates imaginatively. But her success in working out the implications of her impression's horizons on so little evidence only goes to show the strength of the test of harmony and agreement that we all apply in everyday perception to assure ourselves of the identity of objects given us in a variety of aspects. Where we recognize an identical object from two different perspectives if both of these aspects harmonize and agree, Ritchie reverses the process and comes up with a variety of aspects that her object might have since they harmonize and agree with her original perspective. James's concern with displaying his subjects through "the multiplication of aspects"—and with giving these a certain "consistency" while "making them amusingly various" (AN, p. 90)—is the correlative in his theory of fiction to Husserl's theory of aspects. Neither James's notion of the impression nor Husserl's theory of aspects guarantees certain and complete knowledge, since neither abolishes the possibility of error, incomplete perception, or extravagant speculation. Quite the contrary, all of these possibilities are not only allowed but explained. But both theories do shed light on the extraordinary power coupled with inherent weakness that characterizes phenomenal knowing.

So far I have tried to explain the workings of the impression by comparing it with ordinary perception. But James's theory of the impression does more than merely account for how the strengths of phenomenal knowing overcome certain limits to perception. Rather, James positively revels at those limits as an opportunity for the imagination to show off its special powers. Although Ritchie's example indicates that imagination participates even in ordinary perception, James invokes her case not to show that she can consequently discover by imagination what empirical testing would reveal just as well but, instead, to contend that imagination enables her to discover more. She illustrates "that odd law which somehow always makes the minimum of valid suggestion serve the man [or woman] of imagination better than the maximum" (*AN*, p. 161). In his own artistic practice, James wanted life to give him only "the germ"—"the prick of inoculation" (*AN*, pp. 120, 121) that would set his imagination to work. As Blackmur observes, James "never wanted all the facts, which might stupefy him, but only enough to go on with, hardly enough to seem a fact at all" (*AN*, p. xv). James always feared the danger of being overwhelmed by "the fatal futility of Fact" because too much information, too full a report would only smother the "tiny nugget" of suggestion he wanted (*AN*, pp. 122, 120). For him, the imaginative knowing that he and Ritchie practice has greater power than any empirical, literal-minded approach. It is better able to reveal the essence of what something really is because an overwhelming abundance of facts can do more to obscure that essence than to display it.

James takes a stand in line with phenomenology when he claims certain privileges for the imagination over a naive empiricism in disclosing the essence of something. When he applies his imagination to a "germ," James engages in an activity with a method and goal similar to Husserl's "eidetic reduction." The "eidos" is the essence of the thing beyond "the realm of facts" or "the world of realities"—"the immutable and necessary complex of characteristics without which the thing cannot be conceived." Husserl's "reduction" is a method of grasping this essence by *imagining* "what changes can be made" on "an arbitrarily perceived or fancied individual sample of this or that kind of thing . . . without making it cease to be the thing it is."[15] Much like Ritchie when she imagines what other aspects follow from the necessary structure of the aspect she has on her sample of French Protestant youth, the phenomenologist practicing Husserl's reduction would spin out an imagined series of aspects on the thing under study to determine the "invariant" that unites them as aspects belonging to an identical object. Unlike James, Ritchie, or any other artist, the phenomenologist undertakes this reduction in the hope of finding formulas to express the ultimate presuppositions that govern our engagement with the world. But this philosophical enterprise finds an interesting artistic correlative in James's attempt to discover a truth that expresses the essence of reality at a level more fundamental than the empirical. James would agree with Virginia Woolf that Mr. Bennett never learns the secret of Mrs. Brown when he concentrates literally and unimaginatively on the facts of her case. Like Woolf—and thus both like Husserl—James claims that "the great thing is to be *saturated* with something" (*Letters*, 1:142) in an exercise of the imagination that does not deny the empirical but is more profound. The echoes of Coleridge in James's phrase are appropriate, since Coleridge's theory of imagination describes an intuition of the thing's essence in the manner of the phenomenological reduction. In any case, James and Husserl both agree—one implicitly and the other explicitly— that we must suspend what phenomenology calls "the natural attitude" of blind engagement with the world of fact before we can get to the truth at the heart of reality.

The paradox, of course, is that the essence of any state of affairs is still only knowable indirectly—that is, phenomenally, on the same inessential level as ordinary reality. Some phenomenologists, including Husserl at certain points in his career, have lapsed into idealism by insufficiently acknowledging this paradox and by hoping, consequently, to uncover a quasi-Platonic realm of transcendental forms.[16] The "reduction" cannot take place without a phenomenologist who, in turn, cannot intuit an "eidos" except as a phenomenon. Ritchie may have "a personal, a direct impression" of French Protestant youth, but it cannot be more than indirectly direct because it is personal and impressionistic. Similarly, James and Woolf can be "saturated" with a state of affairs down to its essence only through the mediation of acts of imagination that are phenomenal in the extreme. As William James insists when refuting idealism and advancing a more modest "radical empiricism," the single "indefectibly certain truth" we have is "the truth that the present phenomenon of consciousness exists."[17] Truth begins and ends with experience, he argues, and experience need not lean on anything more essential than itself.

Although committed to penetrating to the essence of existence, Henry James realizes that the essence of reality is created only by reality itself and that this essence is accessible to understanding only through real experiences of knowing. Hence his protests against "going behind" or "telling about the figures" in a story "save by their own appearance and action" (*Letters*, 1:333). Their experience must be trusted to reveal its own truth. Hence also his concern with making his own characters "phenomenal to a particular imagination" and then making "that imagination, with all its contents, phenomenal to the reader" (*Letters*, 1:326). This technique emphasizes the experiential foundations of knowledge. And hence finally his practice of judging the essential validity of a story, an incident, or a represented individual and type not by unshakable rules but according to the criterion of "that which has life and that which has it not" (*PP*, p. 393). Like his brother the philosopher, James has a deep suspicion of categories and classifications that shows him aware that truth is not laid out in a static, essential, rationalistic scheme beyond or behind the real but is created and discovered in lived experience itself.

Because of the primacy they give to experience, both brothers place great emphasis on the powers of engaged subjectivity by which we construct our worlds. William James argues, for example, that "the world . . . comes to us at first as a chaos of experiences" in which "lines of order soon get traced" because "man engenders truths upon it." Because we select what objects to recognize according to our interests and because we give meaning to these objects according to the attention and purposes we bring to them, he concludes that "in our cognitive as well as in our active life we are creative."[18] Poulet has pointed out that for Henry James as well the "cohesion and even intelligibility" of "the universe" seem to depend on the "organizing power" of the mind.[19] Both William and Henry James emphasize the active, creative character of consciousness that Husserl describes in his theory of intentionality and that Ritchie's story dramatizes.

In any case, as Mark Spilka notes, "Jamesian apprehension is really more aggressive than" indicated by his rather "passive image"[20] of the mind's "immense sensibility" as "a kind of huge spider-web of the finest silken threads suspended in the chamber of consciousness, and catching every air-borne particle in its tissue" (*PP*, p. 388).

Henry James misrepresents his views in this static, purely receptive image, since he would agree with Merleau-Ponty that "I am not the spectator, I am involved"[21] whenever I perceive; as Ritchie demonstrates, the world calls to me, but what I make of its call depends on how I respond. Hence James's contention that "the figures in any picture, the agents in any drama, are interesting only in proportion as they feel their respective situations" and his delight in "the acute, the intense, the complete," in those whose "power to be finely aware and richly responsible" enables them "to 'get most' out of all that happens to them" (AN, p. 62). Hence too—and unfortunately—his rather chilling dismissal of "the stupid, the coarse and the blind" (AN, p. 62) who do not inhabit rich worlds because they do not respond actively to the call of their possibilities. The reverse side of this coin, though, is that an active imagination can compensate for much, so that James objects when Walter Besant claims "a young lady brought up in a quiet country village should avoid descriptions of garrison life" (PP, p. 386). "Greater miracles have been seen than that, imagination assisting, she should speak the truth of some of these gentlemen," James argues, as long as she is "a damsel upon whom nothing is lost" (PP, p. 388). Everything depends, once again, on the powers and weaknesses of engaged subjectivity.

James's faith in the village girl's potential ability to transcend the limits of her circumstances should not lead us to conclude that for him subjectivity is not tied to its situation. Again and again he demonstrates in his novels and stories that the range of observation hinges on the position of the observer. Some of his most dramatic moments turn on the surprise that ensues when a character encounters a new situation and discovers something unexpected that his or her position had previously not allowed to come into view. For James as for Husserl, such surprises occur because we actively fill out hidden sides that the limits of our position keep from our view. Famous examples are Isabel Archer's discovery of the liaison that Osmond and Madame Merle had kept hidden from her and Lambert Strether's revealing encounter with Chad and Madame de Vionnet on a river outing. Milly Theale, Maggie Verver, and many others experience similarly surprising revelations that show the limits of their range of understanding because of the limits of their positions. Accustomed to "hanging over banisters" and wondering about what is happening downstairs, Maisie cannot penetrate the mysteries of the adults in her world in large part because she is poorly positioned for the task. And, in our example, Ritchie's distance from and limited perspective on the scene given in her impression result from her position on the staircase, outside the open doorway.

In all of these instances James dramatizes the meaning of Merleau-Ponty's observation that "the system of experience is not arrayed before me as if I were God, it is lived by me from a certain point of view . . . and it is my involvement in a point of view which makes possible both the finiteness of my perception and its opening out upon the complete world as a horizon of every perception."[22] Perception must start from somewhere, and this starting point limits our otherwise almost infinite freedom for performing intentional acts. But without starting from a position we could not undertake specific, directed acts of perception—acts that cannot give us omniscience but that do give us the privilege and power of revealing our own particular possibilities for understanding. As William James notes, "neither the whole of truth nor the whole of good is revealed to any single observer, although each observer gains a partial superiority of insight from the peculiar position in which he stands."[23] Once again, as with the other limits to perception, the necessary positionality of consciousness is both a weakness and a strength—a weakness because we are confined to knowing from a particular standpoint, but a strength because it gives us a hold on the world we would otherwise lack.

James's image of fiction as a house with many windows captures in polyvalent language what I have been trying to clarify systematically with the univocal terms of phenomenology. But this image, which occurs in the preface to *The Portrait of a Lady*, also points beyond the bare fact of our inescapable positionality to some of its broader implications and consequences:

> The house of fiction has . . . not one window, but a million—a number of possible windows not to be reckoned, rather; every one of which has been pierced, or is still pierceable, in its vast front, by the need of the individual vision and the pressure of the individual will. These apertures, of dissimilar shape and size, hang so, all together, over the human scene that we might have expected of them a greater sameness of report than we find. They are but windows at best, mere holes in a dead wall, disconnected, perched aloft; they are not hinged doors opening

straight upon life. But they have this mark of their own that at
each of them stands a figure with a pair of eyes, or at least with
a field-glass, which forms, again and again, for observation, a
unique instrument, insuring to the person making use of it an
impression distinct from every other. He and his neighbors are
watching the same show, but one seeing more where the other
sees less, one seeing black where the other sees white, one
seeing big where the other sees small, one seeing coarse where
the other sees fine. And so on, and so on; there is fortunately
no saying on what, for the particular pair of eyes, the window
may *not* open; "fortunately" by reason, precisely, of this incalculability of range. (*AN*, p. 46)

Or, as James says elsewhere, "The novelist is a particular *window*,
absolutely—and of worth in so far as he is one" (*Letters*, 1:165).

Each artist has "an impression distinct from every other" because
each stands at a different position which offers a different world with
different horizons and different possible aspects. The position itself is
lifeless and meaningless—a "mere hole in a dead wall"—until the
observer takes field-glasses in hand and puts the intentionality of consciousness to work exploring what is open to his view. Consequently,
what he sees depends in part on the "temperament" of his "particular
mind, different from others" (*PP*, p. 384). This makes him "a unique
instrument" and contributes to his "individual vision." And, together,
positionality and temperament make for an "incalculability of range"
in what can be seen—a veritable plenitude of realities that ensues
from the various placements of different observers all "watching the
same show." Let us take a closer look, then, at what temperament and
plenitude mean for James and phenomenology and how these notions
follow from concepts already familiar to us like positionality and
intentionality.

For phenomenology, "temperament" describes the fundamental and
uniquely individual patterns of intentionality that join the self to its
world. For example, William James claims that a philosopher's "temperament"—his "more or less dumb sense of what life honestly and
deeply means" and his "individual way of just seeing and feeling the
total push and pressure of the cosmos"—"really gives him a stronger
bias than any of his more strictly objective premises."[24] Temperament
includes what Henry James calls the "atmosphere" that "uncon-

sciously suffuses . . . the particular tone" of an artist's "vision"—that
abiding "state of the weather" that so characterizes someone's world
"that the life that overflows in Dickens seems . . . always to go on in
the morning, or in the very earliest hours of the afternoon at most"
where "in Charlotte Brontë we move through an endless autumn" and
"in Jane Austen we sit quite resigned in an arrested spring." This typical, pervasive "color of the air" of "the projected light of the individual strong temperament in fiction," as James calls it, shares much
with what Heidegger describes as the "mood" (*Stimmung*) or "state of
mind" (*Befindlichkeit*) that always accompanies our existence as part
of its basic ground.[25] But more than mood, color, or tone, "temperament" refers both for James and phenomenology to our entire habit of
mind—our total world-design or project of world. Consequently, for
James, if "the novel is simply a vision of the world from the standpoint
of a person constituted after a certain fashion . . . it is therefore absurd to say that there is, for the novelist's use, only one reality of
things" (*PP*, p. 246). Even though the novel is "a direct impression of
life," he argues, "the impression will vary according to the plate that
takes it, the particular structure and mixture of the recipient" (*PP*,
p. 246). James is not suggesting that literary criticism give way to
psychology, then, when he insists that "the deepest quality of a work
of art will always be the quality of the mind of the producer" (*PP*,
p. 406). Rather, he is implying that even the most mimetic art is an
expression of the artist's way of being-in-the-world, a reflection not of
the "real" pure and simple but of the unique and individual reality
created when the artist engages the world according to his temperament and position.

    This is already an explanation of how James comes to believe in the
plenitude of possibilities available in the "house of fiction" and, by
extension, in human existence. "Humanity is immense, and reality
has a myriad forms" (*PP*, pp. 387–88), he claims, because everyone
creates his or her own world with its own array of possibilities. More
exuberant and outspoken than his brother even when they agree, William James frankly rejoices in the plenitude he finds in the open reality of a "pluralistic universe" just as he marvels at how "other minds"
carve out "other worlds from the same monotonous and inexpressive
chaos."[26] There is also a certain plenitude, though, even to that one
world created by one individual with a single temperament and a single position. As James observes, "Experience is never limited, and it

is never complete" (*PP*, p. 388). And he demonstrates the meaning of this observation in those many novels and stories of his which end "*en l'air*," with the expectation of crucial developments yet to come, and all because "the whole of anything is never told." [27] Just as Merleau-Ponty describes an aspect as an "invitation" to discover the other aspects that harmonize and agree with it, so James finds that "relations stop nowhere" (*AN*, p. 5) and that he cannot escape from a "strange sense for the connections of things." [28] This plenum of the possible owes much to the epistemology of the impression (or the phenomenon), since plenitude is implied both by the infinite freedom of intentional activity and by the infinity of aspects that any one object may have. James never ceases to wonder at the multifariousness of a reality where everything suggests so much, where everyone's individual world contains so much suggestive material, and where there are so many worlds that reveal so many varieties of experience.

Still, all I have said about James's awareness of perception's limits should indicate that he doubts the wisdom of trusting uncritically in the powers of consciousness. Wary of solipsism even if delighted by plenitude, neither James nor phenomenology put their faith in pure subjectivity. The impression, like the intentionality of consciousness, mediates subject and object. Ritchie's impression of the pastor's household is neither subjective nor objective. Rather, it is both at once. Her impression seems exclusively objective when her readers praise its authenticity and marvel at her supposed opportunities for probing the concrete circumstances of French Protestant youth. It seems extremely subjective only when James singles out her case to demonstrate the teleology of the impression and the revelatory power of the imagination. [29]

"The Art of Fiction" abounds in hedges against the misapprehensions that might trap an excessively active subjectivity. For example, James places "ingenuity" second to the "capacity for receiving straight impressions" (*PP*, p. 399). And when he admonishes the artist to "try to be one of the people on whom nothing is lost" (*PP*, p. 390), he is advising imaginative, subjective engagement with experience at the same time that he is warning against the danger of getting misled into a world that ignores more than it reveals. The inappropriate passivity of the "spider-web" image that we noted earlier might even be explained as an attempt on James's part to depict consciousness as purely receptive and all-inclusive at its best in order to encourage subjectivity to struggle toward objectivity. The most active, imaginative use of impressions, then, would lead toward a condition of impeccable objectivity where nothing is lost and everything is received.

As we have seen, however, the personal, positioned, and creative nature of perception makes such perfection impossible except as a utopian metaphor. So James always comes back to the dilemma that "the measure of reality is very difficult to fix" (*PP*, p. 387). Every individual world posits a sense of the real different in some ways from every other. In the words of William James, "the breach from one mind to another is perhaps the greatest breach in nature."[30] In fact, though, intersubjective validation—that is, if two or more people find that their worlds agree or at least harmonize about some aspect of reality—is one of the few reasonably trustworthy tests of objectivity. Henry James applies this test when he "say[s] Yes or No, as it may be" to the validity of the represented reality of "what the artist puts before me"—saying "No" to Edmond de Goncourt's portrait of childhood in *Chérie* but "Yes" to "George Eliot, when she painted that country with a far other intelligence" (*PP*, pp. 403–4). Similarly, Ritchie learns that her impression of French Protestant youth has been trustworthy only when others clamor around her saying "Yes, Yes!" James downplays the difficulty of getting agreement about what is objective reality in either perception or art when he claims: "Selection will be sure to take care of itself, for it has a constant motive behind it. That motive is simply experience. As people feel life, so they will feel the art that is most closely related to it" (*PP*, p. 397). But since he knows so well the significance of subjective selection and creative contribution in perception, this assurance sounds more like a wish or a hope than a guarantee that certainty about the real in either life or art can be achieved without difficulty.

Still, James is not a cautious epistemologist anxious to establish the certainty of adequate, apodictic knowledge. Quite the contrary, he openly celebrates "our own precious liability to fall into traps and be bewildered" (*AN*, p. 63). After all, "if we were never bewildered there would never be a story to tell about us" (*AN*, p. 63). He even imagines that "the all-knowing immortals" of ancient Greece led "dreadfully dull" lives (*AN*, p. 64). Every example I have given so far of how James dramatizes one or another of the limits to perception in the plot of a novel or story simply demonstrates how he delights in testing and exploring the problems of impressionistic knowing in his fiction. The material for his tales begins at the boundary where the certainties of knowing end.[31]

In *The Ambassadors*, for example, James decides to let us know about Strether's adventures only "through his more or less groping knowledge of them, since his very gropings would figure among his most interesting motions" (*AN*, pp. 317–18). There and elsewhere James tempts solipsism by adhering single-mindedly to describing one individual's phenomenal world. The narrator of *The Sacred Fount* wonders, indeed, whether he has gone solipsistically mad at the end of that novel because he cannot gauge how much his subtle interpretations owe to accurate, sensitive observation and how much to his own extravagantly lively imagination—that is, because he cannot find anyone he would trust to confirm or deny his theories since he immediately suspects the motives of anyone who agrees with him. Similarly, but with fewer complications and less self-consciousness, the obtuse narrator of *The Aspern Papers* proves himself ignorant of the point of his own story because he fails to understand with any intersubjective sympathy what his intrusion means to the worlds of Juliana and Tina Bordereau. Again, the question of what is trustworthy observation and what is solipsistic, imaginative extravagance is at the heart of the debate over *The Turn of the Screw*. In these and other works, James converts epistemological dilemmas into the stuff of stories that demonstrate the existential consequences of the impression's characteristics. He accepts the pitfalls of phenomenal knowing as an invigorating if dangerous challenge for both art and life.

James is responding to that challenge when he champions the novel's freedom. He describes his essay "The Art of Fiction" as "simply a plea for liberty" (*Letters*, 1:110) for the novel and a defense of its "large, free character" (*PP*, p. 402). The first and fundamental tenet in his argument is that "we must grant the artist his subject, his idea, his *donnée*: our criticism is applied only to what he makes of it" (*PP*, pp. 394–95). It is difficult if not impossible, of course, to separate an artist's "subject" and "what he makes of it"; the treatment helps to shape the idea just as the subject helps to decide the technique. But James makes this somewhat tenuous distinction in order to allow for the widest variety of possibilities in fiction. There are all sorts of *données*, just as "there are all sorts of tastes" (*PP*, p. 397). This plenitude of intersubjective diversity—the same we saw symbolized in the many-windowed house of fiction—makes freedom both a possibility and a necessity. "No two men in the world have the same idea, image and measure of presentation," James explains; so "each of us, from the moment we are worth our salt, writes as he can and only as he can" (*Letters*, 1:289, 288). Every writer's *donnée* and every reader's taste reflect his or her own individual position, temperament, and world. No one enjoys a privileged position that commands all the others, and no one can pretend an omniscient authority about what another's impressions can and should disclose. But since everyone's position and habits of attention, selection, and interest give him unique access to certain aspects of the real, we must remember that "what he leaves out has no claim to get itself considered till after we have done justice to what he takes in" (*PP*, p. 255). James expresses a "horror of dogmas, moulds and formulas"[32] because their absolutism ignores the limits to what we can know. Even worse, it steals away the power we have to convert those limits into an opportunity for getting a unique and revealing hold on some particular aspect of the world. Novels "are successful in proportion as they reveal a particular mind, different from others," and "can only suffer from being marked out or fenced in by prescription," he insists; the novel "lives upon exercise, and the very meaning of exercise is freedom" (*PP*, p. 384). The novel's freedom follows as a necessary and fortunate consequence of the impression's characteristics as a way of knowing.

James would seem to contradict his defense of the liberty and equality of the *donnée* when he concedes that "there are degrees of merit in subjects" (*AN*, p. 309) and advises that "artists should select none but the richest" (*PP*, p. 396). This is only an apparent contradiction, however. As always, James is concerned that freedom be matched with responsibility—that the novelist's great liberty, in this case, not degenerate into license. James feels strongly that "one never really chooses one's general range of vision—the experience from which ideas and themes and suggestions spring: this proves ever what it has *had* to be, this is one with the very turn one's life has taken; so that whatever it 'gives,' whatever it makes us feel and think of, we regard very much as imposed and inevitable" (*AN*, p. 201). By granting the artist's *donnée*, then, James acknowledges the unchosen ground of our freedom. But by urging the novelist to treat the richest possible subject in the most revealing way, James is challenging every writer to make the most of what his position and temperament open to his choice.

Paradoxically, in fact, freedom can help overcome the limits of phenomenality to which it owes its existence. Although the novelist's freedom is a necessity because everyone's grasp of the world is incomplete, its exercise can provide a means for fulfilling our knowledge in an approach toward intersubjective omniscience. In James's estimation, the novel has value most of all because it "helps us to *know*."[33] It does its work best by "flying in the face of presumptions" (*PP*, p. 395) in order to expand the worlds we know by opening horizons we had not expected. We thus get to see beyond our worlds because the novelist tries to open his world to us with the promise that "another point of view will yield another perfection" (*PP*, p. 287). As he says of his favorite Balzac, James "loved the sense of another explored, assumed, assimilated identity."[34] James claims that the novel can provide "a miraculous enlargement of experience" by "mak[ing] it appear to us for the time that we have lived another life" (*PP*, pp. 227–28) —a life revealed to us by another imagination working from another position with another temperament.[35] By granting the artist his *donnée* and thus gaining access to other aspects of the real, we may begin to approach that knowledge of the world as a whole that beckons as a possibility beyond the horizons we have. Practiced to perfection (and, once again, this is only a goal to strive for without hope of attaining it), such intersubjective transparency would create a situation of complete and total knowing, much as if all the observers at fiction's many windows could pool their resources and see all at once what they can actually capture only partially, individually, and diachronically.

Like Peirce when he fears that "fixation of belief" will lock us blindly into our own limited habits of thought,[36] James declares himself fascinated with what other novelists can achieve on much different principles than his because he is "more in dread of any fool's paradise . . . than in love with the idea of security proved" (*Letters*, 2:486). If James maintains confidence in what he can achieve from his own position and with his own habits—insisting all the time that "I don't mean to say I don't wish I could do twenty things I can't" (*Letters*, 2:487)—he bases his integrity on his conviction that he too can contribute to the intersubjective opening up of the world that is the task of the novel's freedom. Peirce's doctrine of "agapasm" claims that complete, unshakable truth lies only at the end of the path that all researchers must undertake with one another in cooperation and exchange. James's doctrine of the novel's freedom is an "agapasm" of fiction.

Our inquiry has moved from epistemology to aesthetics. We began by asking the impression about the way it knows the world. We have just concluded that fiction is a way of knowing in league with the impression. We must now turn briefly to two questions that we have been anticipating: According to James, how does the novelist represent reality in art? And why does the novelist represent? Asking these questions will clarify further how fiction knows, what it can know, and how its way of knowing follows as an implication of the epistemology of the impression.

T H R E E

According to James, "The art of representation bristles with questions the very terms'of which are difficult to apply and to appreciate" (AN, p. 3). One of the questions that most interested James is this: Does successful mimetic art strive to render life as it is, or does it give a simplified, rearranged version of reality? James seems to take the radical stance of arguing an identity between life and representational art. He claims that the novelist "competes with life" (PP, p. 390). One of James's characters asks: "What's art but an intense life—if it be real?"[37] James demands that the novel catch "the very note and trick, the strange irregular rhythm of life" because only insofar as "we see life *without* rearrangement do we feel that we are touching the truth; in proportion as we see it *with* rearrangement do we feel that we are being put off with a substitute, a compromise and convention" (PP, p. 398). In "A Humble Remonstrance," his response to "The Art of Fiction," Robert Louis Stevenson argues the other side of the question: "No art—to use the daring phrase of Mr. James—can successfully 'compete with life.'" According to Stevenson, "Life is monstrous, infinite, illogical, abrupt, and poignant" where "a work of art, in comparison, is neat, finite, self-contained, rational, flowing and emasculate." The novelist cannot stand up to "the dazzle and confusion of reality" unless he determines "to half-shut his eyes" and strive for "a simplification of some side or point of life."[38]

We need not choose between Stevenson and James, however, because at bottom they actually agree. James read Stevenson's essay
with pleasure and wrote to assure him "no one can assent more than I
to your proposition that all art is a simplification" (*Letters*, 1:110).
James is not contradicting himself. He never meant to suggest that the
novel should try to give reality itself but rather "the air of reality" or
"the illusion of life" (*PP*, p. 390)—what Roman Ingarden calls a convincing, compelling "*habitus* of reality." According to Ingarden, represented objects "simply simulate, or, if one will, 'play,' a *habitus* of
reality and in themselves are not and cannot be real."[39] The point may
seem obvious, but it is worth making because of the consequences
that follow from it. That reader would be mad indeed who succumbed
to the delusion that the illusion of reality in a novel deserves the same
credence as life itself. But James finds fault with Trollope for admit-
ting in *Barchester Towers* that he's "only 'making believe'" (*PP*,
p. 379), and the reason for his criticism is that the novelist cannot
achieve the "air of reality" unless he persuades his readers that his
work's *habitus* deserves their unreserved acceptance.

Selection and simplification create a novel's air of reality. They prevent a work's *habitus* from ever attaining the full depth and thickness
of the real as we experience it, but at the same time they overcome
this limitation by conspiring to induce belief in the novel's illusion of
life. Because "really, universally, relations stop nowhere," as we have
seen James contends, the novelist "is in the perpetual predicament"
that "he has at once intensely to consult and intensely to ignore" reality in the "difficult, dire process of selection and comparison, of surrender and sacrifice" (*AN*, pp. 5–6) by which he creates his illusion
of life. But as our study of the impression's epistemology has shown,
this "process of selection" is not at odds with the structure of normal
perception; quite the contrary, the essential characteristics of consciousness are what make representation possible in the first place.
Representation may demand belief in an illusion, but then perception
already depends on a leap of faith. If representation cannot succeed
without selection, neither can intentional, impressionistic knowing.
Although never much of an aesthetician, William James draws an explicit parallel between artistic activity and "the essentially selective
or interested character of consciousness." Just as the "selective industry" of perception "picks out certain [sensations] as worthy of its
notice and suppresses all the rest," so "the artist notoriously selects

his items, rejecting all tones, colors, shapes, which do not harmonize with each other and with the main purpose of his work."[40] All art, whether mimetic or not, owes its effect to selection. But the selection that makes representation work bears a closer relation to perception's "selective industry" than does any other kind of artistic simplification. Perception and representation are not identical, of course, but they are compatible and do cooperate with each other. Henry James can argue that the novel competes with life and yet still agree with Stevenson that art selects and simplifies because perception itself gives us a sense of reality that is selective and simplified.

Ingarden's phenomenological aesthetic provides a theory of representation that may help clarify James's assumptions about selectivity in life and in the novel. Ingarden first notes that it is a small miracle that fiction can imitate reality with any success at all. Language can never hope to duplicate the innumerable, flowing aspects in which, even with the selectivity of perception, the world is given to us. Language can only "ensnare" an object "as in a 'net'"—at best displaying the object in "a discrete manifold of distinct, though connected, states of affairs" that cannot duplicate the flowing roundness of intuitive givenness in original perception.[41] The finitude of language forces what Ingarden calls "spots of indeterminacy" to appear in every literary work of art. For every realistic detail that a writer includes in his fiction, he leaves out an infinite number of others that could define its people, places, and things still more completely. But these indeterminacies can work to a novelist's advantage too. As Iser notes, "it is the unwritten part" of the text "that gives us the opportunity to picture things; indeed without the elements of indeterminacy, the gaps in the text, we should not be able to use our imagination."[42] Although the indeterminacies in a novel might seem at first to be an obstacle to representation, they in fact assist it if they are properly controlled. The novelist can arrange the indeterminacies in his work to present an object in an aspect—that is, from one side and one perspective only, with other sides hidden and other perspectives undeveloped.

Here perception and representation meet. Remembering his experience with objects in aspects in real life, the reader can recognize what kind of object the artist wishes to evoke from the fictional aspect he has created. Since ordinary perception demands that the observer participate in realizing the object before him, the reader does not hesitate to respond to the suggestions held ready in a fictional aspect by intentionally filling out the hidden sides of the object it offers, completing whatever indeterminacies may exist, and endowing the represented object with a quasi-intuitive presence it would lack by itself. Representation succeeds by convincing the reader to borrow from habits of ordinary perception to constitute objects given with a similar inherent incompleteness in art.

Once again, as an artist rather than a philosopher, James does not say all of this explicitly or in the same way. But his explicit remarks and implicit assumptions about representation and epistemology do seem to agree with Ingarden's theory in many important respects. Remember, for example, James's use of imagination to discover the essence of the real in a process much like Husserl's reduction. This search for "the ideal right" (*AN*, p. 122) for representation also agrees with Ingarden's theory that an artistic aspect must capture the essential structure of the thing that underlies all the aspects in which it appears. Because language is finite, fictional aspects are schematic and rigid, not full and flowing; they must contain what is necessary to their objects if they are to allow a reader to recognize these and complete them appropriately. James gives an explanation of how novelists must discover and craft their works' aspects when he argues that "art is essentially selection, but it is a selection whose main care is to be typical, to be inclusive" (*PP*, p. 398).

Like Ian Watt, Erich Auerbach, and other students of realism, both James and Ingarden consider "truth of detail" or "solidity of specification" (*PP*, p. 390) crucial for holding aspects in readiness for the reader.[43] Descriptive detail is part of the material out of which a work's aspects are made. But details help representation only insofar as they help create convincing, suggestive aspects. Too much specification may clutter up the picture that a work's aspects must be carefully arranged to create and thus distract the reader from what he must do to make the picture live. This is why James criticizes Balzac (whom he ordinarily admires) for being too inclusive without being selective and typical enough. In "the positive monstrosity of his effort" to create "a reproduction of the real on the scale of the real," Balzac "sees and presents too many facts" whose "value is thus threatened with submersion by the flood of general reference in which they float." Balzac's representations of the real "may thus at times become obscure from his very habit of striking too many matches."[44] James and Ingarden agree that the novelist struggles in vain and even counterproductively if he tries to copy reality fully. They agree that he should strive instead to offer a selection of reality that inspires perception's own selectivity to acknowledge its authenticity and respond appropriately to its suggestions.

For both James and Ingarden, the success of representation depends as much on the reader as the artist. Without the reader's active participation, the most potentially convincing image of reality would remain just so many lifeless marks on a page. Ingarden's theory of how aspects work in representation is also a theory of reading that explains how readers must "concretize" represented objects from suggestions carefully laid in the text.[45] Perhaps more than any other novelist before him, James openly calls on readers to take an active role when they sit down with a work of fiction. He chides those "many people who read novels as an exercise in skipping" (PP, p. 381) and insists that "in every novel the work is divided between the writer and the reader." In turn, this division of labor influences the artist's task since "the writer makes the reader very much as he makes his characters."[46] James knew that every novel projects its own "implied reader" long before Iser formulated this notion theoretically. The writer "makes" the reader by assigning him the role he must play to fulfill the work, by arranging the work's aspects so that he will respond to them appropriately, and by seducing him to accept the duties of reading willingly and even eagerly. James objected to photographs or illustrations in novels, for example, because they might tempt the writer and the reader to lapse into passivity. He made an exception for the introductory photographs in his own New York Edition only because he kept them suggestive rather than giving them a "competitive and obvious" relation with some "particular thing in the text" (AN, p. 333).

According to James, the writer must manipulate the aspects and indeterminacies in his work "to produce on the reader's mind" an impression that "must have much in common with the impression originally produced on his own mind by the subject."[47] In order to open his world to the reader according to the "agapasm" of fiction, the novelist must try to make the reader's experience with the aspects held ready by the text resemble the perceptual aspects through which the writer understands his subject. But although the writer must persuade his audience to accept his vision of reality, he can achieve this only by adhering to "our general sense of the way things happen" and avoiding "our particular sense of the way they don't happen" (AN, p. 34).

As we have seen, it is finally up to the reader to say "yes" or "no" to a novel by discovering whether he can draw on his own experience to fill out its aspects and indeterminacies as required. The criterion of validation through intersubjective agreement, then, is behind James's argument that "the good old fashion of 'liking' a work of art or not liking it" provides the "ultimate test" of representation's success or failure (*PP*, pp. 395–96). This test decides whether the novel offers a solipsistic vision or a sharable display of the world's aspects. By deferring so much to the reader's "liking," James is not granting his audience the license to accept or reject works according to their whims. Rather, he is acknowledging that agreement between writer and reader provides the most compelling evidence that a novel contains convincing, recognizable aspects that reveal an authentic, "real" world. In all of these ways, then, James elevates the reader to the status of a full partner with the artist in the task of making representation succeed.

Does James ask too much of the reader? Stevenson and some later critics have thought so—not because James asks readers to concretize a work's objects but because he demands that they exercise at the same time the utmost critical attention, what he calls "close or analytic appreciation" (*AN*, p. 227). To Stevenson, though, "the luxury" of reading "is to lay by our judgment, to be submerged by the tale as by a billow, and only to awake, and begin to distinguish and find fault, when the piece is over and the volume laid aside."[48] Ingarden would agree with Stevenson that the attitude a reader must assume to make a representation come alive is not compatible with the critical, self-conscious attitudes he might take to analyze a work. Ingarden distinguishes three possible attitudes in reading. In the "aesthetic attitude," the reader surrenders to the work's suggestions in order to concretize the reality it seeks to represent. But the reader sacrifices the joy of letting a represented world absorb him if he assumes the critical postures of either the "preaesthetic attitude" (where he analyzes the work's artistic structure) or the "postaesthetic attitude" (where he studies the results of his own aesthetic concretization).[49] Now James is certainly right if he is insisting that a work of representation should be able to sustain attention in each of these attitudes. Furthermore, Ingarden may underestimate how closely these three attitudes ordinarily cooperate. The aesthetic attitude requires ongoing advice and support from the pre- and postaesthetic attitudes to make sure it is creating an appropriate and valuable concretization. But James himself realizes that excessive attention to criticism and analysis can spoil the pleasures of immersion. The narrator of "The Figure in the Carpet," for example, finds that his obsessive search for "the buried treasure" in Hugh Vereker's work "damaged" his "liking" and interfered with "charming things" he "had formerly enjoyed."[50]

The problem is how to attain the most advantageous interaction between Ingarden's three attitudes. James failed to solve this problem in his theory of reading, and he often failed as well to solve it in his writing of fictions. Much of the discomfort that some readers feel with James's later style derives from his difficulties here. These readers sense that his late style's complex syntax and indirectness of specification compel a critical, analytic attitude that allows too little for concretization. Nevertheless, the problem of reconciling the various attitudes of reading has no fixed, formulaic solution, since every work will make different demands on the reader according to what it seeks to achieve and since every reader will make different demands on a work according to his interests and purposes. James is closest to a solution when he argues that the successful novel will "appeal to us when we have read it once to read it yet again."[51] Further readings invite us to explore a work's inexhaustible range by taking different attitudes that uncover different possibilities—even though a vivid representational effect might not always result.

Any theory of reading depends on a theory of representation, and representation depends in turn on perception. Here too, though, James's art sacrifices some of its visualizing effect as he becomes increasingly self-conscious in the way he bases representation on perception. Particularly in his later work, James represents objects by presenting them through descriptions of the fulfilled perceptual aspects that his characters have on their worlds. By portraying the impressions of his characters and thus thematizing the aspects that display their worlds, James elevates the implicit epistemological workings of representation into an explicit, formal principle. James portrays the world *in* aspects, where Ingarden argues only that representation must proceed *by means of* aspects. In this sense, James's artistic practice is a running commentary on the workings of representation.

James's practice of thematizing perceptual aspects goes one step further than conventional realism. In traditional mimetic fiction, according to Iser, "the use of simulated reality does not merely denote the desire to copy a familiar reality; its function is to enable us to see that familiar reality with new eyes."[52] James's epistemologically self-conscious approach to representation asks us to see the way we see reality. In the process of disclosing a fresh view of the world, James also displays the very dynamics of vision. James may frustrate the reader's desire to immerse himself in a world of objects by distancing them through the screen of a character's consciousness. The loss of an opportunity for immersion, however, is the gain of an occasion for self-awareness. By observing the acts of knowing through which James presents his worlds, the reader can acquire a new understanding of the workings of consciousness.

F O U R

James argues that "the only reason for the existence of a novel is that it does attempt to represent life" (*PP*, p. 378). But this justification of the novel does not explain why the art of representing life is worthwhile. We have seen that James considers represented experience a source of knowledge much like lived experience and that his unique epistemological realism offers the reader new knowledge about knowing. We have also seen that, in James's view, the impressions given by novelists in their works open our world to other worlds in what I called (borrowing from Peirce's vocabulary) an "agapasm" of fiction. But there is still more to learn from James and phenomenology about why representation matters. What, then, is the value of representation for James, and what kind of value does he expect novels to have?

Ingarden claims to have developed a theory of value to complement his theory of representation. According to Ingarden, the various "strata" of the literary work that combine to allow representation all contain particular "artistic values" that await readers to realize them as "aesthetic values" in a "polyphonic harmony of value qualities."[53] Unfortunately, though, Ingarden remains intriguingly vague about what he means by a "value" or a "value quality." But he does make clear that for him, art's value does not include truth-value—that the worth of literature has nothing to do with moral significance, existential meaning, or intellectual insight. He insists that the statements in a novel or poem cannot "be considered to be seriously intended assertive propositions or judgments" that make a "claim to truth" about some "truly existing" state of affairs. Ingarden concludes that works of art contain nothing but "quasi-judgments" that refer only to each other in the world of the text and do not point beyond themselves to anything else. He therefore warns critics that it is a serious mistake "to carry the judgments spoken by the represented characters beyond the bounds of the world represented in the given work and to interpret them as judgments concerning the real world or as the author's opinions about certain questions pertaining to the real world."[54] Contrary to Ingarden's analysis of quasi-judgments, however, James argues that in attempting "to represent and illustrate the past, the actions of men," the novelist is "looking for the truth" with the same integrity as "the historian" and "the philosopher and the painter" (PP, pp. 379–80). Ingarden may be correct about the quasi-judgmental status of the statements in a novel or poem. But he goes wrong by ignoring how artistic quasi-judgments can help us to know the world just as much as genuine judgments do—although in a somewhat different manner. Ingarden's theory of value is incomplete, then, in ways that James transcends.

James would seem to agree with Ingarden by defending "the purpose of making a perfect work" as the artist's single clear-cut goal (PP, p. 406). In his own artistic practice, James's concern with execution, economy, and form—with braving difficulties and "doing" subjects as they would most take "doing"—led him to regard as "my problem, so to speak, and my *gageure*" in every work how "to play the small handful of values really for all they were worth" (AN, pp. 330–31). But as René Wellek points out, James is not the "'formalist'" or "devotee of art for art's sake for which he is often dismissed."[55] In fact, James even refutes "art for art" when he emphasizes the need to have "moral meaning giving a sense to form and form giving relief to moral meaning."[56] As I have suggested, however, "the moral" for James often has broad existential significance. Heidegger's analysis of care's different levels is consequently helpful in suggesting the relation between values of technique and broader values in James. James's passion for execution is a "concern" (or *Besorgnis*) not for technique alone but for technique in the service of disclosing a subject's possibilities. Technique has to do with the way an artist uses his equipment at the level of the "ready-to-hand" (or *zuhanden*). Exercising the appropriate care at this level is necessary for complementing and supporting art's care (or *Sorge*) for existence at a more profound

level.[57] The relation between concern for technique and care for existence in Heidegger helps to explain James's commitment to organic
unity in art. "There is life and life," James argues, "and as waste is
only life sacrificed and prevented from 'counting,' I delight in a deep-
breathing economy and an organic form" (AN, p. 84). Concern for
technique, for James as for Heidegger, is not an end in itself; it is part
of care for life's possibilities.

Heidegger and other phenomenologists refute the distinction between form and content by pointing to the total, indivisible quality of
our engagement with our worlds. As we saw earlier, this totality is
what the unity of knowing and doing rests on. And this unity gives
another, complementary meaning to the existential significance of
James's aesthetics. Since epistemological and existential issues are
all of a piece in an indivisible pattern, and since James's theory of
representation is so firmly grounded in the workings of perception, it
follows that the value of representation should have an existential significance for him that would reflect the significance of the impression.
An existential aesthetic of value is the appropriate counterpart to a
phenomenological theory of representation that is based on the impression as a way of knowing.

As we might expect, James's existential aesthetic of value is not a
theory of the moral value of literature in any limited sense of "morality." In fact, James's critical writings abound with doubts about the
place of moral value in literature. He takes issue with Besant's insistence that a "conscious moral purpose" must inform all worthwhile
fiction (PP, p. 404). He makes no secret of his impatience with "the
inane" and "dull dispute over the 'immoral' subject and the moral"
(AN, p. 45). James's refusal to link fiction to a didactic mission reflects the concern we have seen him show for the novel's freedom. His
dislike of preaching in art also indicates that he, at least in part like
Ingarden, regards full-fledged judgments as inappropriate for fiction.
But James recognizes "the importance of the moral quality of a work
of art" as "a part of the essential richness of inspiration"[58] that motivates novelists and poets. If James denies the oppressive, literal-
minded "moral purpose" of a Besant or a Mrs. Wix, he does so only
because the strength of their zeal is a weakness in disguise—a "diffi-
dence," "a cautious silence on certain subjects," and an "aversion to
face the difficulties with which on every side the treatment of reality
bristles" (PP, pp. 405–6). "The essence of moral energy is to survey

the whole field" (*PP*, p. 406) and thus to confront experience openly, resolutely, and self-consciously. "Every out-and-out realist who provokes serious meditation may claim that he is a moralist," James explains, "for that, after all, is the most that the moralists can do for us."[59] Direct moral propositions have less value in art than indirect (or quasi-judgmental) statements not because truth-value is irrelevant to fiction but because indirect statements can embrace a greater range of experience and may enjoy greater power to provoke reflection. For James, the "moral" value of representation is that it can give rise to meditation on existence.

Paul Ricoeur explicates the relation between indirect expressions and reflection in his theory of symbols. Ricoeur describes symbols as polyvalent expressions that disguise in order to reveal—that "mean something other than what is said" by "designating an indirect meaning in and through a direct meaning," and that "thus call for something like a deciphering, i.e. an interpretation."[60] The quasi-judgments of a story have a symbolic function because they indicate a multitude of indirect meanings through a surface meaning that calls for interpretation and provokes reflection. According to Ricoeur, man makes symbols in order to understand paradoxes that in themselves are "insupportable for thought." But symbols also participate in our striving for self-transcendence by serving as a "surveyor's staff and guide for 'becoming oneself.'"[61] Reflecting on symbols is "the appropriation of our effort to exist and of our desire to be, through the works which bear witness to that effort and desire."[62] In a concession to Ingarden's position, Ricoeur acknowledges that fictional statements do not have "ostensive reference"—that, unlike spoken exchanges in a dialogue, for example, they do not refer to a "situation common to the interlocutors" or "aspects of reality which can be shown or pointed at." But Ingarden fails to see that the language of literature loses this only to gain what Ricoeur calls "nonostensive reference"—"the nonsituational references" that disclose the world of the work and explore the ways of seeing and being depicted within it.[63] The quasi-judgments of literary art suspend situational reference in order to speak all the more broadly and profoundly about man's being.

James shares Ricoeur's sense of the relation between literature and human existence. James describes this relation in his well-known assertion to H. G. Wells: "It is art that *makes* life, makes interest, makes importance, for our consideration" (*Letters*, 2:490). Art "makes" life in many ways, but not the least of them is its power to help us understand ourselves. The language of literature expresses, as James puts it, "the general multifold opportunity, . . . the dignity and integrity, of our existence."[64] Representational art provides us with images of who we are and who we might be. Interpreting them can thus be an aid to deciding who we are to become. For James, making art out of life and reflecting on the life disclosed by art are crucial aspects of man's effort and desire to transcend himself by understanding himself. In James's view, reflecting on art is among the noblest speculations that can engage the human mind because such critical activity makes "the mind as aware of itself as possible" and constitutes "the very education of our imaginative life."[65] Like Ricoeur, James believes that the symbol-maker—in this case the novelist whose work has value insofar as it has symbolic value—serves the rest of us by creating expressions that cultivate our ability to reflect on ourselves by challenging us to interpret images of ourselves. According to James, "so long as life retains its power of projecting itself upon his imagination," man "will find the novel work off the impression better than anything he knows. . . . Till the world is an unpeopled void there will be an image in the mirror."[66] Representation has value for James, then, not so much because the novel is a mirror carried along a road as because it is a mirror in which we see an image of ourselves and try to make sense of what we see.

This is the way in which, for James, the novel has the value of helping us know ourselves and our worlds. The epistemological and existential function of art here relies heavily on the imagination. Epistemology and imagination meet in the activity of projecting life into art and reflecting on art's meaning for life. They meet when we try to understand "the image in the mirror" held up to us by the novel. By asking how the impression is related to representation and artistic value, we have moved from the realm of perception and epistemology toward the domain of existential issues. The next step in this direction is to inquire further into the imagination as James understands it.

IMAGINATION AND
EXISTENCE: EXTRAVAGANCE
IN *RODERICK HUDSON*

ONE

Henry James claims that few subjects interested him more than "the personal history . . . of an imagination, a lively one of course, in a given and favourable case." He delighted in exploring the "endless crisis" of the "man of imagination at the active pitch."[1] By James's own testimony, then, the imagination deserves to be considered one of the intentional foundations supporting his achievement. Roderick Hudson is one of the first of the many men and women of active imagination in James's canon whose interest for him and for us lies precisely in that lively faculty. The imagination is fascinating because it is a pivotal yet elusive, even contradictory aspect of experience. The imagination is all-powerful, since there is no limit to the range of images it can create. But it is also impotent, since these images are pure nothingness—with no substance, no independence, no durability. The imagination is pivotal in the sense that it is deeply implicated in both perception and existence but without being identical to either. As Sartre points out, imagination and perception are "irreducible attitudes of consciousness" that "exclude each other," inasmuch as perceiving something is not at all the same as imagining it.[2] Yet as James shows again and again, heightened powers of imagination contribute to and draw support from heightened powers of perception. Imagination and existence are similarly separate but inseparable. Imagining a world is hardly the same as being-in-the-world. But men and women with lively imaginations do share a manner of being-in-the-world different from others—a particular structure of existence that Roderick Hudson exhibits and that we shall explore with the aid of Binswanger's studies of extravagant world-designs. Even those who live less imaginatively must still exercise imagination to exist in freedom and with care, since both require that we move out of ourselves in a kind of imaginative transcendence. By taking the imagination as a central theme, then, James opens horizons of significance for his art that extend from the perceptual to the existential. Consequently, by asking what the imagination means for James, we will be exploring how this aspect of experience forms a bridge that leads from the phenomenological significance of the "impression" to the existential dynamics of his "moral vision."

We have already seen how, for James, perception and imagination can cooperate. According to his story in "The Art of Fiction" about the powers of the impression, Anne Thackeray Ritchie knows French Protestant youth both perceptually and imaginatively. She begins with a purely perceptual impression of an after-dinner gathering that she observes while glancing through a doorway from a staircase. But then she translates this limited view of her object into a wonderful revelation through acts of imagination that spin out the possibilities contained in the aspect her observation provides. Although Ritchie begins in the realm of perception, she ends with an impression that is largely imaginal—one that has not left the perceptual completely behind but has incorporated the perceptual in the imaginal and put the imagination to use for perception. What I called the "teleology of the impression"—that is, the impression's impulse pointing beyond and ahead of itself to reveal more than it immediately gives—can take the form of one act of perception inviting others to complete it; but, as in Ritchie's example, it can also take the form of perception inviting imagination to put the advantages of its greater freedom to work at the same task. Ritchie's story shows that, each in its own way, perception and imagination are both transcendent in structure because both involve the process of "going beyond." It is only because both imagination and perception involve transcendence that we can pass back and forth between them, that they can contribute to and draw support from each other, and that, in short, there can be a certain continuity uniting these two different aspects of experience.

Transcendence also supports the bridge that extends from the imagination to existence—and particularly to freedom and personal relations, the next two aspects of experience beyond it. If we define freedom, following Kierkegaard, as the "possibility for possibility," then imagining what we might become given what we are can play an important role in the process of transcending ourselves toward our possible futures. Maisie's overly active imagination not only hopes to provide her with a fuller knowledge than the limited view given to her by perception; it also tries to disclose possibilities that she can project herself into. But because the impressions she generates are too purely imaginal, she commits herself with unfortunate consequences to possibilities that turn out to be mere wishes, hopes, and dreams. Maisie's many failures to penetrate the meaning of the mysteries that oppress her show that imagination alone cannot completely close the gap that separates the Self and the Other and that prevents perfect transparency in personal relations. But an imaginative grasp of worlds beyond our own can be a first step toward reducing the Other's opacity by transcending the limits of our personal horizons. Because of the imagination's relevance to problems of freedom and personal relations, Roderick Hudson's extravagant imagination—like Maisie's—has consequences not only for his perceptual faculties but for his experience in these areas of existence as well.

The imagination has such wide relevance to existence because its being is nothingness. As Heidegger, Sartre, and other existential phenomenologists have argued, existence itself is a tissue of negativity. According to Heidegger, existence is the "null projection" of a "null entity" on "the basis of a nullity."[3] The purpose of existential anxiety (or *Angst*) is, in his view, to call us out of the false security that characterizes inauthenticity by confronting us with the nothingness that is the essence of existence. Sartre argues that existence (the "for-itself") is free, unbound, and even volatile because consciousness is a nullity—that is, because consciousness is a "lack," an absence radically different from the dense presence of things (the "in-itself"), an emptiness that strives self-contradictorily and thus futilely to fill itself by incorporating things without sacrificing its freedom.[4] All consciousness is nothing, in Sartre's terms, but the imagination is most radically negative and negating. "Alive, appealing, and strong as an image is," he notes, "it presents its object as not being." Because of the "absence in actuality" or "essential nothingness of the imagined object," Sartre claims that "I grasp *nothing*, . . . I posit *nothingness*" when I imagine. The negativity of the imagination is for Sartre a proof and guarantee of human freedom; by positing not-being, the imagination negates the in-itself and transcends it. The power of negating the real is the origin of man's ability to create meaning and pursue possibilities. Hence Sartre's sweeping assertion that "every concrete and real situation of consciousness in the world is big with imagination in as much as it always presents itself as a withdrawing from the real."[5] The nothingness of the imagination, then, captures in an especially revealing manner the negativity that permeates existence in all its aspects.

The imaginative life is fragile in a way that reflects the frailty of existence as a whole—the tenuousness of all human projects because our worlds are constructed on a foundation of nothingness. As Matthiessen observes, Henry James "kept throughout life the sense of the abyss always lurking beneath the fragile surface."[6] This sense of the fragility of existence is a major link between *Roderick Hudson* and Hawthorne's *The Marble Faun*, two works that many critics have connected because both portray the American art colony in Rome as the backdrop for their narratives.[7] On a deeper level than setting or subject matter, though, both novels convey an understanding of "that pit of blackness that lies beneath us, everywhere"—to borrow from a speech that Miriam makes in a chapter entitled "On the Edge of a Precipice" to another of the four major characters in Hawthorne's work: "The firmest substance of human happiness is but a thin crust spread over it, with just reality enough to bear up the illusive stage scenery amid which we tread. . . . By and by, we inevitably sink!"[8] Both novels turn on an event that renders Miriam's meaning symbolically—a disastrous fall from a height into an abyss that reveals the tenuousness of existence. As we shall see, Roderick Hudson's fall from an Alpine cliff acts as a culminating metaphor for his existential trials as a man of imagination at the active pitch.

For James, as for existential phenomenology, the life of imagination is a marvelous adventure—but an adventure with perils that underline its significance as they endanger its outcome. Imagination is both a blessing and a curse, a sign of nobility and the mark of an outcast. The tension between the imagination's risks and values is, of course, a theme of central importance to the Romantic tradition from Goethe and Schiller through Coleridge and beyond. James's concern with the imagination takes up this tradition and makes it his own. Those who exercise imagination at an active pitch can climb to heights of possibility inaccessible to those who do not. But they also risk falling to depths that less daring souls will never know. Imagination can also help create care, or it can lead to solipsistic fantasies. Similarly, imagination can enable miraculous revelations, but it always carries the risk of delusion. The extravagant imagination is a borderline case that reveals most about the tension between these risks and values by taking it to the breaking point. Roderick Hudson is just such an extravagant, borderline case whose marvelous but perilous adventure reveals much, I think, about James's understanding of the imagination's wonders and dangers and of the relation between imagination and existence.

Roderick Hudson is not one of James's greatest artistic achievements and, consequently, might not in itself seem to justify my claim for its heuristic value among his studies of the imaginative life. Although Edel argues that "few first novels in American literature" can "equal it," Dupee states the conventional critical wisdom when he identifies *The American* as James's first great novel and calls *Roderick Hudson* "a museum-piece . . . possessing some very good points but being dead in the center."[9] This "deadness" is Roderick himself who, if he is imaginative, is also at times too egotistical and tempestuous to be interesting or, perhaps, believable. For my purposes, though, Roderick's weaknesses as a character are his strengths as a symbol of the imagination's risks and values. As we shall see, his shallowness and volatility reflect a fundamental structure of the imaginative life— a structure described by Binswanger as the basic world-design of extravagance. As an extreme case of the imaginative life, Roderick embodies this structure almost too rigidly. But James's later, subtler treatments of the active imagination still retain this structure as their foundation, even though they build on it with greater creative variation. We might expect young Henry James, writing *Roderick Hudson* in his early thirties with his own artistic future still uncertain, to show a revealingly heightened preoccupation with the darker fates possible for the man of imagination. In any case, the novel's peculiarities make it a borderline case in James's canon with particular revelatory value precisely because of its extreme position.

T W O

What, then, is the structure of Roderick Hudson's world, and how is it symbolic of the rewards and pitfalls of the imaginative life? Edel describes Roderick as "the romantic artist of tradition, the artist who 'lives dangerously.'" Cargill calls him "spectacular" and "immature," and Dupee remarks on "his ruinous self-indulgence."[10] These representative observations about Roderick's character describe the surface of his world, but they do not penetrate to its underlying structure. His patron Rowland Mallet thinks Roderick "impulsive, spontaneous, sincere" as well as "moody, desultory, idle, irregular, fantastic"—a man driven, as the sculptor himself claims, by "a restless fiend" to extravagant extremes.[11] Rowland is mystified "at the extraordinary incongruities of [Roderick's] temperament" (p. 286), the contradictions in his ways of feeling and behaving that seem to defy coherent explanation. Sometimes Roderick is the fresh, exuberant genius, inspired with boundless powers of imagination and eager to embrace the possibilities for living and creating that unfold before him. At other times, though, and alternating with his times of high spirits, he feels hopeless and powerless and acts out his frustration with an irritating petulance and a disillusioned restlessness. Rowland finds his friend's world confusingly contradictory because Roderick actually inhabits two different, mutually exclusive worlds. Although contradictory, these worlds are still united, however, inasmuch as they both go back to the same existential structure of what Binswanger calls "extravagance." An "extravagant" world-design generates two opposed but fatally united worlds—an "ethereal world" of boundless possibilities and a "tomb world" of hopeless despair.[12] In order to understand Roderick better than Rowland does, we must describe his two opposing worlds more fully, explain how they arise from the same worlddesign, and discover what outcomes their contradiction offers.

Roderick's "ethereal world" is a realm where his imagination plays free and opens up to him a seemingly endless horizon of value. Binswanger describes the ethereal realm as "a bright, light, wide, nonresisting world," an "infinitely vast, mobile, radiantly lighted, warm, and colorful" sphere where "'winged' wishes and 'highest ideals'" are at home. We enter this world by flying upward beyond the mundane through "fantasy or imagination" or by "being carried" beyond our everyday concerns on "the 'wings' of moods, wishes, passions." Everyone has a world "of fantasies, wishes, longings, hopes," just as everyone has the faculty of imagination. But those like Roderick with imaginations keyed to an unusually active pitch have more extravagant ethereal worlds that they inhabit more single-mindedly.[13] When Roderick has his periods of inspiration, his "indefatigable fancy" (p. 87) lifts him beyond the limits of the ordinary to a world where his wishes, hopes, and ideals engage him with a most intense reality. For example, even before he leaves the confines of Northampton for the wide horizons offered by Rome, Roderick has already embarked on an ethereal adventure by "dreaming of the inspiration of foreign lands"; almost "as if his thoughts had lent him wings," his "spirits" rise "to incalculable heights" with "the pledge of a brilliant future" (p. 65).

His miraculous success at the start of his career in Italy merely confirms his commitment to such fantasies because, as in a dream, nothing seems to resist him. Sartre describes the imagination as perfectly free because its engagement with the unreal suffers none of the resistance of the real.[14] Roderick's fairy-tale rise to prominence shows him powerfully free because all resistance seems to vanish at the touch of his artistic imagination. After Rowland's liberating patronage almost magically clears the way, the sculptor's imagination takes over and miraculously makes everything possible for himself by flying over hurdles that trip up those more earth-bound than he is. Like Ritchie, for example, Roderick enjoys heightened powers of perception because of his heightened imagination. Rowland wonders at "the rate at which" his friend, thanks to "the instinctive quickness of his observation and his free appropriation of whatever might serve his purpose," manages to do "intellectual execution on the general spectacle of European life"—at how "the vivacity of his perceptions" and "the audacity of his imagination" give Roderick "experience rapidly and easily assimilated" with "the intellectual comfort of genius which can arrive at serene conclusions without disagreeable processes" (pp. 77–78, 75).

Fascinated by the immense possibilities that the ethereal flight of his first "high aesthetic revel" (p. 79) seems to put within his grasp, Roderick makes a radical statement of self-confidence that reveals his faith in the magical omnipotence of his wishes: "I care only for perfect beauty," he declares. "For me, it's either that or nothing. . . . I mean to go in for big things; that is my notion of art. I mean to do things that will be simple and vast and infinite. You shall see if they won't be infinite! . . . I mean to thrill the world again!" (pp. 94–95). Roderick's boast shows that, as Binswanger explains, the ethereal world is the world of the unlimited future into which the imagination projects itself with "unbounded, unimpeded, unrestrained, ambitiously optimistic wishing and yearning."[15] But Roderick would seem to have the right to believe in this infinite future because, at first, his imagination seems able to deliver on what it promises. The sculptor's early, dreamlike flight blesses him with all the advantages that, according to James, the imagination can offer on the brighter side of its wonders and dangers.

As an artist, Roderick creates in just as ethereal a manner as he lives. "Genius," notes Rowland, "is a kind of somnambulism. The artist performs great feats in a dream" (p. 39). Many theorists of the creative process before and after Freud have compared artistic inspiration to dreaming. The phenomenological critic Gaston Bachelard attributes the birth of the poetic image to "reverie" and advises readers that they too must dream in response to the image if they wish to enter its sphere of "reverberation." [16] Roderick sounds like Bachelard when he identifies his creative inspiration with "reverie"—even announcing to Rowland before retiring to his studio that "I want to dream of a statue" (p. 77). Bachelard might approve when Rowland confounds Mr. Striker, the down-to-earth New England lawyer, by defending Roderick's habit of "sitting by the hour with the page unturned, watching the flies buzz, or the frost melt on the windowpane": "It is very possible . . . that he will prove some day the completer artist for some of those lazy reveries" (pp. 60–61). Again and again James pictures Roderick lying flat on his back, staring up into the air in idle reverie, searching the sky for inspiration from some muse. Even more, though, Roderick produces in just as inspired a manner as he conceives—working in a dreamlike trance at a fever pitch of excitement and involvement. He almost flies when he works; he creates in an ethereal way that knows no resistance to translating his ideas into clay or stone. He can only create by letting himself be carried away by a passion for his project. The wings of inspiration are everything for Roderick—his only hope for getting an idea and his only means for executing it.

Still, Roderick's ethereal mode of production is problematic and even paradoxical. An inherent contradiction exists between the substance of his dreams and the material in which he creates. The inspiration of his reveries is light, airy, free, and insubstantial. But the stone he sculpts is hard, solid, resistant, and massive. How can a sculptor embody a divine inspiration in an earthly substance? Or, even more, how can Roderick bridge the gap between these contradictory realms without ever leaving his ethereal world—that is, without interrupting the dream he lives when he creates? No artistic creation can succeed without resolving this contradiction between imagination's call to the unreal and the demands of the reality of form. By portraying Roderick as a sculptor, James accentuates the divide between the poles of this paradox; the substance of sculpture is more evidently resistant than, say, the substance of words, and as Nietzsche observes, statues represent the discipline of Apollonian form at its most rigorous.

Even Bachelard, the champion of reverie, admits that in art "the function of the real and the function of the unreal" must be "made to co-operate." Or, as Binswanger observes, art must involve "a mutual permeation" of the ethereal world and the world of reality.[17] In fact, then, Roderick may inhabit a sphere of unreality when he imagines, but he must return to reality in several ways when he creates—to the reality of the medium in which he works, to the reality of the human form that even the most idealized statue of a man or woman represents, to the reality of the tradition of cultural significations in which his work has a place, and to the reality of the worlds of others who must acknowledge the truth of his art if he is to be considered an artist with vision rather than a mad solipsist. In art—but also in life—the ethereal world cannot be self-sustaining. It is incomplete in itself. This is the danger implicit in its wonders—the danger Roderick runs when the passion of his early, dreamlike abandon blinds him to the necessary difficulties of creativity and existence.

James points up the wonder and danger of Roderick's adventure by contrasting him with the less ethereal members of the American art colony in Rome. The young sculptor's high flights of creative inspiration and daring execution raise him far above the amateurish Augusta Blanchard who tries to disguise her limitations by painting figures with their "back turned"—"she did backs very well, but she was a little weak in faces" (p. 90). His miraculous creativity even lifts him above the more professional Sam Singleton, who makes up in "modesty and patience" (p. 90) for what he lacks in genius, and above the masterful Gloriani, who embraces the corrupt and the ugly because ideal beauty exceeds his grasp. Gloriani substitutes "skill unleavened by faith, the mere base maximum of cleverness" (pp. 98–99) for the elusive gift of inspiration. Still, although less wonderful than the more imaginative Roderick, Gloriani and Singleton have each answered the dangerous paradox of creativity by taking its vicissitudes into account with a practicality impossible for the extravagant young sculptor.

Gloriani's resignation to the earthly over the heavenly seems to betray a certain cynicism that may be a residue of frustration from the disappointment of higher hopes and ideals. Nonetheless, his "definite, practical scheme of art" (p. 88) stands as a "warning against highflown pretensions" (p. 97) of Roderick's kind. Binswanger points Gloriani's moral less cynically when he observes that the ethereal world cannot long survive because, in denying the powers of the earthly, it "does not stand 'with both feet firmly on the ground.'"

Securing such a foundation means engaging the real in "practical activity" that confronts resistance resolutely, and this is the moral pointed by Sam Singleton's modesty and his dedication to improving himself by constant practice.[18] Through "hard work" and "patient industry," he succeeds in a small way even though he "gave no promise of talent" at the start (p. 89). Aesthetically, Singleton is not perhaps an entirely satisfactory foil to Roderick since the contrast between them is made almost mechanically at times. Even if less powerful than Roderick's extravagance, though, Singleton's happy steadiness is also less dangerous and more complete because it makes a virtue of consenting to the necessities that Roderick's imagination defies. Roderick may seem justified at times in describing his fellow artist as "a watch that never runs down" and in exclaiming that Singleton's incessant "tic-tic, tic-tic" maddens him (p. 323). But Singleton's delight in "equable" productivity seems less an obsession than an expression of what Bachelard calls that "joy in accepting limitations" that can make practical activity invigorating rather than stifling.[19] Gloriani advises Roderick that he would do well to retreat from the ethereal to the safer ground of the practical when he warns "you can't keep it up—you can't keep it up!"—"you stand on tiptoe, very gracefully I admit; but you can't fly; there's no use trying" (pp. 98, 96). As Binswanger argues and as Singleton demonstrates, existence must confront constraints through practical activity; imaginative flights like Roderick's cannot scoff at the claims of the real forever.

To be sure, Roderick's wings do fail him, and he does plummet back down to earth when his ethereal world collapses. He experiences what Binswanger calls the "tomb world"—an abyss of meaninglessness that "smells of the grave, of that lifeless, decaying odor of a past no longer having a future." The world of the tomb is the reverse side of the ethereal realm; "the more radiant and animated the ethereal world becomes, the more the world in and beneath the earth consolidates" and asserts itself.[20] The higher we fly ethereally, then, the more the world of the tomb threatens to pull us back to the dull, mundane sphere that our hopes, dreams, and ideals would rather deny. Roderick exhibits this dismal side of extravagance when, after his first flight of inspiration, he finds that "all of a sudden I hate things. My old things look ugly; everything looks stupid" (p. 100). From an airy height where everything interests and invigorates him, Roderick falls into an abyss where everything bores and disgusts him. "Everything is mean and dusky and shabby," he despairs during one period in the tomb: "My illusions are all broken-winded; they won't carry me twenty paces" (p. 190). When his illusions break down, he cannot fly effortlessly to achievement; worse still, he cannot dream even of some modest possibility, and if he could, he could not move toward its realization even at a crawl. Trapped in a world where nothing seems possible, he feels restless and hopeless—all because his imagination betrays its fragile unreality.

Roderick demonstrates the horrible irony of extravagance by showing how an exhilarating sense of freedom may alternate with a desperate sense of bondage. Because the tomb always threatens the ether, Roderick is "a man of moods" who "applies himself . . . by fits and starts"—who seems fated to go around in a "circle of" such uncontrollable, unpredictable "metamorphoses" that he is faced with a "damnable uncertainty when [he] goes to bed at night as to whether [he] is going to wake up in an ecstasy or in a tantrum" (pp. 113, 191). In fact, his genius as a whole is a state of bondage rather than freedom; even when airily free, an extravagant existence like Roderick's is trapped into patterns that are determined by its world-design and that doom it to fall. "Do I succeed—do I fail?" Roderick asks. "It doesn't depend on me" (p. 164). Roderick does not believe "in purpose, in will" but believes instead that the "will is destined" (p. 109) not only because he experiences the tomb world as hopeless and unfree but also because he experiences the entire alternating pattern of his existence as fated rather than chosen. Roderick is indeed fated to alternate between the ether and the tomb, with the tomb gaining in power, as long as he remains trapped in extravagance.

The history of Roderick's conflict with the unreality of the ether and the horrible reality of the tomb tells itself in the kinds of works he creates at various points in his career. He begins with imaginary, ideal, or allegorical subjects. But eventually he turns to subjects that acknowledge the claims of the earth. In Rome, his first statues are an Adam and an ideal Eve—before the Fall, no doubt, since their unreflective innocence then would complement Roderick's naive sense of his own perfect freedom. Soon after, he imagines himself pursuing the unreal even further by making statues of the "divine forms":

> They shall be Beauty; they shall be Wisdom; they shall be Power; they shall be Genius; they shall be Daring. . . . Then there are all the Forces, and Elements, and Mysteries of Nature. . . . I mean to do the Morning; I mean to do the Night! I mean to do the Ocean and the Mountains; the Moon and the West Wind. I mean to make a magnificent statue of America! (p. 95)

Gloriani points out the extravagance of all these capital letters when, with cutting understatement, he notes that Roderick "will find it rather hard . . . to compress such subjects into classic forms" (p. 96), and Roderick himself soon discovers their lack of substance. After tomb-like despair has shattered his dreams, he admits that these unreal conceptions do not inspire "a completely plastic vision" (p. 163). Their all too imaginary being does not allow for adequate mediation with the real—a mediation that would bring together a subjective "vision" with the objectively "plastic."

Roderick turns to more realistic subjects that are inherently incarnate: "a woman leaning lazily back in her chair" (p. 110), "a *lazzarone* lounging in the sun" (p. 206), and busts of his mother and Christina Light. His turn to representation means a return to reality after the abyss shows the emptiness and illusion of the heavens. Although he is never satisfied with the compromises forced upon him when his dreams collapse, the perhaps unwitting goal of his attempts at representation is to merge the real and the ideal—to portray "the poetry of fidelity," for example, in his "perfectly unflattered" bust of Mrs. Hudson (p. 246). Such a merger might mediate the claims of the air and the earth and thus allow Roderick to transcend their conflict. At least the skeptical Gloriani thinks so, since he changes his prophecy about Roderick's prospects and declares: "I believe in you"—"I was a great ass" when "I told you last year you wouldn't keep it up. . . . You will!" (p. 246). In any case, the direction in which Roderick's art moves is also the direction his existence must take for him to reconcile the imaginary and the real so that they cease to war with each other in the caricatured form of the ether and the tomb.

The question for Roderick's existence is whether he will go on "standing passive in the clutch of his temperament" (p. 158) or whether he can somehow free himself from the fatefully alternating pattern of his divided world. For Binswanger, Roderick will liberate himself when he "strides forth" and "mounts upward"—keeping his feet in touch with the ground in practical activity that addresses the real even as it seeks self-transcendence by imagining the unreal. Roderick must overcome the "disharmony in the relation between rising upward and striding forth" that characterizes extravagance and that divides his existence between the flights of the ether and the standstill of the tomb.[21]

Now that we have examined the structure of Roderick's imaginative genius, we must study in greater detail his response to the dilemma posed by the extravagant design of his world. In this way we shall move a step closer to understanding the resolution James projects for the wonders and dangers of the imagination. We must take up the question that faces Roderick: How can an existence secure the wonders that the imagination offers without falling victim to the dangers it also holds?

THREE

Ultimately, though, what we discover with Roderick is how *not* to achieve this resolution. Roderick does not learn to "stride" and "mount" but, instead, continues to let himself be carried away on ever higher, more dangerous flights until he literally falls disastrously into an abyss, never to rise again. His death in the Alps acts as a metaphor for his extravagant existence. It expresses the futility of his alternating pattern of ascents into the ether and descents into the tomb. Binswanger uses a remarkably similar metaphor when he refers to extravagance as *"Verstiegenheit"*—a term that defies translation because it compares the danger of rising upward too far and too fast on the wings of an overly active imagination with a danger of mountain climbing. If a mountaineer climbs too high and too far, he runs the risk of becoming *"verstiegen"*—that is, of getting stuck at a point from which he is less likely to descend safely than to plummet dizzily back to earth.[22] This is essentially what happens to Roderick when, on his last lonely climb through the mountains, he gets caught on a dizzying cliff during a violent storm and makes "the inevitable slip" that plummets him from a precipice down into "the stony Alpine void" below (pp. 349, 374). As Rowland explains, "Roderick's passionate walk had carried him farther and higher than he knew" (p. 349). But this description suits the fate of his existence as fittingly as the circumstances of his death.

Images of falling from a precipice occur throughout the novel and, by foreshadowing Roderick's death, contribute to the existentially symbolic value of his demise. Roderick is like a terrace garden that Rowland visits in Florence and that "hangs in the air" so precariously that you "wonder how it keeps from slipping down . . . into the nakedly romantic gorge beneath" (p. 217). At one point, Rowland has "a vision of Roderick, graceful and beautiful as he passed, plunging like a diver into a misty gulf. This gulf was destruction, annihilation, death" (p. 216). This is the abyss that awaits the man of active imagination who fails to respond adequately to the challenge of extravagance by resolving the conflict of the ether and the tomb.

Roderick's failure to resolve this conflict is due largely to his involvement with Christina Light. His obsession with her plunges him into his final episode of tomb-like despair during his last weeks, and her reappearance at the end motivates the events leading up to the "passionate walk" that kills him. Roderick loves Christina, and Binswanger claims that love can transport a person "beyond-the-world" in a transcendence that "transforms the individual existence" by opening "a finite being-in-the-world" up to "the infinite fullness of homeland and eternity."[23] But here again it is also possible to go too far—and to go wrong by extravagance. Ironically, perhaps, Roderick gets too far ahead of himself by caring so extravagantly for Christina that he becomes fantastically solipsistic about her. Never achieving an intimate mutuality, they appear to each other as ethereal objects that inspire an imaginative investment of meaning and value. Roderick fascinates Christina, for example, because, as "a man of genius," he is "not a common mortal"; his "sacred fire" makes him different and "defiant" (p. 153). He has many values for her imagination—including, among others, the value of a stimulus to incite her interest when everything else has grown tediously ordinary. Christina excites

Roderick's imagination as much as he does hers. When he first encounters her, she seems the incarnation of a dream—"a vision . . . of transcendent perfection" who excites him into exclaiming that "she's beauty itself—she's a revelation. I don't believe she is living—she's a phantasm, a vapour, an illusion" (pp. 81–82). Reviving his enthusiasm for life after a period of disillusionment, she incites in him a flight of imagination that frees him from the tomb so that he insists on sculpting her bust.

Edel misnames the cause of their effect on each other when he argues that "the moral" of Christina's and Roderick's relationship is "that a great physical passion can be fatal to art."[24] Their relationship is passionate but hardly physical. They appeal to each other less at the level of anything so substantial as the body than at the level of the insubstantial image whose power to excite desire is more formative, even in Freudian terms, than the power of the libidinal alone. When Roderick confesses "an almost unlimited susceptibility to the influence of a beautiful woman" (p. 109), he reveals less about his libido than about his tendency to let a woman's beauty act as an easy substitute for artistic beauty. It is easier to fall in love than to make a statue, after all, but both a woman and art can give wings to his imagination just as both can flatter his vanity. When he abandons art and, in his desire for Christina, commits his imagination to its most passionate ethereal flight, Roderick does not realize that love can offer as much resistance to wishes, hopes, and dreams as the stone he sculpts.

Their desire for each other cannot succeed because it is an extravagant illusion based on imagination and fed by vanity. Actually, it is not a "love" at all but, rather, a rivalry of two "transcendent egotist[s]" (p. 337)—to borrow Rowland's description of Roderick—who are too wrapped up in themselves to care about the Other except as this serves the Self. Christina and Roderick do not want intimacy; although they desire each other, they desire even more to be desired by the other and thus, in a manner described by René Girard, to be transformed into the other's god. In line with Girard's model of the "rivalry" of "vanity," both experience "the failure of a more or less conscious attempt at an apotheosis of the self"—Roderick whenever he falls into the tomb world and Christina when she becomes disillusioned about her prospects. Then, finding the promise of perfection apparently unbroken in another, they make that other their deity be-

cause "they are not able to give up infinity." Vanity cannot rest at wor-
shiping another, however, and tries instead to get its god to worship it
because it thus achieves a divinity greater than its idol. Extravagant
imagination is the foundation of this roundabout search for transcen-
dency. "Men become gods in the eyes of each other" only because
vanity "transfigures its object" by "confer[ring] upon it an illusory
value."[25]

Tired and indifferent because she is idolized by everyone and is
left, consequently, with nothing to desire, Christina still feels restless
and unsatisfied. All too conscious of personal inadequacies no one
sees as clearly as she does, she has no deity of her own who might
offer something more. Roderick fascinates her as a possible god
whose promise seems unbroken. He secures his ascendancy over her
by refusing at the beginning of their relationship to idolize her like the
others. "Mademoiselle, you almost satisfy my conception of the beautiful," he tells her, and she feels that "that *almost* should be re-
warded" (p. 126) because it seems to share in her own secret knowledge of her disappointments and failings. When he directs her to
rearrange her hair "with a peremptoriness of tone" while sculpting her
bust, his fault-finding sets off her coquetry in response—"'Do it your-
self then'! she cried, and with a rapid movement unloosed the great
coil of her tresses and let them fall over her shoulders" so that "she
looked like some immaculate saint of legend being led to martyrdom"
(p. 132)—all because his aloof manner makes him seem like a god
whose desire is worth capturing. But later, when he fawns over her
like everyone else, her illusions disappear and his desirability van-
ishes because he makes himself ordinary.

Roderick also plays the game of vain desire to win the power that
belongs to a transcendent god—and plays it with a characteristic "extravagant folly" (p. 186). There is, for example, the episode in the
coliseum where he frightens Christina and Rowland and foreshadows
his own death by proposing to undertake an impossible climb for a
little flower in a lofty niche above a deep drop. When she taunts him
by claiming "it's highly probable" that he's "a failure," "a third-rate
talent," "terribly small," and "after all rather ordinary," he can defend
his status as a deity in her eyes only by performing some feat that
reasserts his ascendancy and expresses "the voice of a conqueror"
(pp. 182–84). Although typically romantic, a little flower is an absurd object for such a magnificent deed. But its pettiness merely em-

phasizes Roderick's actual object—that is, to recapture Christina's desire by regaining her awe-struck respect—at the same time as it points up the awful extravagance of their entire rivalry. Rowland intervenes, of course, and Roderick does not get the flower. But that matters little because he gets what he wanted when Christina's facade of indifference crumbles in a fit of hysterical fear at his danger, thus reestablishing his ascendancy; he has revealed her weakness, where she had threatened to reveal his. It is relevant that "the language of absolute decision" (p. 184) that Roderick uses to win here is also the language of extravagance where, according to Binswanger, "the 'absolutizing' of a single decision" creates a rigidity that is weakness disguised as strength.[26]

The ethereal nature of their meaning for each other shows itself conclusively in the horrible nature of the tomb that envelops them when their volatile relationship finally breaks up. Even if she never completely overcomes her own vanity, there is something noble in Christina's attempt to defy the tyranny of her mother's designs. But, predictably, "this ethereal flight of her moral nature" is "rudely jerked down to the base earth" by the "sinister compulsion" that Mrs. Light exercises to enforce her daughter's compliance (p. 275). The dark secret about Christina's illegitimate origin that compels her submission acts as a specter from the world of the tomb that announces the extravagance of any such defiance and points up the ultimate futility of the struggle for ascendancy she and Roderick wage. When her world collapses, Roderick's does too, and he plummets into his last but deepest pit of despair. Showing all the by now familiar signs of the tomb world's awful bondage, he experiences "extreme restlessness" and "irritation and *ennui*" and goes through "long silences, fits of profound lethargy, almost of stupefaction" (p. 297). Trapped in a world emptied of possibilities, Roderick reveals the meaning of Binswanger's claim that "the tomb-world is ruled by the unauthentic (because it is without future), ever present past." Roderick declares that "the future is a dead blank" (p. 294) to him and that, even more hopelessly, "for one hour of what I *have* been I would give up anything I may be" (p. 310). He lives in "the mere Now," equally cut off from the past and the future. His temporal isolation offers no future that might proceed in an invigorating way from his past.[27] As he and his group travel from Rome to Florence and then the Alps, Roderick's lack of attention or interest makes it seem as if he were "waiting for" some "spiritual miracle" that might bring "his redemption" (p. 297)—some magical influence that, as in the past, might lift him out of the abyss. His despair here does indeed prepare for one final ethereal flight— but one that leads to his death.

The living death that impoverishes Roderick's last weeks also pre- pares for his actual demise in another way. I have already alluded to the rigidity, narrowness, and loss of freedom that characterize extrav- agance. Roderick's rigidity increases as his extravagance escalates, in a process that Binswanger calls "*Verweltlichung*"—that is, "a shrink- ing and simultaneous narrowing of existence" marked by "the narrow- ing and leveling of the significance of the world."[28] "The fault of the young man's whole structure was an excessive want of breadth" (p. 37), Rowland notes near the beginning in an observation about Roderick's physique that applies just as well to his existence. But Roderick's narrowness is most striking because most severe at the end when he feels "dead, dead; dead and buried . . . in an open grave, where you lie staring up at the sailing clouds, smelling the waving flowers and hearing all nature live and grow above you" (p. 310)— where he yearns for the world of meaning and value all the more in- tensely because it is lost to him in his miserably constricted *Verweltli- chung*. A narrowing of existence goes hand in hand with a feeling of helplessness, a paralysis of the ability to choose from possibilities. And so when Rowland admonishes his friend to "choose, select, de- cide" (p. 292) a course for the future, Roderick sees little open to him except to be shot and buried dead or to be taken back to Northampton and buried alive.

Thanks to this lack of openness and agency, Binswanger explains, the narrowness and rigidity of *Verweltlichung* prepare for the fall of *Verstiegenheit*; they make its victim vulnerable to sudden shocks, to "the breakthrough . . . of the unexpected." These can be too much to handle for an existence that has reduced itself to so little.[29] The nar- rowness of Roderick's extravagance makes him susceptible to the sud- den throughout his career. But he is most vulnerable in the extreme rigidity and constriction of his last few days when the unexpected breaks through to such overpowering effect with Christina's sudden appearance in the Alps, Rowland's surprising (at least to Roderick) confession of his love for Mary Garland, and the violent storm that catches him unprepared during his final climb.

The dangerous power of the sudden and unexpected over Roderick gives existential significance to the melodramatic turns of plot with which James concludes the novel. Many readers—including James himself, when he reviewed his earlier work for the New York Edition—have regarded the sudden turns of fortune that lead to Roderick's death as arbitrary and unconvincing. James wonders in his preface whether Roderick's unusually "large capacity for ruin" might not point "too stern a moral" and thus deprive him of interest by rendering him "a morbidly special case":

> My mistake on Roderick's behalf . . . is that, at the rate at which he falls to pieces, he seems to place himself beyond our understanding and our sympathy. These are not our rates, we say; we ourselves certainly, under like pressure,—for what is it after all?—would make more of a fight. . . . [T]his young man must either have had less of the principle of development to have had so much of the principle of collapse, or less of the principle of collapse to have had so much of the principle of development.

Now James may be right that Roderick fails to emerge as a fully satisfactory "fictive hero," if such a character "successfully appeals to us only as an eminent instance, as eminent as we like, of our own conscious kind."[30] Roderick belongs to "our conscious kind" as an extreme case rather than "an eminent instance." But, as I have argued, it is the truth of this extreme to have an extreme "principle of development" alternating with an extreme "principle of collapse."

The storm that surprises Roderick in the mountains draws meaning from the two other events just before—that is, again, Christina's reappearance and Rowland's confession—which also overpower him and catch him off guard. When Christina unexpectedly reenters his world near the end, Roderick once more feels her power to release him from despair by launching him on a flight of inspiration and enthusiasm. "She makes me feel as if I were alive again," "she makes my heart beat, makes me see visions" and "feel excited," he exclaims: "she has waked me up" and "it is such a huge refreshment to find myself again desiring something" (pp. 332–33). But if Christina's reappearance sets him off on a heady flight, Rowland's confession brings Roderick crashing down to earth again in a by now all too familiar pattern of rising only to fall. Rowland's confession surprises Roderick by revealing a hidden side he had never expected to a state of affairs he had construed quite differently. There was no place in Roderick's view of his patron for motives or desires other than simple benevolence in service of his artistic career. He is paralyzed because he could not assimilate such motives or desires without a radical reordering of his world of the kind that the inflexibility of his *Verweltlichung* renders impossible. The storm that traps Roderick on a cliff reflects his helplessness throughout because of his incapacitating extravagance. The storm seems melodramatic because it has demonic qualities. But the demonic epitomizes the powerlessness man experiences when unfreedom overwhelms freedom.

Before his death Roderick has a chance to rescue freedom from unfreedom but fails to rise to its challenge. Substituting insight for blindness as Rowland's confession calls on Roderick to do can have good effect by leading to self-reflection and then, in turn, to a change in world-design to accommodate the new revelation.[31] Roderick seems on the road to a liberating self-awareness when he confesses himself "damnably stupid" and asks, "Isn't an artist supposed to be a man of perceptions? I am hugely disgusted" (p. 340). But when Rowland declares, "Well, you understand now, and we can start afresh" (p. 340), Roderick does not hear him because, still trapped in his old patterns, he is busy nursing his vanity instead of replacing it with humility. Where, in his vanity, Roderick felt complete ascendancy over his unspectacular patron, he has suddenly discovered in him a rival with a certain superiority all his own because of the apparent nobility of his self-sacrificing resignation. Instead of entering into Rowland's situation sympathetically or evaluating the error of his own ways self-critically, Roderick delivers a series of stinging blows that show his egotism still asserting itself—discrediting Rowland's experience by declaring he could not "have suffered so much as some other men would have done," disclaiming his threat as a rival for Mary by announcing "it's a pity she doesn't care for you," and destroying his hopes once and for all by proclaiming "she idolizes me, and if she were never to see me again she would idolize my memory" (p. 340). Roderick's tragedy shows how preoccupation with the Self in vanity can prevent reflection on the Self in the responsible exercise of the freedom to change our worlds.

Still, Roderick does confront death in the Alps, and some existential thinkers argue that facing up to death resolutely can have a liberating effect. Accepting the absolute contingency of existence can make us stop escaping the responsibilities of freedom and care.[32] We do not know what happens to Roderick during the storm, however, and the restlessness with which he walks off after his encounter with Rowland makes it seem unlikely he is near to overcoming his extravagance. Throughout the novel, Roderick takes off on restless wanderings whenever despair strikes. His final hike refers back to these "long rambles, generally alone" and very often "into dizzy places" near "the edges of plunging chasms" (pp. 314, 311)—walks that, in their aimlessness, show Roderick unable to direct himself toward a resolution of his problems. Restlessness like this shows that we are not at home with ourselves.[33] When we last see him, Roderick is restless and not resolute, vain and not courageous. On the level of plot, then, Roderick's death would seem more likely to reflect the bankruptcy of his existence than to herald his salvation. This in turn, on a metaphoric level, would indicate that Roderick's death is a sign of *Verstiegenheit* in Binswanger's sense and that a resolution for extravagance has not been won but lost.

FOUR

As we expected, then, we have learned from Roderick how not to resolve extravagance. But has this approach by virtue of the negative brought us any closer to understanding a positive resolution of the risks and values of the imaginative life that we might then attribute at least implicitly to James? We have seen, for example, that Roderick's failure to overcome his extravagance points up the value of critical self-reflection in the exercise of freedom, the virtue of engaging in practical activity with both feet on the ground, and the necessity of mediating the unreality of the imagination's subjectivity with the reality of various objective factors. We have seen these projected resolutions to the imagination's crisis dialectically, by virtue of the negative—because, namely, their absence in Roderick's case implies a call for their presence. The dangers he falls victim to speak persuasively for the value of the paths he does not take. These preliminary findings warrant us, I think, in applying our dialectical procedure to a few other areas of the novel as we seek to project James's most overarching resolution of the imagination's risks and values.

One major hope for transcending extravagance that Binswanger proposes lies in the help that the care of others can provide. We have already examined the negative side of this hope in the way that Roderick's and Christina's vain rivalry, instead of bringing them together in intimacy, keeps them apart at a distance necessary to sustain their illusions about each other's seemingly unbroken promise. According to Binswanger, someone "detached from loving *communio* and authentic *communicatio*" runs the greatest risk of extravagance because he lacks "the challenge and correction that can only be derived from such intercourse" with others. "Love and friendship have, in these airy heights, lost their power," he explains, so that a return from the peaks of extravagance must include "a return to the world of others and to actual, authentic communication with them." Or, in the metaphoric terms of *Verstiegenheit*, "rescue from the extravagant position" may be "possible only by means of 'outside help,' as is true of a mountain-climber who has climbed too far out upon a precipice."[34] Recall, for example, the incident in the coliseum where Rowland's intervention rescues Roderick from an extravagant attempt to impress Christina by preventing him from undertaking an absurd climb. Echoes of this incident reverberate near the novel's ending. Just as Roderick is departing on his final walk, Rowland feels "a singular and most illogical impulse" to intervene again—"a desire to stop him, to have another word with him—not to lose sight of him" (p. 341). He has a premonition, in other words, of the need to save his friend from going too far and getting caught irretrievably in *Verstiegenheit*. Binswanger's theory about the relation between extravagance and care depends on the relation between imagination and intersubjectivity. The imagination can either help narrow the gap between ourselves and others or lock us in solipsism by feeding the vanity of extravagance. Losing care is one of the consequences of extravagance, then, and restoring care is a necessary part of its resolution.

Roderick's example demonstrates the loss of community that extravagance entails, but his tragedy also shows the difficulty of restoring the power of love and friendship once they have lapsed. In becoming extravagant, Roderick isolates himself from others in an all but solipsistic existence where "sympathy" and "compassion" have turned into "things to which he seemed perfectly indifferent and of which he could make no use" (p. 288). As Rowland notes, "The great and characteristic point with him was the perfect exclusiveness of his emotions. He never saw himself as part of a whole; only as the clear-cut, sharp-edged, isolated individual, rejoicing or raging, as the case might be, but needing in any case absolutely to affirm himself" (p. 288).

Parading in the guise of proud independence, Roderick's fearful isolation makes him immune to the influence of others. For example, the arrogance that deprives him of friends in the artistic community also prevents him from understanding Gloriani and Singleton as potentially helpful examples of roads to creativity other than ethereally inspired genius. But his vanity isolates him equally from those closer to him. The love of Mrs. Hudson and Mary Garland is all one-way, from them to him as their idol but with never a hint of similar devotion in return. When, near the end, Mary has the audacity to claim her "rights" for some show of "reciprocity," Mrs. Hudson reacts to this "arrogant doctrine" with an outrage that reveals it is the young woman's part not to care for her future husband and what becomes of him but to act "as a kind of assistant priestess at Roderick's shrine" (pp. 302–3). This absence of reciprocity in his relations with others proceeds from Roderick's extravagance, then, and at the same time reinforces it by isolating him from the possibly saving influence of others. Solipsistic in his extravagance, Roderick is thus closed off from the care he needs to end his solipsism.

Although equally capable of proud aloofness, Christina reaches out to Rowland for help in a way that sheds light on the relation between intersubjectivity and extravagance and illuminates a major obstacle to replacing isolation with care. She regards Rowland as a paragon of moral integrity—everything she is not since she thinks herself "corrupt, corrupting, corruption" (p. 273). Apparently taking the very road that could lead Roderick to salvation, she pleads with Rowland for guidance and trust to help her overcome the limits of her character and situation. Only with his assistance, she claims, can she attain her "stifled ideal" of "moral sublimity" (pp. 280, 201). But what Rowland must first decide is whether to believe her. "I *was* sincere," she finally declares (p. 329)—but was she? When Christina demands "begin and respect me," "believe in me," and "show confidence in me" (pp. 201, 213, 214), should Rowland regard her plea as an earnest expression of moral concern or, on the contrary, as a clever gambit to enlist him among the worshipers at the altar of her vanity? These questions are vexing even for critics of the novel who in general conclude ambivalently (and no doubt correctly) that "good and evil impulses" are at war in her.[35] Rowland faces the dilemma of determining first how to read her call for understanding and sympathy and then how to respond without slighting her yet also without overextending himself on her behalf. At times he seems "grossly obtuse" and "thick-skinned" (p. 335) about her, as Roderick claims, because he often tries to evade and never satisfactorily resolves this problem. Still, the dilemma Rowland wrestles with here is as thorny as it is significant. The exercise of intersubjective sympathy and understanding—including any effort to rescue a victim of extravagance—faces no obstacle more stubborn than the question of how to mediate the conflicting calls of suspicion and faith that Rowland finds so vexing with Christina.

This same quarrel of suspicion versus faith frustrates Rowland's relationship with Roderick. If Rowland often seems overly suspicious of Christina, his hesitancy may reflect his fear of once again trusting too much as he did when he staked his faith in the sculptor. His problems with Roderick—and, indeed, the vicissitudes of the artist's entire adventure—come about because, at the beginning, Rowland trusts too blindly in himself and his friend. When asked for "guarantees" about the success of his project by Roderick's family, Rowland replies, apparently with all due caution, that "one can't *know* in such a matter save after proof, and proof takes time. But one can believe" (p. 61). And since Rowland does believe, the counsels of caution about the risks of such faith are overruled. Habitually prudent and hesitant, he may wonder "at his temerity" in "meddling" so self-confidently with the established security of other lives "in the interest of a far-away fantastic hypothesis" (p. 64). But only at the end, when all his expectations lie in ruin about him and he feels "like a restless trustee who has speculated with the widow's mite"—only then does Rowland fully comprehend the extravagance of the hopes and dreams in which he had believed (p. 298). Roderick's fall from the extravagance of his aspirations is also Rowland's fall from the extravagance of his faith. Ironically, perhaps, where the intervention of others can curb extravagance, Rowland's intervention in Roderick's life has quite the opposite effect.

When Rowland attempts to reverse his course and offer Roderick assistance based more on caution and suspicion than on liberality and faith, he finds himself caught in a contradiction that renders him powerless to rein in the extravagance he unleashed. On the one hand, Rowland would like to make Roderick more skeptical of his own weaknesses in order to warn him away from the dangers he risks; as Roderick's sponsor, Rowland considers himself accountable when things go wrong. Yet, on the other hand, he realizes that Roderick is ultimately responsible for himself and must first help himself if anyone is to help him; even when filled with suspicions about his friend's inadequacies, then, Rowland must trust to Roderick's doubtful ability to overcome them. When Rowland tries nonetheless to rescue his friend with level-headed advice, Roderick puts him off by telling him *"you don't understand me!"* (pp. 158–59; original emphasis) and complaining: "I resent the range of your vision pretending to be the limit of my action. You can't feel or judge for me" (p. 335). Part of this protest is self-indulgent stubbornness. But part of it too is an expression of the truth that there are limits to how much someone can help someone else by intervening on his behalf. Roderick's complaint is justified to the extent that well-intentioned assistance becomes meddling when it oversteps the line where trust in the other must take over. No one can ever understand someone else fully, and Roderick's failure to understand himself does not mean that anyone else has a better vantage point for seeing into him than he does if he would only make proper use of it. Furthermore, as Roderick indicates by resisting Rowland's attempt to "feel" and "judge" for him, no one can take another's responsibilities away from him because no one can take another's freedom upon himself.[36] Rowland can only succeed in his solicitude for his friend's welfare by resolving the conflict of suspicion and faith that faces him here—that is, by finding a way to instill self-criticism in Roderick while nonetheless trusting him as required in a free and unmanipulative and thus truly caring relationship.

Even if he could reach Roderick with his help, however, the advice Rowland has for him does not contain a perfectly satisfactory resolution for the wonders and dangers of the imaginative life. He urges Roderick to substitute self-discipline for self-indulgence, to take his responsibilities more seriously, and to "set to work" even if he does not "feel like it" (p. 165). These prudent suggestions seem to agree with Binswanger's views on curbing extravagance by engaging in practical activity. Still, even though Roderick may need to pull himself up as abruptly as Rowland suggests, the cautious patron's advice is in itself just as one-sided as the extravagant behavior it aims to correct. Most critics of the novel seem to sense the limitations of the attitude this advice reflects. Almost unanimously they give Rowland praise with one hand by calling him "a morally responsible individual" with a "cool, measuring mind" at the same time as they take it away with the other by faulting his "stuffy sobriety," his too "dispassionate heart," and his "somewhat priggish" demeanor.[37] Rowland is incomplete because he is too cautious in the face of the imagination's risks to enjoy its values in full measure. He would have Roderick avoid the imagination's dangers, but at the sacrifice of too many of its wonders—its openness, freedom, and possibility.

The contrast between Rowland's disciplined moral sense and Roderick's uncontrolled extravagance, both one-sided and incomplete in themselves, has much in common with the contrast Kierkegaard establishes in *Either/Or* between the ethical attitude of Judge Wilhelm and the aesthetic attitude of this solid burgher's pleasure-seeking young friend. Kierkegaard regards both the aesthetic and the moral attitudes as limited and thus in need of a dialectical transcendence to what he calls the religious attitude, which, in existential terms, would still embrace the freedom and openness of the aesthete's position while incorporating the responsibility and resignation of the judge's.[38] Now Rowland is more aesthetically inclined than Judge Wilhelm, and Roderick is more productive than Kierkegaard's aesthete. But we can still recognize a fundamental identity between James and Kierkegaard here that amounts to a call for transcending the limits of both the aesthetic and the moral positions. Rowland acknowledges his incompleteness in the very act of becoming Roderick's patron and thus seeks to open himself at least vicariously to a world of imaginative possibility that would otherwise remain closed to him. When he retreats later, Rowland's defense of duty and work reveals his own inadequacies as much as Roderick's and, consequently, needs to be transcended as much as the extravagance it seeks to overcome. Suspicion and faith are once again the central issues here because Rowland's ethical sense is too long on restraint and too short on openness to the inspiration of possibilities—just as Roderick's aesthetic enthusiasm can be exactly the opposite.

What kind of resolution to the wonders and dangers of the imaginative life would transcend the limits of a cautious moral attitude and yet still avoid the excesses of extravagance? Although no such resolution appears in the pages of the novel itself, the one projected by virtue of the negative according to Rowland's and Roderick's failure to discover it seems equivalent to the resolution that Ricoeur finds to a similar problem in what he calls a dialectical hermeneutics of suspicion and revelation. Ricoeur wonders how to reconcile demystifying interpretive methods that emphasize the "discipline of the real" and the "ascesis of the necessary" with revelatory, restorative approaches that stress "the grace of imagination" and "the upsurge of the possible." He proposes to resolve these conflicting opposites into mutually enhancing complementaries by means of a dialectical hermeneutics that would make suspicion and faith work together rather than fight each other. This dialectic would give a progressive movement to the otherwise regressive action of doubt and suspicion. It would have demystification serve revelation in order to ground hope, faith, and trust more securely without destroying them. Suspicion must criticize the limits of faith, he argues, just as faith must reveal the limits of suspicion.[39]

Such a dialectic would transcend Rowland's worries about the imagination's risks by applying his suspicions to the work of establishing a critically grounded revelation of its values. This dialectic would similarly overcome Roderick's extravagance by justifying faith in the imagination's wonders through doubts that would disclose its dangers. Rowland seems to be struggling toward Ricoeur's dialectic when he battles with the conflicting demands of suspicion and faith that his relations with Christina and Roderick impose on him. Furthermore, the antagonism of ether and tomb that plagues Roderick represents an extreme disharmony that is the reverse image of Ricoeur's dialectical harmony—a harmony that can only come about when progressive and regressive movements like those that tear the sculptor apart are made to cooperate instead. Ricoeur's dialectic of suspicion and revelation would seem to provide an overarching resolution, then, to the crisis of the imagination's wonders and dangers—the crisis that lies behind the many conflicts portrayed in *Roderick Hudson*.

Still, some doubts may remain as to whether Ricoeur's resolution is truly James's too. It may seem that we have risked illusion in speculating by virtue of the negative about a dialectic projected by but not actually present in a literary work. To begin with, however, this resolution—so gracefully simple in theory—is, no doubt, so difficult to put into practice that James would have risked extravagance himself by portraying it at work triumphantly. James avoids this danger by refusing to specify his dialectic positively—by leaving the reader to discover it on his own as an unwritten implication of the written text. Textual indeterminacy is unavoidable, and this is one way of manipulating it. According to Iser, many narratives invoke a similar practice: "Instead of being expressly stated, the criteria for such judgments have to be inferred. They are the blanks which the reader is supposed to fill in, thus bringing his own criticism to bear. In other words, it is his own criticism that constitutes the reality of the book." [40] Speculating by virtue of the negative about implied resolutions to the imagination's crisis is not an unusual procedure, then. It is one of the tasks assigned to the reader as he responds to the perspectives through which James's novel unfolds. In evaluating them, the reader transcends them to achieve a more adequate, more encompassing viewpoint. *Roderick Hudson* is not one of James's most innovative narratives. Later works like *The Turn of the Screw* and *The Golden Bowl* deploy indeterminacies much more ingeniously to create greater ambiguity and to challenge the reader more strenuously. But even this early work manipulates the reader's role to encourage active analysis and projections that may in turn transform his consciousness by the discoveries they lead to. In using his imagination to fill a major blank that *Roderick Hudson* leaves unspecified—a resolution to the risks and values of extravagance—the reader receives training in the responsible exercise of the imagination.

James's dialectical attitude toward the imagination's wonders and dangers is part of a more global dialectical vision of the relation between faith and suspicion. Richard Poirier has identified one form of this dialectic in his interpretation of the function of comedy in *Roderick Hudson* and other of James's early works. Poirier argues that James's comic sense demystifies by tearing off the masks that disguise tyranny in order to defend and reveal the possibility of freedom. [41] James is better known for his tragic than his comic sense, however—his tragic sense of how life persistently disappoints because it fails to reach all it might be. But his tragic sense acts in a similar manner to uncover the horrible in order to project the marvelous that it stifles. This double movement of suspicion united with revelation makes James no simple skeptic but, rather, a persistent if tough-minded affirmer of existence who says "yes" dialectically by saying "no." Applied to the crisis of the imagination, the dialectical action of James's tragic sense makes him suspicious of its dangers because he rejoices in its wonders. A tragic sense of the imagination's double-sided nature, then, is itself a resolution of its crisis.

F I V E

James's tragic sense and its hermeneutic counterpart in Ricoeur's dialectic of suspicion and revelation involve much more than the imagination alone. Their relevance extends over a wide domain that encompasses the imagination but that also reaches from perception to all aspects of existence. Only because the crisis of the imagination at the active pitch turned out to have such wide implications did it become necessary to project so broad a resolution for it. The range of problems and possibilities raised by the vicissitudes of the imagination confirms its role as a bridge between perception and existence.

Roderick Hudson's extravagance is basically a crisis of imagination, but it is also inextricably a crisis of epistemology, freedom, and care. His extravagant manner of being-in-the-world involves two contradictory ways of knowing the world. When he knows ethereally, he is inspired by vivid, bountiful impressions; but when the tomb takes over, his perceptual horizons contract violently. A dark cloud separates him from the wonderful world he had envisioned before. As we saw, Roderick's ethereal world represents freedom and his tomb-world bondage; as his perceptual horizons expand or contract, his possibilities open themselves up or close themselves off. We also saw that Roderick would have to secure a steadier, more responsible freedom by liberating himself from the grasp of his fate-like extravagance if he were to resolve the crisis of his imagination. A more responsible freedom would steady his volatile perceptual worlds. It would also help intersubjectivity and care because a prideful isolation from others is, as we learned, one of the major consequences of the alienation from himself brought about by the bondage of vanity and extravagance. Ricoeur's dialectic can respond to the imagination's crisis only because it also speaks to these questions of epistemology, freedom, and care. We worked up to this resolution of the imagination's wonders and dangers because we encountered the same conflict of suspicion and faith in all three areas—in how to know with skepticism as well as revelation, how to be with restraint as well as freedom, and how to care with criticism as well as trust.

The relation between the imagination's wonders and dangers and those of perception and existence shows again the unity of knowing and doing in James. Because of the imagination's wide-ranging significance, this chapter bridges the studies of epistemological and existential matters that flank it. In our study of the imagination, we have crossed over from the epistemology of the "impression" in James to the existential dynamics of his "moral vision." Even in the epistemological researches of the last chapter we were involved with matters of freedom and care; elucidating the significance of the impression led us to James's appreciation of the perceptual and aesthetic possibilities that follow from its way of knowing as well as to his concern with the threat of solipsism that endangers its ability to know. But now, closing in on what the impression and the imagination have brought us to anticipate, we must fill out the existential significance of James's insight into freedom and care, the next two aspects of experience that we must consider. How does James understand the dilemma posed by the conflict between freedom's call to the possibility of possibility and responsibility's reminder of the limits posed by various kinds of necessity? And how does he regard the obstacles to care created by the opacity of the Other? These two questions will take us further down the paths that the imagination has charted for us.

• 4 •

FREEDOM AND NECESSITY:

THE SERVILE WILL AND

THE PORTRAIT OF A LADY

ONE

James the moral dramatist never tires of exploring the conflict between freedom and necessity in his fictions. As a dilemma of defining
importance to his moral vision, this conflict ranks as one of the intentional foundations that help to explain how his artistic world organizes
itself. On the one hand, James could declare his confidence in "*a
mighty will*, there is nothing but that! The integrity of one's will, purpose, faith."[1] On the other hand, though, this true believer in the
freedom and power of the will could feel with equal conviction that
"the very stuff" of "human life" is revealed in "the discovery by each
of us that we are at best but a rather ridiculous fifth wheel to the
coach, after we have sat cracking our whip and believing that we are
at least the coachman in person."[2] James can delight in the exuberance with which Strether declares: "Live all you can; it's a mistake not
to." But he can also demonstrate that it's the better part of freedom "to
submit to the inevitable" and "assent to destiny"—to consent willingly to the limits that establish how much we "*can*" live.[3] How are we
free, and how are we constrained? And what is the relationship between our will and our fate, our possibilities and their limits, our freedom and the demands of necessity? These are questions James is forever posing in his fictions as he probes this paradoxical aspect of
existence.

It is widely known that existentialism from Kierkegaard through
Sartre has taken freedom as one of its central concerns. But existential phenomenologists have always attended equally to the claims of
necessity. They argue that, at bottom, we are inalienably, inevitably

free inasmuch as we exist only because we make ourselves by choosing how to project ourselves toward the future. But, as Merleau-Ponty observes, "the choice which we make of our life is always based on a certain givenness."[4] This "givenness"—the unchosen element in all our choices—is what we refer to when we talk about "necessity." It comes about because, to recall Heidegger's terms, we always find ourselves already "thrown" (geworfen) into a world already decided for us in many respects. As Maisie finally discovers in her quest for a meaningful freedom, our "thrownness" confronts us with a certain "ground" that our freedom must accept as a limit to its possibilities.

Now our "ground" limits us, according to Heidegger, but it also lends us power. It grants us a particular hold on the world by allowing us a position from which to make choices and to realize our "potentiality-for-Being" (Seinkönnen).[5] It denies us an unlimited range of possibilities, but it makes possible what Merleau-Ponty calls a "field of possibility" for us to disclose to ourselves and decide what to make of.[6] We always have the freedom to take a critical posture toward our ground and thereby to accept it as a field that allows the option of striving to change it. To give a somewhat un-Jamesian example, but one that Merleau-Ponty uses, this is what workers do when they acknowledge the alienation of their labor in order to become revolutionaries. But if, in what Ricoeur calls a "dream of innocence," we refuse to "consent to necessity," we not only delude ourselves about our possibilities but, even worse, actually sacrifice our freedom by fleeing from its conditions of possibility.[7]

It is necessary to consent to the givenness that confronts us but— and this is key—such consent is itself a free act, a choice. It is always possible to attempt to deny the claims of our ground (as Sir Claude does in his wishful declaration of freedom), and many different ways of assenting to them are open to us. Only because we are free can we, in James's words, "assent to destiny" and "submit to the inevitable." Necessity is nothing in itself but brute, meaningless facticity. It becomes "necessity" only as we give it meaning by a free act of constitution (or Sinngebung, in Husserl's vocabulary). But by acknowledging our givenness as a limit, we transform it into a part of our "situation"—that theater of operation that our freedom makes for itself so that it can exercise itself. Ricoeur summarizes this reciprocity between freedom and necessity in what he calls "the paradox of the servile will." Servitude and the will go hand in hand, he argues, because we can be free only if we are bound just as we can be bound only if we are free.[8] In order to understand the existential significance of this aspect of James's moral vision, then, we must ask whether his understanding of the relationship between freedom and necessity incorporates the dialectic of the "servile will."

Perhaps nowhere does James explore the relation between possibility and limitation more tellingly than in *The Portrait of a Lady*, that story "of a certain young woman affronting her destiny" who in turn finds her destiny affronting her.[9] Almost every critic who has written about Isabel Archer's tragedy has interpreted it in terms of freedom and necessity. Dorothy Van Ghent summarizes the critical consensus when she explains that the novel is "deeply informed with the tragic view of life" because it displays the "tension between the power of willing (which is 'free') and the power of circumstances ('necessity') binding and limiting the will." This is also the point of those critics who, like Cargill and Poirier, identify Isabel's tragic flaw as her extreme "American idealism"—that is, the almost "pure Emersonianism" behind her insistence at the beginning that her possibilities know no limits. The novel seems to exemplify what Morton Dauwen Zabel calls the "implicit paradox" central to James which pits "liberty and possibility" against "an opposing law . . . of limitation, of necessity and sacrifice."[10]

We have here another instance where an issue that concerns us for its existential and phenomenological significance has already received considerable attention from other perspectives because of its importance for James's achievement. My contribution to the consensus will be twofold. My reading of *The Portrait* will try to lay bare the experiential underpinnings of this issue—the origins of the dialectic of freedom and necessity in the basic structure of existence as James understands it. I will also be trying to show how James's attitude toward possibility and limitation contributes to his overall existential and phenomenological significance insofar as his assumptions about them are consistent with the other intentional foundations supporting his artistic project.

Our studies of epistemology and imagination in James have already shown us that the paradox of the servile will is thoroughly implicated in his other major concerns. For example, the impression's amazing power despite inherent weakness can be seen as a particular instance of how possibility and its limits work together. The impression is weak because it presents no more than a particular "aspect" (or *Abschattung*) of an object, but it is wonderfully powerful because its restricted view points toward an array of possible revelations implied in its particular hold on the world. James's faith in the novel's freedom consents to the restrictions of each writer's vision in order to open the genre as a whole to the possibility of disclosing a complete picture of the world. The wonders and dangers of the imagination also exhibit the existential paradigm of freedom and necessity. Roderick Hudson revels in the imagination's wonders only to run amok in its dangers as he seeks freedom without bondage only to find bondage without freedom. Ricoeur's dialectic of suspicion and revelation can resolve the conflict between the imagination's risks and values because it reconciles the discipline of necessity and the grace of possibility. The affinities between these aspects of experience offer more evidence of the unity between James's epistemological concerns and his moral vision—a unity noticeably similar, as I have argued, to the unity that joins phenomenological views on such problems as perception and imagination to existential views on such issues as possibility and its limits.

The relationship between freedom and necessity should also recall the link between Henry and William James that I suggested earlier. With an almost Emersonian faith in the power of self-creation, William insists that nothing can determine freedom but freedom itself and declares for himself that "my first act of free will shall be to believe in free will."[11] Still, despite his allegiance to the possibility of possibility, William has a roughly dialectical understanding of how freedom and necessity go hand in hand. And this dialectic informs the well-known categories he suggests in *The Varieties of Religious Experience*: the "healthy-minded" and the "sick soul," the "once-born" and the "twice-born." These two dyads actually combine to make up a single triad that consists of a thesis (possibility), an antithesis (limitation), and a synthesis (the servile will).

William describes once-born healthy-mindedness as a naive condition of expansive, confident faith in the power to realize possibilities. But he regards this attitude as woefully "inadequate" and thus in need of having itself transcended because it fails to acknowledge "sorrow, pain, and death" or any of "the evil facts" of human limitation that are at least "a genuine portion of reality" but may even "be the best key to life's significance" at "the deepest levels of truth." In their disillusionment with healthy-minded dreams of innocence, the sick souls have "a profounder view" of the challenge to freedom of bondage and necessity. But their emphasis on "pity, pain, and fear, and the sentiment of human helplessness" may lead them into an equally one-sided loss of faith in any possibility at all. The twice-born have recovered their belief in freedom but with a sober understanding of its relation to limitations. They have been born again into a condition of "firmness, stability, and equilibrium succeeding a period of storm and stress and inconsistency"—that is, into what Ricoeur calls the "post-critical faith" of the servile will where freedom has grounded itself in the necessary.[12] William's account of how innocence must suffer disillusionment to secure a more profound freedom shows how such existential concepts as freedom and ground, choice and givenness, possibility and thrownness take on actual meaning in experience. His triad represents the rite of passage that must be traversed to realize the lived truth of the servile will.

I have reviewed William's categories at such length because they provide an illuminating and convenient first approximation of the stages Isabel Archer passes through in her struggle with the conflicting claims of freedom and necessity. As we shall see, her career takes her through three phases that William's triad can help to describe. At first, with the buoyant healthy-mindedness of the once-born, Isabel regards her possibilities as limitless and relishes an almost giddy sense of her freedom and power. Then, trapped by circumstances she has helped to create in a misguided attempt to ground her freedom in a meaningful situation, she learns the horrible reality of bondage and necessity as she undergoes the trials of guilt and despair. Ultimately, though, she seems to break through to the integrity of the twice-born in the liberating act of acknowledging her limits freely, fully, and resolutely. Now of course Isabel's story is not this simple. But William's categories can and will act as interpretive guideposts to lead us through the complex dilemmas that the contradiction between possibility and limitation results in for her. Our goal will be to discover how *The Portrait* shows Henry James's understanding that freedom and necessity depend on each other in a kind of existential dialectic—to reveal, that is, how Isabel's story dramatizes the paradox of the servile will.

TWO

Isabel Archer is the very image of once-born healthy-mindedness when James begins to paint her portrait. She regards "the world as a place of brightness, of free expansion, of irresistible action." [13] She is "too young, too impatient to live, too unacquainted with pain" (1:72–73) to suspect that the world might not live up to her great expectations. According to Kierkegaard, "freedom is precisely the expansive." [14] Isabel, then, is the perfect embodiment of freedom in the eagerness with which she opens herself to the possibilities that Mrs. Touchett has almost magically made available to her by whisking her away from Albany to Gardencourt. Freedom starts with the disclosure of possibilities (what Heidegger calls *Erschlossenheit*). Isabel's invigorating sense of the freedom offered by her new situation begins with the prospect that Europe has much to disclose to this wide-eyed American girl. She has "an immense curiosity about life" and is "constantly staring and wondering" (1:45)—gathering impressions that confirm and inspire her sense of the possibilities opened to her by her suddenly expanded horizons. She likes unexpectedness because it discloses the possibility of still more possibilities and gives promise that her horizons have yet to reach their limit. Freedom and possibility are essentially futural. And as Isabel begins her adventure, she is a creature of hopes, aspirations, and anticipations—with no sense that her future has any necessary boundaries but, quite the contrary, with complete trust that her possibilities will continue to grow.

Her sense of freedom is naive and one-sided, however, because, among other things, it does not include "sustaining a felt purpose against felt obstacles"—what William James calls the will's requisite "feeling of effort," or what Sartre and Bachelard call the need for freedom to engage its "coefficient of adversity," all referring to the requirement that freedom confront its situation resolutely. [15] As Dupee points out, Isabel does have "a premonition of the fact of evil and suffering, of the quantity of defeat that is involved in any success, of the necessary limitations of life." [16] But she still insists at this early stage that "it's not absolutely necessary to suffer; we were not made for that" (1:65). With once-born healthy-minded confidence—and Isabel has "a great deal of confidence, both in herself and others" (1:17)—she believes according to her dream of innocence that possibility need suffer no limit, that freedom need concede no necessity, and that the will need not humble itself to the servility of effort and suffering. The drama before her will be the testing of this conviction.

Isabel's faith in possibility without limit sustains and is sustained by a lively, perhaps even somewhat extravagant, imagination. She may not share Roderick Hudson's volatile *Verstiegenheit* and thus does not get caught in the vicious circle of the ether and the tomb. Still, "her imagination was by habit ridiculously active," and it shows a tendency to transport her too far ahead of herself—"when the door was not open it jumped out of the window" (1:42). As James notes, she has "a certain nobleness of imagination which rendered her a good many services and played her a great many tricks" (1:68). Her imagination can be dangerous because it covers up limits by leaping beyond them without notice. It obscures the resistance of reality because the absolute freedom of fantasy knows no "feeling of effort" or "coefficient of adversity." These "tricks" and dangers are the reverse side, though, of the imagination's "services" and wonders; it covers up limits in order to reveal possibilities and, in ignoring resistance, asserts that we make ourselves more than we are made by our circumstances.[17] In his sympathetic portrait of the ennobling character of Isabel's imagination, James shows essential agreement with his brother William's view that an important sign of our freedom is "the exuberant excess" of our "subjective propensities"—"the fantastic and unnecessary" but marvelous "quest for the superfluous" that defies restrictions.[18] Isabel may "live too much in the world of [her] own dreams" (1:310). But the extravagant, once-born, healthy-minded faith with which Isabel trusts that it's possible "to see some dream of one's youth come true" (1:286) is evidence too of how the imagination serves freedom by assisting self-transcendence. Looked at from both sides, then, Isabel's initial sense of freedom and her exuberance of imagination reinforce each other powerfully—although at the expense of her awareness of the constricting claims of necessity.

According to Isabel's understanding of freedom, limits can signify only an oppressive, even tyrannical threat to her possibilities. The question of what freedom means to Isabel plays so central a role in her fortunes that it is raised at the same moment she enters the novel—in the telegram from Mrs. Touchett announcing their arrival. Ralph quotes the message and then ponders its meaning:

"'Changed hotel, very bad, impudent clerk, address here. Taken sister's girl, died last year, go to Europe, two sisters, quite independent.' Over that my father and I have scarcely stopped puzzling; it seems to admit of so many interpretations.

". . . who's 'quite independent,' and in what sense is the term used?—that point's not yet settled. . . . [I]s it used in a moral or in a financial sense? Does it mean that they've been left well off, or that they wish to be under no obligations? or does it simply mean that they're fond of their own way?"

"Whatever else it means, it's pretty sure to mean that," Mr. Touchett remarked. (1:13–14)

James invites us here to take up Ralph's hermeneutic quandary by asking how Isabel asserts her "independence" and, at the next level of interpretation, what "independence" means as a definition of freedom. Isabel is introduced as "the independent young lady" who is "very fond of [her] liberty" and—all credit to Mr. Touchett's perspicacious punch line—very "fond of [her] own way" (1:17, 24, 35). This means, in the positive terms of healthy-minded optimism, that "she herself will do everything she chooses" (1:59). But this positive definition rests on a negative premise. For Isabel, to be "independent" means that she will *not* be dependent on anyone or anything; she will *not* be limited or tied down in any way. One small step further. this "independent spirit" would rather *not* commit herself to any person or project because "she must suffice to herself"—hence her "great fondness for intervals of solitude" (1:215) since only when alone can she be reliant on only herself. Isabel's "independence" denies the bondage of the will in order to preserve herself from dependence; she does not realize that, since only a free will can bind itself, she could bind her will without sacrificing her freedom. In the first phase of her history, at least, Isabel does not understand that the will can be both servile and free. Her definition of "independence" completely contradicts what freedom means according to the servile will.

Isabel puts her theory of independence into practice by refusing, as she describes it, "to tie myself" (1:212) by marrying Caspar Goodwood or Lord Warburton. Her attitude toward both suitors is *noli me tangere*—"leave me alone" (1:220) and don't tread on me or my independence. Goodwood and Warburton are exact opposites in many respects, as several critics have noticed.[19] But to Isabel they seem more similar than different because they both pose the threat of limitation to her defiant will. (In this regard it is significant that James yokes them together by having Warburton arrive to propose just as Isabel finishes reading a disagreeably presumptuous letter from Goodwood. The letter and the proposal cannot help but be associated in her mind as similarly oppressive intrusions.) Warburton represented "an aggression almost to the degree of an affront" to "her self-sufficiency," and Goodwood "seemed to deprive her of the sense of freedom" (1:143, 162). As she sees it, her choice in both cases is between marriage on the one hand and "the free exploration of life" on the other (1:155). She has no sense that intimacy with either might affirm her identity in the complementary manner Erik Erikson describes.[20] She feels, rather, that to marry at all would mean to enter an alienating situation. "I like my liberty too much" and "my personal independence," she explains; marrying would put an end to her power "to choose my fate" while forcing her "to give up . . . other chances" (1:228–29, 186). Isabel's sense of her "other chances" is compelling if not intoxicating because, as she confesses, "I like so many things" (1:130).

The problem here, as Heidegger would point out, is that these "other chances" will remain empty possibilities until some of them are actually engaged. Such actualization will inevitably sacrifice the chances not chosen just as marrying Goodwood or Warburton would.[21] As James demonstrates in "The Jolly Corner," the unlived life always haunts the life we have lived as the ghost embodying the possibilities we have not selected. But as he shows in "The Beast in the Jungle," we sacrifice everything if we attempt to forfeit nothing by not choosing at all. There is certainly something ennobling and even endearing in the healthy-minded courage and once-born idealism with which Isabel defends her "liberty" and rejects her two suitors as too little a challenge. The question she leaves unanswered, though, is how she will respond to the need to commit herself eventually—a need she neither feels nor understands while enthralled by her one-sided "independence."

A large part of Isabel's concern about her independence involves a desire to achieve and maintain perfect freedom of self-expression. Consider, for example, this oft-quoted exchange with Madame Merle, who takes the view—anathema to Isabel—that "our 'self'" includes a "whole envelope of circumstances" that form us as much as we form them and that are, consequently, an "expression of one's self." Isabel protests:

> "I don't agree with you. I think just the other way. I don't know whether I succeed in expressing myself, but I know that nothing else expresses me. Nothing that belongs to me is any measure of me; everything's on the contrary a limit, a barrier, and a perfectly arbitrary one. Certainly the clothes which, as you say, I choose to wear, don't express me; and heaven forbid they should!
>
> ". . . To begin with it's not my choice that I wear them; they're imposed upon me by society."
>
> "Should you prefer to go without them?" Madame Merle enquired in a tone which virtually terminated the discussion. (1:287–88)

Madame Merle's rejoinder aptly demonstrates that Isabel deceives herself if she claims to concede no cultural boundaries. But the larger point here is that all expression depends to some degree on conventionally established means of expression—like, say, language. These conventions may limit our freedom of signification but, as the condition of possibility for any creation of meaning, they enable us to speak freely when we accept their necessity.

Because we are committed to an arbitrary system of signs (or *langue*), we are bound in a way that the structuralists emphasize by claiming that language speaks us. Conversely, though, and in a way that the structuralists neglect, we are thereby free to create an infinite variety of speech acts (*parole*) that reveal our power as speakers and that can show this power by even changing the linguistic system.[22] Just as we are "thrown" into language as the unchosen ground of our freely chosen speech acts, Roland Barthes and other semiologists have shown that we are similarly always and already, without our full awareness, active participants in a complex of cultural "codes" that lend expressive possibility to such things as the clothes we wear, the food we eat, or the furniture we own by organizing them into a conventional system of signs.[23] Isabel protests too much, then, when she denies the necessity of binding herself to "perfectly arbitrary" structures of signification in order to "succeed in expressing" herself. Reflecting earlier on Madame Merle's felicitous combination of the original and the conventional, Isabel conceded that language is at bottom "a convention" and admitted the wisdom of her friend's "good taste not to pretend, like some people, . . . to express herself by original signs" (1:274). Their disagreement later, though, shows that Isabel would prefer "original signs" for herself; and what Poirier calls her sometimes "fuzzy use of language" may reflect the self-defeating character of such dreams of linguistic independence.[24] Once again, Isabel rebels against limits in the name of independence when consenting to their necessity would seem the price of meaningful freedom—here the freedom of meaningful self-expression.

Isabel's resistance to the limits of semiotic conventions is consistent with that failure to understand the situated nature of freedom that we are coming to see as the main flaw in her definition of independence. As Heidegger argues in the analysis from which all other existential descriptions of freedom's situation derive, existence is *"Dasein"* or "being-there"; this means that existence is always delivered over to a particular "there" and can disclose real possibilities for itself only by resolutely engaging its "there."[25] For James, engaging the "there" of our situation means first and foremost developing the "point of view" by which we have a hold on the world and make it our world. Isabel seems to agree with Heidegger and James when she tells Mrs. Touchett that everyone, including the two women themselves, "should have a point of view" (1:81). Still, and predictably, Isabel is reluctant to take her own advice because committing herself to one point of view would exclude her from the possibility of others and thus limit her independence. She can often be inconsistent and even self-contradictory because of the "sudden change of point of view with which she sometimes startled and even displeased her interlocutors" (1:160). Isabel's "general disposition to elude any obligation to take a restricted view" (1:152) reveals a commendable openness to possibility. But it overlooks the difficulty created because, as we saw in the case of Anne Thackeray Ritchie, the broad view is open to us only as an implication of the sharply limited view we have from the particular "there" of our position as observers.

The "tangle of vague outlines" (1:67) in the confusion of Isabel's thoughts reflects, at least in part, this impatience with the particular; clarity can be achieved only by resolutely confronting and rigorously following out the implications of a limited point of view, the situation it discloses, and the horizons it offers. Isabel's inveterately abstract approach to everything—her interest in "specimens," her habit of "summing people up," and her penchant for theorizing (1:89, 111)—is attributable as well to an insufficient commitment to the claims of the "there." Only at such an abstract level can Isabel enjoy the independence of flying from possibility to possibility without the resistance of a committed point of view. Isabel's inconsistency, vagueness, and abstractness all give further evidence, then, of the inadequacy of any definition of freedom that refuses the limits of freedom's situation.

The many flaws in Isabel's notion of "independence" do eventually assert themselves, however, and they contribute to the passing of her once-born healthy-mindedness. Ironically, what leads to Isabel's disillusionment with her "independence" is the fortune she inherits that Ralph intended to "make her free" (1:261). "I should like to put a little wind in her sails" and "see her going before the breeze," he tells his father (1:260, 262). But then Isabel discovers that she does not know what course to set or how to navigate it because the negative character of her independence has made her more concerned about what commitments to avoid than what projects to undertake. Although "to be rich was a virtue because it was to be able to *do*," Isabel's "new consciousness" of her sudden wealth "was at first oppressive" (1:301) because she had not thought seriously before about *what* to do. "She lost herself in a maze of visions" about "the fine things to be done" (1:321), but she soon finds that "doing all the vain things one likes is often very tiresome" (2:17). She discovers, in other words, that an invigorating sense of freedom is not the same as the independence to indulge in possibilities without limit.

What does she do, then? She decides to travel—which is more a metaphor for her dilemma than a solution to it. As an experienced tourist, Henry James could be expected to understand that travel can have many meanings, some salutary and others not. In one of its less felicitous forms, travel can provide a way of changing our position frequently enough to give the illusion that we have avoided situating ourselves. By moving rapidly from one "there" to another, we can persuade ourselves that our thrownness need not limit us. I might seem to be reading too much into an innocent adventure here—except that James takes care to have Madame Merle note that Isabel is "restless" when she decides to take her trip to the eastern Mediterranean and then "travelled rapidly and recklessly" during it: "[E]ven among the most classic sites, the scenes most calculated to suggest repose and reflexion, a certain incoherence prevailed in her. . . . [S]he was like a thirsty person draining cup after cup" (2:37–38). In Isabel's case, traveling was a sign of restlessness that was in turn, as Heidegger points out and as we saw with Roderick Hudson, a sign of deficiency in our freedom's engagement with its world. This is a problem that she must take with her wherever she goes, and so she returns from her trip without having either escaped or resolved the dilemma that motivated her departure. "Grave she found herself, and positively more weighted" than before she left but "with the vagueness of unrest" still her prevailing mood (2:31). Isabel's disillusionment with the meaninglessness of her independence is not quite the despair of a sick soul, but it does mark the end of the limitlessly exuberant and expansive vision of the first phase of her history.

Her disillusionment is the prelude to a decision that would seem, at least on the surface, to promise a resolution for her dilemma. She decides, simply, to marry Gilbert Osmond. For the moment, we must ask only how this decision seems to respond to her dilemma, even though (as we shall see shortly) it proves itself to be the product of flawed reasoning. Before her travels, Isabel had resisted Osmond's presumptions as an encroachment on her independence just as troublesome as Warburton's and Goodwood's previously. She "retreated before" his advances "as she had retreated in other cases before a like encounter" because she felt a "dread of having, in this case too, to choose and decide" (2:18). In Kierkegaard's sense of the word, Isabel's "dread" is a fear of nothing but freedom itself—a fear, that is, of having "to choose and decide" how and where to commit herself to engagement with a situation.[26] Her decision to travel was, in part, an attempt to escape Osmond's threat and its accompanying anguish. But when she returns, she marries him because she positively wants to consent to a limiting necessity, to bind herself to a situation.

Ralph cannot understand why she wants "to be put into a cage" when she had earlier "valued [her] liberty beyond everything" and had "wanted only to see life" (2:65). But Isabel replies, "I've seen it" and "it doesn't look to me now, I admit, such an inviting expanse"— "I've seen that one can't do anything so general" (2:65). In an apparently unimpeachable formulation of the claims of the "there," she tells him: "One must choose a corner and cultivate that" (2:65). A hard-won realism seems to have convinced her that, as Ricoeur points out in describing the consequences of the servile will, "to become oneself is to fail to realize wholeness"; we can never be more than part of all we wish for.[27] Only by binding her will, then, will Isabel be free to exercise her will and realize her "potentiality-for-Being" (or *Sein-können*, Heidegger's term for what we "can-be" and "can-do"). Only by giving up the false possibility of unlimited possibility will she gain a particular field of possibility that she can engage with a particular project. Ralph is disappointed at her willingness to quit "soaring and sailing" in what he calls "the bright light over the heads of men" (2:69). But Isabel has found that "if one marries at all one touches the earth" because, at the very least, "one must marry a particular individual" (2:74). Convinced that her "rather roving disposition" was leading nowhere, she has decided "to choose something very deliberately, and be faithful to that" (1:380–81)—advice she had given herself earlier but could not follow until her restlessness lends it compelling significance. Now that she has seen the limits of once-born healthy-mindedness and decided to transcend them, the only question that remains is whether she has bound her will as "deliberately" and properly as she thinks.

THREE

The unfortunate answer to this question takes Isabel, in the second phase of her history, through unexpected trials to the despair of a sick soul. Although Isabel marries Osmond with "ardent good faith" (2:74), she is actually a victim of Sartrean "bad faith" (*mauvaise foi*) because a basic self-deception undermines her project.[28] Isabel fools herself when she thinks she is consenting to necessity in marrying Osmond; she is, in fact, attempting to defy limitation in the guise of accepting it. Her old self prevails even though she believes a new self has taken over. There is, for example, something suspiciously abstract about her way of marrying Osmond (as Ralph puts it to himself) on the basis of "a fine theory" she has "invented" about him (2:75). As we shall see, then, Isabel undertakes her project of marrying Osmond with more healthy-minded optimism than she would like to admit since she prefers to think herself solidly grounded in a tough-minded resignation to the necessity of limitation. Isabel's blindness to her own motives (which, in turn, contributes to her ignorance about the motives of others), combined with the extravagance of seeking to defy limitation, leads her into enslavement in a bondage worse than any limits her independence ever imagined.

The contradiction bedeviling her plans—the contradiction, that is, of attempting to defy limitation in the guise of accepting it—is not easy to see because it is hidden under an all too plausible rhetoric of realism. She justifies herself with arguments valid in themselves but invalidated by her way of putting them into practice. Apparently quite self-conscious about the futility of dreaming about boundless independence, she finds that "the desire for unlimited expansion had been succeeded in her soul by the sense that life was vacant without some private duty that might gather one's energies to a point" (2:82). Espousing the cause of practical activity, Isabel accepts Osmond because "she should be able to be of use to him. . . . [S]he was not only taking, she was giving" (2:82). She plans to engage her freedom in the service of an unselfish care. With "a tenderness which was the very flower of respect," she finds that the "helpless and ineffectual" Osmond evokes "a kind of maternal strain" in her and makes her feel "that she was a contributor, that she came with charged hands" (2:192). Isabel's inheritance had raised the question "what to do," and she has found an answer in this "poor and lonely" man who "seemed to give her her opportunity . . . to do something finely appreciable with her money" (2:192–93). What could be more fulfilling than to fuse together freedom and care in such a noble and ennobling project? From an existential perspective, her theory seems perfect. But that is just the problem—it is too much a theory, and it is simply too perfect. Although she is binding her will by devoting herself to Osmond, Isabel's pride in accepting restraints blocks any sense that she is actually going to be limited. Romantically imaginative still, she senses only the possibilities of which she will avail herself. To recall Ricoeur's dialectic, she exercises too much revelation and too little suspicion; she does too much grandiose theorizing and too little skeptical probing of her own motives, the designs of others, or the frustrations inherent in the servile will under even the most congenial circumstances. She finds Osmond attractive, though, precisely because his apparent combination of nobility and need allows her this romantically self-deceptive way of accepting limits without feeling their pinch.

Much of what Isabel finds noble in Osmond is the high aesthetic cultivation that he has achieved and that she wishes to share. Such high culture is alluring because it seems to promise the transcen-

dence of restrictions through a consent to them. Isabel resists the limiting power of conventions—even of conventions necessary for expression. But Osmond seems to have overcome this problem completely by
being "not conventional" at all because he is, paradoxically, "convention itself" (2:21). He claims to have transcended conventions by
cultivating conventions, which is one definition of what art and culture do. Art is marvelous because it defies the paradox of the servile
will by exploiting it. It is a special, borderline case of how accepting
limitations may open possibilities. The literary work of art, for example, consents to the necessity of technique, structure, and language—in short, all the elements of its medium—all the better to reveal possibilities of meaning and value. As a general rule, the more it
confronts the difficulties of its medium, the more it deepens and expands its capacities for expression. (Consider, for example, the difference between poetry and prose. If one must employ *langue*, how
much better it is to make one's *parole* poetic rather than prosaic because of that highly disciplined art's greater freedom and power of signification.) Osmond and Madame Merle fascinate Isabel because they
seem to have mastered art's secret of combining abundant possibility
with strict constraints. "To be so cultivated and civilised, so wise and
easy, and still make so light of it"—this way of being so restrained
and yet so free, so laden with manners and yet so rich with meaning
and value, has "to Isabel's imagination a sort of greatness" (1:272).

In marrying Osmond to make this "greatness" her own, however,
Isabel misleads herself. She makes culture the object of an extravagant dream of innocence that idealizes and idolizes it. Although art
can transcend limits by accepting them, this is harder work than Osmond's and Madame Merle's facile ease of manner makes it seem.
These two may pretend to have captured the secret of art in their perfect cultivation, but this pretension is actually a false pride. For Osmond, art is more a frivolous pastime than a serious quest, and his
cultivation of beautiful manners is more a useful strategy for abetting
his egotism than a sincere attempt to enrich the meaning and value of
his life. Neither he nor Madame Merle show that serious engagement
of artistic freedom with the limits of structure without which art's transcendent powers lapse and only banal conventions remain—as Isabel
discovers when she finds herself "ground in the very mill of the conventional" in her marriage to Osmond (2:415). All this is not to suggest that art and life are identical but, rather, to argue that both have
similar dynamics that can go wrong in similar ways.

Given the many attractions of Osmond's apparently noble cultivation, Isabel admires him most of all because his way of life seems to have made him absolutely sufficient unto himself. Osmond seems perfectly self-contained because he shows "such dignity" and "such independence" and because he "has never scrambled or struggled—he has cared for no worldly prize" (2:73). With all the self-assurance of proven integrity, he declares to Isabel that he has found complete satisfaction by following resolutely a decision taken many years ago "to resign" himself "to be content with little" (1:381). His "studied" and even "wilful renunciation" (1:381) of all but a select set of possibilities that he cultivates avidly offers Isabel an intriguing alternative vision of the road to independence when a more expansive view of freedom had led her only to a restless discontent. Even though she claims to be self-consciously binding herself by marrying Osmond, then, we see once again that she still clings to her dream of independence; she accepts him in order to discover the secret of self-sufficiency that she fails to find on her own.

Osmond's "renunciation" is less a consent to limitation than a refusal of servility. This insistence on having defeated the limiting influence of ordinary circumstances makes Osmond "a mock version of the transcendentalist," as Poirier points out, and of the Emersonian ideal of independent self-creation that Isabel aspires to.[29] His self-sufficiency makes him less of a threat and more of a fascination than Goodwood or Warburton who press their claims too actively and who express their desires too openly. Important as it is that he need her so that she can devote herself to him, it matters just as much that he *not* need her so that he not impose a limit on her own ideal of independence. She admires "the success with which he had preserved his independence" (1:383) and trusts that he will help her maintain hers with equal felicity since he does not seem to demand its sacrifice. Now of course, as we shall see shortly but as Isabel learns too late, Osmond's self-containment is more apparent than real. He needs her more than he lets himself show, and he will demand greater sacrifices than she foresees. But the point here is that Isabel's marriage to Osmond invokes the notion of the servile will in a self-deceptive way. She chooses him precisely because he seems to have preserved independence for himself by willfully refusing servility of any kind.

What James calls the "sweet delusion"[30] that marks Isabel's self-deception is inherently doomed, then, and the shock of its collapse finds a structural correlative in the three-year narrative break between

Chapter 35, which ends before her wedding, and Chapter 36, which takes up her marriage in medias res. This break is a way of emphasizing how Isabel deceives herself thanks to the workings of imagination and perception. The sudden discontinuity in the narrative suggests the shock Isabel feels in finding her extravagantly imaginative dreams about her future brutally destroyed by the harsh reality of her marriage—a shock, that is, similar to the disillusionment of someone overextended imaginatively who finds the freedom of the ether unexpectedly replaced by the bondage of the tomb. Isabel's disillusionment is also like the surprise that accompanies the appearance of an unanticipated hidden side—the surprise that shows how much of a contribution our intentional acts of consciousness have made to constituting the object we misconceived.

James has let us know what is coming better than Isabel does. Although mild and sympathetic, the oft-noted irony that the narrator occasionally directs toward Isabel pulls the reader back from her perspective and suggests a more detached evaluation of its limitations. This alternation between immersion and observation is similar to the epistemological double vision that James's ironic voice sets up in *Maisie*. The superiority of the reader's perspective is further guaranteed, of course, by the other points of view we have shared but from which she has been excluded. The chapter break reverses this hierarchy because now Isabel knows what the reader can only guess. But this reversal simply emphasizes the role of hypotheses in understanding by putting the reader in the position of having to make them. All reading is a dialectic of anticipation and retrospection, as Iser points out.[31] By interrupting the time-line of his narrative, James calls on his readers to sum up all that they have anticipated about her marriage in order to fill in the blank years—guesses that the narrative retrospect will later confirm or modify. The temporal disruption thus dramatizes in the reader's own concretization of the text the extent to which understanding is formed and guided by expectations. The discontinuity in the narrative is a way of highlighting in the experience of reading many of the epistemological processes that are revealed by the emergence of an unexpected hidden side. These processes are also a central dramatic theme in the novel because Isabel has been intentionally active in filling out the hidden side behind Osmond's carefully cultivated facade with hypotheses that gave her great expectations.

Isabel has claimed to feel that "the more information one has about one's dangers the better" (1:359). She even sensed at one point that something about Osmond "signified more than lay on the surface" (1:368). But she is so pleased with the prospects their marriage promises that she disregards her doubts and suspicions. And so, after her dreams and expectations have had a chance to prove (or disprove) themselves, Isabel finds that she "had been mystified to the top of her bent" (2:145); she had imagined too much and trusted too blindly in an impression of Osmond and their marriage that she herself had creatively constituted. As she discovers, "she had seen only half his nature" before their marriage, and "she had mistaken a part for the whole" (2:191). She had seen only one side of him through a limited set of aspects, and she had gone wrong in the way she spun out a series of hypotheses about the hidden side that she assumed was implied by the side she saw. Her mistake is complementary to the success Ritchie enjoys in teleologically working from the part to the whole. Enthralled by a "wondrous vision" of Osmond—a vision "fed through charmed senses and oh such a stirred fancy"—Isabel "had not read him right" but had "married on a factitious theory" (2:192–93). She had leapt too eagerly beyond the horizons bounding her perceptual situation and had come up empty-handed. Isabel's healthy-minded trust in her perceptual assumptions and imaginal expectations about Osmond helped to mislead her into a trap where she feels with full force the disillusionment of a sick soul.

The reversal that plummets Isabel into despair traps her in a particular kind of bondage with special significance for the paradox of the servile will. Borrowing from Kant, Ricoeur contends that our freedom seeks to express itself in three basic areas that he calls "having, power, and valuation or worth (*avoir, pouvoir, valoir*)"—categories that may help to illuminate Isabel's situation. Isabel's quest for independence stakes a claim in each of these territories because, in marrying Osmond, she seeks the value of culture, the power of self-sufficiency, and the satisfaction of putting the wealth she possesses to meaningful use. But these three areas also act as "the successive regions of our alienation" and "our helplessness" when our bondage asserts itself. They then take on meaning "under the distorted mask of fallen figures" as "avarice, tyranny, and vanity (*Habsucht, Herrschsucht, Ehrsucht*)"—the "threefold *Sucht*" or passion that represents the trap that our "authentic *Suchen*" or search for fulfilling self-transcendence can fall into.[32] Isabel overextends herself in the demands that her quest for independence would make on the regions of having, power, and value. Horribly but fittingly, she becomes in consequence the prisoner of a villain who is the living embodiment of avarice, tyranny, and particularly vanity. Osmond avariciously covets her inheritance, and he tyrannically demands the same submission from Isabel that he has exacted from Pansy in molding her to be a self-effacing instrument for his will. But Osmond's hallmark is his vanity. His avarice usually expresses itself as a greed for the envious regard of others, and his tyranny desires absolute power over others as support for his sense of superiority. Actually, though, Osmond's vanity is only an awful caricature of Isabel's own vain wish to defy the inherent servility of the will. The reign of avarice, tyranny, and vanity under which she suffers in their marriage results not only from the trickery of Osmond and Madame Merle but also from the excessive claim that Isabel makes for the freedom of *avoir, pouvoir,* and *valoir.*

It would be wrong, of course, to understate the extent to which Isabel loses her liberty because others take it away from her. Osmond does indeed deprive her of her freedom by denying her subjectivity and treating her as an object. For him, Isabel's "real offense, as she ultimately perceived, was her having a mind of her own at all" (2:200). Sartre argues that this is how others always offend us— namely by having a subjectivity different from ours and beyond our control. According to Sartre, the Other's gaze threatens our freedom by regarding us as an object. The Other thus transcends our power of transcendence even as we struggle to preserve our subjectivity by responding in kind.[33] But Osmond takes the cruel logic of Sartre's battle between the Self and the Other to an absurd extreme. In order to satisfy his vanity's voracious will to power, he insists that Isabel have no will of her own; rather, she must humble herself so completely as to become a pliant agent for and even an absolute expression of his will alone. He goes so far in denying her subjectivity that he even gives reified terms to the limited powers of mind he would allow her. Her "intelligence was to be a silver plate" (2:79), which, like an object in his collection, would gratify his aesthetic sense. He expects her to be "as smooth to his general need of her as handled ivory to the palm" (2:11)—a deceptively aesthetic simile whose harsh reality Isabel states more bluntly when she discovers that "she had been an applied handled hung-up tool, as senseless and convenient as mere shaped wood and iron" (2:379). In Heideggerian terms, Osmond violates the integrity of her being by regarding her as a tool "ready-to-hand" for his use instead of respecting her as a free individual to "be-with" in mutual care.[34]

If Osmond steals Isabel's freedom from her in these ways, he himself is also "unfree" in a certain sense. According to Kierkegaard, "unfreedom" is "shut-upness." Osmond epitomizes unfreedom because he has shut himself off from open intercourse with the world and from any possibility except the possibility of advancing the cause of his vanity. He also shuts Isabel up in a number of ways. Their house in Rome seems to Ned Rosier more like "a dungeon" or "a kind of domestic fortress" than "a palace" (2:100)—a prison that confines his beloved Pansy. It is thus the physical equivalent of the metaphor Isabel invokes to describe Osmond's temperament: "[I]t was the house of darkness, the house of dumbness, the house of suffocation" where "she seemed shut up with an odour of mold and decay" (2:196, 199).[35] The constraints that Osmond seeks to impose on what she can do, whom she can see, and even what she can think have collapsed her world's horizons down to almost nothing in stark contrast to the limitlessly expansive sense of freedom that marked the once-born healthy-mindedness of her history's first phase. To be married to Osmond is to be imprisoned in the hopeless, unfree world of the sick soul.

It would also be misleading, though, to suggest that Isabel is all the suffering victim and in no way the active, responsible agent of her destiny. To her credit, she shows a generosity and humility inconceivable in Osmond—and perhaps in the earlier overconfident Isabel as well—when she acknowledges her guilt for helping to create their mutual misfortune. "Yes, she *had* been hypocritical," Isabel confesses to herself, "for if she had not deceived [Osmond] in intention she understood how completely she must have done so in fact" (2:195, 191). With all the best intentions, because "she had liked him so much," Isabel "had done her best to be what he would like"— to seem eager to learn from him, for example, and to disguise any "possible grossness of perception" she might commit (2:195, 190; 1:379). It is partly her fault, she admits, if "he had thought at first he could change her" in the ways he desired only to discover "that she was not what he had believed she would prove to be" (2:190). In a certain sense, then, Osmond finds himself just as surprised by Isabel's hidden self-assertive side as she finds herself by the emergence of his avarice, tyranny, and vanity.

Even more, however, Isabel bears responsibility for her fate because, although she may be bound terribly, she did choose freely to bind herself. According to Ricoeur, "the bad choice that binds itself" is "the ultimate symbol of the servile will"—the "bad choice," that is, "by which the act of binding oneself is transformed into the state of being bound."[36] Her choice is "bad" for a number of reasons, including her blindness to her own motives and Osmond's and Madame Merle's. In terms of her self-deception about freedom and limitation, though, the mistake that binds her so desperately is her attempt to defy limits in the guise of accepting them by marrying Osmond in the hope of discovering perfect freedom. By dreaming about "the infinite vista of a multiplied life," she runs into "a dark, narrow alley with a dead wall at the end." By wanting to settle for nothing less than "the high places of happiness, from which the world would seem to lie below one, so that one could look down with a sense of exaltation and advantage," she ends up falling "downward and earthward, into realms of restriction and depression" (2:189). On her own responsibility, then, Isabel learns that to seek possibility without limit means to find limits without possibility. This hard lesson about the relation between freedom and necessity culminates the second phase of her history.

FOUR

How can Isabel transcend the bondage of a sick soul without reverting to the fallacies of her demand for independence? This question and her attempts to answer it dominate the third phase of Isabel's story as she struggles to achieve the integrity of the twice-born by resolving the contradiction between freedom and limitation. Isabel seems trapped between the alternatives of submission and defiance. To defy Osmond is a great temptation, but outright rebellion would not resolve her dilemma. Defiance would contradict the responsibility she accepts for the mutual misfortune their marriage results in. It would also run the risk of once again denying the limits of her situation, of ignoring the claims of the ground on which she now finds herself placed due to the events that have unfolded in her history's first two stages. A rebellious Isabel might seem to be fleeing a problem she must confront resolutely.

Isabel seems to understand the dangers of defiance when she tells Henrietta that she cannot leave Osmond because "one must accept one's deeds" (2:284). Or, as she reflects earlier, "when a woman had made such a mistake" as she had in marrying him, "there was only one way to repair it—just immensely (oh, with the highest grandeur!) to accept it" (2:161). But if she refuses to rebel, Isabel would seem to have no alternative other than to submit to Osmond's tyranny—like Pansy, that piteous tribute to her father's will to power who fails in her single attempt at defiance and then "bow[s] her pretty head to authority and only ask[s] of authority to be merciful" (2:385). By accepting submission so completely, Isabel would be conceding too much to limitation and allowing too little for freedom. Somewhere beyond flight and submission, though, there must be a third alternative—the resolution of the paradox of the servile will as it pertains to her situation. Submission and defiance take the poles of the paradox to their extremes. But Isabel's task is to bring the claims of necessity and freedom into some kind of reciprocal relationship.

Isabel might seem to take too much upon herself in accepting her plight with such stoic resignation. The conspiracy of Madame Merle and Osmond to ensnare her would seem to invalidate Isabel's assumption that she must accept responsibility for her situation because she had been "perfectly free; it was impossible to do anything more deliberate" (2:284) than she had in marrying him—"if ever a girl was a free agent she had been. . . . There had been no plot, no snare; she had looked and considered and chosen" (2:160). As we shall see, Isabel's discovery of their plot does give her more room for freedom and less need for resignation. Nevertheless, Isabel did help to create her own situation by deceiving herself in the ways we have just examined. She also chose, as part of her self-deception, not to listen to the warnings that Ralph and Mrs. Touchett give her. No matter how we evaluate Isabel's responsibility, this conspiracy has established Madame Merle and Osmond as elements of her situation, even if imperfectly chosen and misunderstood ones; and Isabel can only project herself toward a freely chosen future by accepting the field of possibilities established for her by her past involvements, whether active or passive. We embrace possibilities in our situation by joining what will be to what has been.[37] Isabel's dilemma is that her field of possibilities is stiflingly narrow as a result of what has been in her history.

Isabel might be said to get to work seriously for the first time on the task of resolving her dilemma during the "extraordinary meditative vigil" in Chapter 42 that James calls "a landmark" in his heroine's career and "obviously the best thing in the book."[38] It is a turning point in her history because, more than any other single event, it launches her project of building a firmly grounded freedom for herself beyond submission or defiance. In itself, though, it hardly seems a monumental occasion, and its provocation seems slight at best. Simply stated, she comes home unannounced one afternoon, momentarily spies Madame Merle and Osmond positioned strangely (her standing, him sitting), and then stays up most of the night thinking. Her provocation is little more than "the impression" that "she had received" at "the threshold of the drawing-room" where the "anomaly" of "their relative positions" and "their absorbed mutual gaze" first "arrested her" and then "struck her as something detected" (2:164–65) because of the unexpected intimacy it implied between her husband and their friend.

Here, as in the case of Anne Thackeray Ritchie, a single "impression" acts as the gateway to wide expanses of knowledge. But it does its work of revelation in a somewhat different although not inconsistent way. The "anomaly" of Osmond's and Madame Merle's "relative position" is a "gestalt shift" for Isabel—a rearrangement in the order of things contrary to her perceptual expectations because it is discontinuous with the way her world ordinarily reveals itself through a predictably harmonious unfolding of its aspects. As Merleau-Ponty observes, the intentional activity by which we construct our worlds proceeds by way of "gestalts" which structure what we perceive in a meaningful manner.[39] These gestalts become sedimented as habits of perception as they are assimilated into the customary patterns of meaning-creation that we build up over the history of our engagement with our worlds. But the gestalt that Isabel experiences in her momentary, anomalous "impression" suggests that she needs to rearrange her accustomed patterns of perception. Its unexpected appearance indicates a limit to the ability of her ways of making sense of her world to account for things that they need to understand. It is a surprising hidden side that offers itself as a clue for making sense of the other hidden sides that have surprised her in the unexpected turns her marriage has taken.

That night, in her "vigil of searching criticism,"[40] Isabel reexamines the structure and meaning of the events that have overtaken her in the hope of interpreting more adequately their order and significance. She does not concentrate on that afternoon's impression, and she does not unlock its full meaning quite yet. Rather, she roams reflectively back over her history in recognition of the call made by her anomalous impression for a change in the way she has structured her world's meanings. By studying how her expectations have been surprised in the past, she begins to reshape her understanding of her world so as to know better what to expect in the future. She reflects in general about the failure of her hopes and in particular about Osmond's vanity, her motives for marrying him, how the two deceived each other, and how he stifles her freedom. Her "meditative vigil" demonstrates how, as William James and Kierkegaard both claim, "we live forward, but we understand backward."[41] Or, to recall Merleau-Ponty's notion, Isabel's vigil starts the work of converting the "unreflected" into reflection—transforming experiences vaguely and inadequately understood at first flush into more meaningful patterns through self-conscious acts of interpretation.[42]

As we saw with Maisie, the more that the unreflected prevails over the reflected, the less free we are; but we become more free as we clarify the ambiguities and obscurities of our original experience and thus take charge of it by assimilating it into self-conscious understanding. Madame Merle and Osmond can take advantage of Isabel because there are more areas of obscurity than she suspects in her experience with them. Similarly, Isabel can deceive herself because her motives for marrying are too little reflected upon. The surplus of the unreflected over the reflected in our experience makes us vulnerable to lies from others and from ourselves. As Isabel's experience shows, this surplus alienates us from ourselves to the extent that it allows events to control us more than we control them.

Of course Isabel takes longer than a single night to complete the task she begins here of clarifying the unreflected and reworking the meanings she has given to her world. For example, it is not until Countess Gemini tells all about her brother's shady past and until Madame Merle hints too boldly at her hopes for Pansy and Lord Warburton that Isabel fully grasps the depths of intimacy and intrigue suggested by her initial "impression" of the "anomaly" of her husband's and their friend's "relative position" in the drawing-room—not until then that "she seemed to wake from a long pernicious dream" by moving from vague suspicions to an adequate understanding of "what they all meant" (2:323, 365). But these revelations are, ultimately, less significant than the first step from blindness toward insight that makes them possible. James is right to call Isabel's "meditative vigil" a "landmark" in her history because it marks the moment when she moves from bondage toward a better grounded freedom by taking up a new attitude toward her situation and confronting it critically and self-critically as never before.

Chapter 42 has long been recognized as one of the earliest and finest examples of James's epistemological realism. As in *The Ambassadors*, where he focuses on Strether's "groping knowledge" of people and events, James concentrates here just as much on *how* Isabel sees as on what she sees. Instead of presenting objects to the reader by means of representational aspects holding them ready for our concretization, he depicts the epistemological aspects (in this case reflective rather than perceptual) through which his heroine struggles to know her world adequately. The objects of her contemplation are both absent from the scene and present to her consciousness; to the extent that they are deferred, the reader's attention is directed to the processes through which they are construed. James's portrait of Isabel's consciousness is not an amorphous stream. Filtered through the narrator's controlling voice and structured into a syntax of sentences and paragraphs, her consciousness is depicted as composed and composing. But the composition is shifting and unfinished. The delicate balance between structure and fluidity that the chapter maintains is appropriate to the processes of consciousness James depicts—the attempt Isabel is making to discover new hypotheses for organizing her world as well as her still unfinished search for better guesses about sides hidden from her perspective. These processes themselves are a dialectic of order and movement.

The temporal structure of the chapter also reduplicates the temporality of understanding. The narrative present holds Isabel sitting motionless in her chair as she roams back over the past. The chapter is both an advance in the current development of her consciousness and a recapitulation of her history. This temporal duality is the narrative equivalent of the dialectical relation between the unreflected and reflection—the original experience she seeks to clarify coupled with the present of self-conscious inquiry directed at its obscurities. Once again we see in James a correlation between narrative structure and fundamental epistemological processes.

The work of moving from bondage toward freedom through self-consciousness that Isabel undertakes in her marriage to Osmond bears a revealing resemblance to the workings of Hegel's "master-slave" relationship.[43] As Osmond's slave in the bondage of their marriage, Isabel might be said to come to self-consciousness through "fear" and "labor"; she becomes conscious of her consciousness, namely, as the object of her master's will and as the ultimate stake in their struggle over his claims to power. Like Hegel's master, Osmond objects to and objectifies Isabel's consciousness and, in his superiority, never attains the self-consciousness she does because he never suffers so radically. Just as Hegel's slave is more free than his master, Isabel's trials make her more free because she is more humbly self-aware than Osmond.

I have introduced Hegel here in order to raise a question about his master-slave relationship that bears on the consequences of Isabel's night-long vigil. This question has been raised by Hegel's readers from Marx through Sartre who, after crediting his analysis of the evolution of self-consciousness, go on to ask: How free is the self-conscious slave after all? Although generally not one of Hegel's more insightful readers, William James states this problem pointedly when he notes that the convict cannot be said to transcend the walls of his prison in any meaningful way just by understanding them as a limit to his freedom.[44] Does Isabel actually become more free, then, simply because her "meditative vigil" makes her more reflective? Sartre contends, in apparent contradiction to William James, that "the slave in chains is as free as his master" because "there is no situation in which the for-itself would be *more free* than in others." For Sartre, existence is always free. But Sartre then argues that the slave is free less because he can become self-conscious about his bondage than because he can choose to attempt to break his chains. Confronting "the ground of slavery" self-consciously as his "coefficient of adversity," he can choose "to remain a slave or to risk the worst in order to get rid of his slavery."[45]

Isabel begins to move from bondage toward freedom during her meditative vigil, then, but she must still apply the self-consciousness she is beginning to develop to the difficult task of transforming her situation. The twin dangers of submission and defiance still remain. If she overreaches herself in rebellion, she risks losing all she has gained by outstripping the possibilities available in her situation and returning to the extravagant posture of independence. But if she does not struggle at all, she will remain a slave no matter how self-conscious she becomes.

Isabel's new mastery of the meaning of her situation and the events that have led to it shows its power in her altered relationship with Madame Merle. In this case, at least, knowledge alone does have the power to transform a situation. Madame Merle had used her superior understanding to lure Isabel into marrying Osmond; the success of her intrigue depended on her friend's ignorance of her hidden motives and of her machinations behind the scenes. But when they meet at Pansy's convent, Madame Merle finds that "the person who stood" before her "was not the same one she had seen hitherto, but was a very different person—a person who knew her secret" (2:378). By knowing her "secret"—including, most damagingly, Madame Merle's real relationship to Pansy and her early liaison with Osmond—Isabel gains ascendancy over her one-time friend. Her consciousness has rendered transparent the mysterious opacity that enabled Madame Merle to transcend Isabel's subjectivity without allowing this young woman to respond in kind.

Since Madame Merle's opacity was a limit to Isabel's freedom, here is a situation where knowing a limit is the same as transcending it. Faced with Isabel's knowledge, this "most accomplished of women faltered and lost her courage" and, despite futile attempts to avoid "betraying herself" by conceding herself vanquished, finally makes "a confession of helplessness" by her demeanor (2:378, 379). Isabel's knowledge is power here because it allows her to transform her situation by engaging it practically—confronting Madame Merle rather than fleeing her or submitting to her passively. For example, when Madame Merle attempts to regain the epistemological upper hand by claiming to know that "at bottom" Ralph is to blame for Isabel's marriage because he gave her his inheritance, the courageous young girl shows herself willing to fight back if she needs to. Asserting the full force of her ascendancy, Isabel vanquishes the older woman with her reply: "I believed it was you I had to thank" (2:389).

Still, although Isabel is not submissive, she is not defiant either because she refuses the temptation to take "revenge" on Madame Merle. Countess Gemini advises Isabel to be "nasty" and "feel a little wicked, for the comfort of it" (2:371). Instead, she shows more sympathy than resentment in her pity for "poor, poor Madame Merle"— that "poor, poor woman" (2:331, 366) whose disappointments in life appeal to Isabel's compassion. At their first encounter in the convent, "there was a moment during which, if she had turned and spoken," Isabel "would have said something that would hiss like a lash"—but, since Madame Merle has not yet forced an open confrontation, her "only revenge was to be silent" (2:379). Revenge would be little more than self-indulgence since her power is secure without it. But her compassion for Madame Merle reveals that Isabel knows all too well how disappointments ensue because our limits prevent us from realizing the possibilities we desire. In resisting the temptation of defiant revenge, Isabel shows herself able to bind her will with a restraint admirable for someone whose will has been bound so by the constraints of others. With Madame Merle, Isabel has changed from an unwitting slave to a sympathetic master still self-conscious enough to limit her power.

Knowledge alone will not vanquish Osmond, however. Even after the transforming experience of her meditative vigil, Isabel remains uncertain about how to resolve the dilemma of submission and defiance that her marriage presents her with. After realizing that Osmond had married her in large part for her money, Isabel wonders "whether, since he had wanted her money, her money would now satisfy him. Would he take her money and let her go?" (2:331). No such easy way out lies open to her, though—not only because the complex motives of her avaricious but also tyrannical and vain husband will not allow it but also, and perhaps even more, because Isabel herself is not certain that she is willing to let go of her marriage so easily. Although Isabel "gazed at moments with a sort of incredulous blankness" at the fact that Osmond "was her appointed and inscribed master," she also considers herself duty-bound to uphold "all the traditionary decencies and sanctities of marriage"; she feels great reluctance "to take back something she had solemnly bestown" when, in "the most serious act—the single sacred act—of her life," she had given Osmond her hand (2:245–46).

The marriage tie is not a binding necessity in and of itself but, rather, imposes itself on Isabel as a limit to her possibilities because she accepts it as such. Paradoxically and perhaps surprisingly, then, we can say that Isabel binds herself just as much as if not more than Osmond binds her because she chooses to regard the "tremendous vows" of "the great undertaking of matrimony" as a profound responsibility (2:360–61). There is some lingering idealism in Isabel's tremendous sense of "duty" here, but it is an idealism informed by the tragic understanding she has developed of how limitation must necessarily accompany possibility even if we do play a role in choosing where and how to recognize the constraints on our freedom. Isabel feels that duty binds her to Osmond less because marriage is a divine sacrament or because social custom demands obeisance to it than because her decision in the past to commit herself to him has an abiding claim on her for the present and the future. When we turn to the enigmatic and in some ways unsatisfactory ending of the novel, we shall discover that there is still something arbitrary and incompletely chosen about Isabel's consent to the obligations of marriage. Nevertheless, her acceptance of marriage as a necessary, even compelling, convention differs radically from her earlier naive resistance to all cultural restraints.

Even though Isabel wants to consent to the necessity of her commitment to Osmond, however, her dilemma is that such a consent, rather than freeing her to embrace possibilities, only subjects her to the bondage imposed by his vain and tyrannical will to power. With him, she can be either servile or willful—either submissive or defiant— but not a freely bound agent of the servile will. For example, Isabel finds herself almost crippled by ambivalence over Osmond's strategy for capturing Lord Warburton through her influence because she can only defy him or submit, and she cannot win either way. She cannot give in to his desires without playing false to her old friend and former suitor or without binding herself even tighter to Osmond as a self-effacing agent of his will. But she cannot defy him without bringing down his wrath, which, despite her subtle strategy of discouraging Warburton while seeming to encourage him, is exactly what happens. Isabel faces a similar plight in their quarrel over her wish to visit Ralph at his deathbed. To give in to Osmond's opposition to her trip would mean to submit finally and absolutely to his tyranny as well as to violate the bonds to her cousin that their past involvements have made almost as deep a commitment as marriage. But defying her husband would seem to put an end once and for all to the marriage she feels duty-bound to preserve. Osmond warns her that deciding to go to Ralph "will be a piece of the most deliberate, the most calculated opposition" (2:354). The days have passed when "opposition" to constraints in the cause of independence seemed a viable definition of freedom to Isabel. But she cannot seem to avoid situations where she must say "no" to limitation even when she would prefer to say "yes."

When Isabel chooses to go to her cousin despite her husband's opposition, her defiance does not decide the question of how she can discover a meaningful freedom. Even though she denies her bonds to Osmond in order to acknowledge her commitment to Ralph, her act of leaving Rome for Gardencourt is more negative than positive. She is rejecting the limiting claims of her marriage more than she is resolutely embracing grounded possibilities that open up an invigorating future to her. Even as she travels to England and thus moves toward the goal posited by her act of defiance, Isabel feels "all purpose, all intention, was suspended" and completely gives herself over to "the sense of being carried" in a "motionless" and "passive" attitude (2:391). Although "the quick vague shadow of a long future" occasionally flits before her to remind her she is still "a woman who had her life to live," she mostly feels that "the grey curtain of her indifference" blocks any prospect of meaningful possibilities she might project herself toward (2:392–93). Earlier, Isabel's independence— although ultimately a negative definition of freedom—had at least offered the positive hope of a bright, expansive world whose challenge she welcomed. But in the negative act of defying Osmond, she flees to Gardencourt as to "a sanctuary" where she might succumb to the temptation "to cease utterly, to give it all up and not know anything more" (2:391). After the one positive goal of her trip has been surpassed by Ralph's death, Isabel is "the image of a victim of idleness" with "a singular absence of purpose" who, "very tired" and "restless and unable to occupy herself," lets the days pass aimlessly (2:429). This empty, meaningless dissipation is the danger Isabel avoided as long as she resisted the temptation of defiance and accepted the limitations of her marriage, however stifling, in order to preserve a situation for her freedom.

Like Roderick Hudson in the restless apathy of the period before his fatal fall, Isabel is particularly vulnerable at this point to an outbreak of the sudden and demonic because of her inability to take hold

of her freedom resolutely. Enter, suddenly, the demonic Caspar Goodwood—the very figure of unfreedom in the way he takes her by surprise in the garden and forces her to hear his plea. After the initial
shock of his entrance, though, Goodwood seems the perfect "apostle
of freedom" (2:245)—to borrow a phrase used to describe Ralph—
because he proposes to restore Isabel's lost independence. Goodwood
claims to care for her freedom with a liberating solicitude that he describes as a charge entrusted him by Ralph. Offering to support her in
defying Osmond's tyranny, he insists that "we can do absolutely as we
please; to whom under the sun do we owe anything? . . . If you'll only
trust me, how little you will be disappointed! The world's all before
us—and the world's very big" (2:435). Still, to recall the title of the
work James quotes here, Isabel has long ago lost such hope of paradise. This call for independence might have appealed to the early, expansive Isabel; but it cannot speak to the dismally experienced
woman whose disappointments have come about precisely because
she insisted on owing nothing to anyone and trusted too blindly that
her horizons were limitless. His offer only makes her feel more root-
less and ungrounded: "The world, in truth, had never seemed so
large; it seemed to open out, all round her, to take the form of a
mighty sea, where she floated in fathomless waters" (2:435). The
boundless independence Goodwood offers risks the same dissipation
Isabel suffers whenever she fails to accept limitation as the price of
making possible actual engagement with possibility.

     Goodwood's true appeal lies less in the vision of freedom he de-
scribes than in the possibility of escape he represents: "[S]he believed
just then that to let him take her in his arms would be the next best
thing to her dying" (2:435) and joining Ralph in eternal rest from the
struggle of existence. (There are marked sexual overtones in this wish
and throughout Isabel's encounter with Goodwood that I will take up
later.) Despite his offer of liberation, then, Goodwood would in fact
take her freedom away from her—an appealing proposition because
of the surrender of responsibility it would allow, but a distressing one
because it would mean nothing more than exchanging masters without
breaking the chains of slavery. In the absolutism of his insistence that
Isabel abandon herself to his custody, Goodwood is true to his character as "a person destitute of the faculty of compromise, who would
take what he asked for or take nothing" (2:291). Only apparently an
apostle of freedom, then, Goodwood is really the very figure of un-

freedom that his sudden entrance first made him seem. In deciding how to respond to him, Isabel must determine whether she can discover a more satisfactory alignment of possibility and limitation than the false freedom and renewed tyranny he offers.

She makes this discovery at the moment she decides to return to Osmond. Before her decision, Isabel had "felt herself sink and sink" under the temptation of giving herself up to Goodwood, and "in the movement she seemed to beat with her feet, in order to catch herself, to feel something to rest on" (2:435). She falls until she reaches the ground on which her freedom must take its stand. This is what I have called, with Heidegger, the "there" of her situation—including all of the limitations and commitments involved in her relation with Osmond that she cannot deny but must confront because she has been inextricably "thrown" into them by past choices she has made and others have made for her. When Isabel begs Goodwood "to go away" and "leave me alone" (2:436), her pleas have an entirely different meaning from the protests she made earlier in the *noli me tangere* attitude of her independence. By resigning herself to the constraints of her marriage (and of her commitment to Pansy as well), Isabel resolutely takes hold of her situation with the result that "she was free" (2:436). Finding strength by discovering the truth of the servile will, Isabel freely consents to being bound and becomes free because bound.

James portrays Isabel's new resolute freedom in her attitude when, after escaping Goodwood's clutches, "she looked all about her" with "her hand on the latch" of the door to the house: "She had not known where to turn; but she knew now. There was a very straight path" (2:436). Isabel experiences what Heidegger calls a "moment of vision" (or *Augenblick*) where we disclose our situation to ourselves in anticipatory resoluteness and bring together the past and the present by projecting ourselves toward the future.[46] Threatened by despair, she has achieved instead that sense of integrity that comes from accepting the irreversibility of what has been in one's history.[47] For better and for worse, she realizes that her life is her own responsibility. Neither defiant nor submissive, Isabel has emerged, then, from healthy-minded naiveté and the depression of a sick soul into the integrity of the twice-born. In her moment of vision at the end, she shows a resoluteness and resignation achieved by mastering the paradoxical reciprocity of freedom and necessity.

Even though Isabel's decision to return to Rome rests on the solid
logic of the servile will, there is still something unsatisfactory about
the novel's conclusion—in part because of James's attitude toward the
politics of social reality. Isabel is never given the chance to regard her
marriage as a cultural contingency that she might choose to criticize
and struggle against without losing touch with the "there" of her situation. For example, in a play first performed in England during the
same decade *The Portrait* appeared, Ibsen's Nora engages her situation with an open-eyed anticipatory resoluteness when she leaves her
husband and slams the door on her doll's house.[48] According to the
terms established in James's novel, though, Isabel could not follow a
similar course without risking rootlessness by overstepping what her
limits permit. The rootlessness and dissipation of the adults in *What
Maisie Knew* may provide a glimpse of the dire consequences James
envisions if the marriage bond is not regarded as a necessary limitation. In any case, Isabel never really enjoys the possibility of attack-
ing critically the institutional arrangement that justifies Osmond's
power over her. Such an attack would make her appear to be reverting
to a negatively independent attitude. Only part of this problem can be
explained by crediting James with a realistic sense of the power of
cultural institutions or, following William Veeder, by regarding Isabel's plight as "a paradigm" of "Victorian woman's terrible dilemma"
in marriage and thus as a criticism of prevailing social conditions.[49]
We have here a rare instance where James's political conservatism
limits his novelistic imagination.

Another aspect of the ending's inadequacy is sexual. As many have
noted, the language of Isabel's and Goodwood's encounter is all but
unsublimated: "[T]his was the hot wind of the desert. . . . [T]he very
taste of it, as of something potent, acrid and strange, forced open her
set teeth. . . . His kiss was like white lightning, a flash that spread,
and spread again, and stayed. . . . [S]he felt each thing in his hard
manhood that had least pleased her, each aggressive fact of his face,
his figure, his presence, justified of its intense identity and made one
with this act of possession" (2:434, 436). When Isabel flees Goodwood's embrace, it is possible to regard her—and many have done
so—as a frigid young girl who, although she realizes "that she had
never been loved before" (2:433), finds the only kiss in the book hys-
terically disturbing because of her intensely ambivalent enjoyment
and fear of passion.[50]

Now according to Freud, Isabel would not do well to surrender blindly to the overwhelming libidinal force that Goodwood invokes in her. Like the id to the ego, Goodwood's sexual power presents a threat to Isabel's freedom and thus contributes to making him a demonic figure. Still, for Freud, consciousness must accept the body's libidinal endowment as an inescapable part of its situation and attempt to tame its force to the control of meaning. To flee from one's sexual impulses (as Isabel does) is to increase one's bondage to them. Isabel will not have confronted her situation resolutely until she has consented to the necessity of her sexual constitution. She must accept, as part of her ground, that she has been thrown into a body with libidinal desires—and one that can be an object for the passion of others. The sexual and social inadequacies of the novel's ending, then, do not refute the existential truth of the servile will but, rather, indicate only that Isabel still incompletely understands the reciprocity of freedom and necessity when she returns to Rome. Like the limits of her attitude toward marriage, though, the flaws in Isabel's sexual understanding are undoubtedly to some extent James's too.

It would be wrong, however, to find the ending inadequate because it refuses to give a definitive statement about Isabel's future. For one thing, to give Isabel too complete a triumph would bring James close to a false because extravagant idealism much like the healthy-minded optimism that brings his heroine to grief. Such idealism mars the conclusion of "Madame de Mauves," an early story that is in many ways a study for *The Portrait*. Trapped in a marriage to a man of low morals, Madame de Mauves asserts her ascendancy by maintaining a noble moral integrity that so unnerves her husband that he commits suicide. In her integrity, resoluteness, and resignation, Isabel may enjoy a similar ascendancy over Osmond in Rome. But James could not grace her with Madame de Mauves's triumph without imposing a false finality on her existence by giving her a facile victory.

The dismal, difficult future that Isabel can probably look forward to in Rome reinforces the novel's sense of the great gulf between the expanse of the possible and the limits of the actual. In William James's words, "the actually possible in this world is vastly narrower than all that is demanded; and there is always a pinch between the ideal and the actual which can only be got through by leaving part of the ideal behind."[51] As Henry James comments in his *Notebooks*, though, "the obvious criticism" of *The Portrait* "will be that it is not finished—that

I have not seen the heroine to the end of her situation—that I have left her *en l'air*."[52] But this state of affairs simply serves to emphasize that, as Merleau-Ponty notes, "our world" is always still "an 'unfinished task.'"[53] Isabel's return to Osmond presents her with a test of what she will make of her newly discovered well-grounded freedom. The end of Isabel's story is nothing more than a new beginning for her existence. Our existence is a constant unfolding of new beginnings in search of an ending that never comes until death. Commencing her existence anew with the anticipatory resoluteness of her moment of vision at Gardencourt, Isabel must continue the "unfinished task" of deciding her fate by responsibly confronting and grappling with her situation. As a figure of the servile will, Isabel shows that discovering a right relation between freedom and necessity does not end our conflicts; it only grants recognition to the terms within which we must struggle to decide our existence.[54]

F I V E

Isabel's trials over freedom and necessity again and again center on questions of intersubjectivity and care. While enthralled with her vision of perfect independence, for example, Isabel defends her freedom by refusing relations with others. But then, when possibility without limit proves ungratifying, Isabel marries in the name of freedom. She wants to bind herself to another in order to ground herself in a situation, and she hopes not only that caring for Osmond will prove fulfilling but also that being with him will enable her to share the secret of accepting while defying limits that he seems to have discovered. Osmond and Madame Merle plot to entrap Isabel by taking advantage of the opacity of the Other in order to hide their motives. Isabel's night-long meditative vigil stands as a landmark for her freedom because it begins to loosen the ties that bind her by providing initial insight into relations between herself and others that had hitherto been obscure to her. Her bondage is bondage to an Other. Her marriage to Osmond imprisons her because the Other does not care as he should; he regards her as a tool to manipulate to serve his vanity and not as someone to take care of with solicitude as well as to be with in loving intimacy. Furthermore, when Isabel marries, she is separated from the sympathy and understanding of others like Henrietta and Ralph who, although imperfect in the way they care, at least wish to help her. In consenting to necessity in order to establish a ground for her freedom, Isabel must accept involvements with others who are hostile or solicitous as part of the situation into which she is thrown. In her search for a meaningful freedom, she must struggle with all the difficulties inherent in the relation between the Self and the Other that stand in the way of absolute intersubjectivity and perfect care. Her history shows that finding a right relation between freedom and necessity is so troublesome in large part because finding a right relation between the Self and the Other is so trying.

Once again exploring one of James's intentional foundations opens up new territory beyond the domain it governs. Asking about freedom and necessity has led us to questions about intersubjectivity and care. The intimate connection between problems of freedom and problems of personal relations in Isabel's history shows again that James understands experience in all its aspects as a unified field. In accord with the oneness of experience that, as I noted earlier, leads William James to deny the division between subject and object, Isabel Archer's experience is a seamless whole, not divided into compartments like "freedom and necessity" or "intersubjectivity and care" except as we isolate these aspects of her story retrospectively for purposes of analysis. Furthermore, as interrelated aspects of experience, both freedom and personal relations involve the dilemma of transcendence and its limits—the dilemma of how to go beyond ourselves toward our possibilities and toward others, limited in both cases (as Isabel discovers to her sorrow) so that perfect transcendence escapes us. Following up questions about the relation between Self and Other that we have begun to ask, we must continue to inquire: How does James understand the opacity of the Other, the difficulties it gives rise to, and the likelihood of their resolution? What does he make of the existential significance of care, its various manifestations, and the demands of practicing it authentically? We can expect, too, that the answers to these questions will also tell us more about James's understanding of the relation between freedom and necessity as we fill out our understanding of his existential and phenomenological significance.

• 5 •

SELF AND OTHER:
CONFLICT VERSUS CARE
IN *THE GOLDEN BOWL*

ONE

Other people are limitlessly fascinating to Henry James. His readers attest that this fascination holds an important place among the intentional foundations on which he built his house of fiction. Philip Rahv, for example, claims that "there never was a writer so immersed in personal relations." When André Gide complains that James's characters are "desperately mundane," it is because they "never live except in relation to each other."[1] Gide's complaint only emphasizes how deeply James understands that we are always inextricably involved in and even defined by relations between ourselves and others. James never wavers from his conviction that "all life comes back to the question of our relations with each other."[2] This question brings James both joy and despair. It can bring joy because the relation between the Self and the Other offers possibilities for expanding our experience of the world, for enriching our understanding of ourselves, and for exercising a fulfilling care. But it can bring despair because the Other must ultimately remain a mystery—a disturbing state of affairs that makes misunderstanding more likely than understanding and conflict more probable than harmony. As much as any of his fictions, *The Golden Bowl* shows James's understanding of this aspect of experience. As he observes in his preface, the novel deals for the most part with "a group of agents who may be counted on the fingers of one hand." But what James calls "the fundamental fewness"[3] of his characters acts more as a help than a hindrance for exploring the relation between Self and Other because this very economy emphasizes the variety of problems and possibilities inherent in that relation.

The relation between ourselves and others has been as much a fascination for existential phenomenology as for James. This fascination begins with Husserl's observation that the world is both the same and different for different subjects. The objects in my world belong to your world too, and one reason why I anticipate no surprise from their hidden sides is that I assume they present themselves to you as I expect they would to me if I stood where you stand. Still, you know my objects differently than I do not only because you are positioned differently but also because we have had different histories that have left us with different habits of creating meaning and have attached different meanings to the same objects. Something that is strange to me, for example, may be familiar to you. The Other threatens me with solipsism because my world can never agree perfectly with his world. But the Other is also my main hope for securing a hold on "reality" because "reality" is largely a matter of agreement between observers. At first, Husserl thought that the gap between selves could be bridged by acts of "empathy" and "analogy"—acts that would allow me to transport myself to the Other's position and to understand the world as it exists for him in his situation.[4] But Merleau-Ponty, Sartre, and other later phenomenologists have shown that "empathy" and "analogy" cannot guarantee intersubjectivity. To begin with, as Merleau-Ponty points out, the self-presence of another human being is ultimately unknowable.[5] The Self and the Other are not transparent but opaque to each other because I can never experience what another is to himself just as he can never experience what I am to myself. Furthermore, according to Sartre, I can never completely understand my "Self-for-Others"; and the object that I am for the Other can never coincide with the subject that I am for myself.[6]

In sum, then, perfect intersubjectivity is impossible, and the Other must always remain somewhat obscure. We can never understand each other perfectly, and our very status as "Self" and "Other" establishes an insuperable gap between us. But, paradoxically, this impossibility of intersubjective transparency is also proof against solipsism. After all, the Other would not pose problems for me if I did not realize that he is a Self with a world that claims at least equal rights with mine. Language could not exist if solipsism prevailed. And, in fact, dialogue offers the best possibility of reducing the opacity and narrowing the gap that separate the Self and the Other.[7] Solipsism is inescapable but absurd; intersubjectivity is impossible but inevitable to some degree and attainable to a more considerable extent than most of us achieve. That is the paradoxical conclusion phenomenology has reached about the problematic relation between the Self and the Other.

James's readers generally agree that *The Golden Bowl* takes as its major theme the question of personal relations. They disagree radically, though, over what it makes of this theme. Some argue that the novel reveals the possibilities that care and understanding hold for working our salvation. Among these critics, for example, Dorothea Krook calls the novel "a great fable . . . of the redemption of man by the transforming power of human love," and she identifies Maggie Verver as "the instrument of the redemptive act." [8] On the other hand, many claim that conflict and misunderstanding dominate in the relations portrayed in the novel. For example, J. J. Firebaugh calls Maggie a "Machiavellian creature" and "an all but unmitigated tyrant"— a "mistress of shades" who deceitfully carries out "machinations in support of self-interest." [9] Some critics would resolve this dispute by a kind of compromise that would regard Maggie as "neither Saint nor Witch." [10] That view is certainly true as far as it goes, but perhaps it does not go far enough. Perhaps, that is, we can cut beneath the controversy over *The Golden Bowl* by understanding how the opposing sides argue that the novel demonstrates opposing aspects of the relation between the Self and the Other, neither of which alone is adequate to describe it completely. We have already seen that this relation is itself contradictory and that the conflict and misunderstanding of solipsism are as much a part of it as the care and understanding of intersubjectivity.

The meaning of the controversy over *The Golden Bowl* may become clearer if we examine a similar dispute in existential phenomenology. Heidegger and Sartre disagree about the essence of the relation between Self and Other in much the same way as James's readers disagree about his novel. For Heidegger, "care" (*Sorge*) is the fundamental structure of existence, and "being with" others (*Mitsein*) is the basic dimension of personal relations. He finds manifestations of "care" in the ways we comport ourselves toward the people we are involved with, the instruments and tools we handle, and the things we encounter in the world. These manifestations reflect the "care" we show toward Being as beings-in-the-world. [11] Sartre, on the other hand, denies the priority of "care" or "being-with" and argues instead that "conflict is the original meaning of being-for-others." The Self and the Other are perpetually locked in combat, he explains, because another's gaze threatens to take my freedom away from me. Transcending my transcendence, the look of the Other solidifies my subjectivity by regarding it as an object.[12]

Now Heidegger and Sartre are both right; the relation between selves cannot be described adequately without taking both "care" and "conflict" into account. Heidegger understands that ordinarily most of us practice degenerate forms of care that actually signify conflict—manipulating others like tools, for example, in violation of their being. Sartre's theory of conflict acknowledges similarly the claims of care. The Self and the Other can engage in battle only because they *care* about each other and are somehow fundamentally *with* each other in such a way that their gazes matter to each other. Furthermore, Sartre believes that harmony could replace strife as the basis of personal relations if the Self and the Other could open themselves in the mutuality of dialogue and render transparent the opacity that divides them.[13]

The critics in the controversy over *The Golden Bowl* do not share Heidegger's and Sartre's—and, as we shall see, James's—understanding that no view of personal relations that exclusively emphasizes either conflict or care can do justice to the problem of Self and Other. Those readers who stress Maggie's Machiavellian side see only James's portrayal of Sartrean warfare, while those who proclaim her a loving redeemer see only his intuition of the Heideggerian significance of care. But *The Golden Bowl* is neither a sordid account of tyrannical manipulation nor a great fable of the redemptive power of human love. To claim that it is either exclusively is to ignore how the novel explores and exhibits both Sartrean conflict and Heideggerian care.

The phenomenon of lying illustrates particularly well the epistemological and existential questions about personal relations that have concerned us so far and that will guide our reading of *The Golden Bowl*. The lie is a borderline case in the problem of Self and Other that throws into especially bold relief the problems of transparency and opacity, conflict and care. As we saw in our analysis of the duplicity that permeates Maisie's world, a successful liar takes advantage of the gap between the Self and the Other and manipulates it for his own ends. I can lie to you because I can disguise my thoughts, feelings, and motives; they are ordinarily somewhat opaque to you, and I can make them more so. The lie is possible because what I am for others is never the same as what I am for myself. Because we present a surface to others who read our depths from its signs, the liar can control his surfaces to disguise his depths; he can present to us a side that leads us to assume a hidden side different from what is actually behind his facade—hence our surprise when a lie is revealed and we discover it hid something we had not expected. Still, although lying depends on the solipsistic aspect of our relations with others, it is essentially an intersubjective activity. The liar must understand others well enough to control how they know him through his Self-for-Others, and his deception cannot succeed unless others think they understand him as he wants them to.

Existentially, lying would seem to regard strife as the meaning of personal relations. According to Sartre, lying "spoils relations among people" because harmony will not prevail over conflict as long as opacity prevails over transparency—that is, as long as "each keeps something hidden from the other, something secret."[14] But, perhaps paradoxically, lies may also serve and show care under certain circumstances. For example, although lies usually go hand in hand with falsehood, lying may also facilitate the truth. Fiction and other art forms deceive in such a manner inasmuch as they follow what Sartre calls "the law of rhetoric" that says that "one must lie in order to speak the truth."[15] In this and other ways, lies can show solicitude for another's welfare. If James is fascinated with the lie, it may be because duplicity exhibits in extreme form many of the problems that complicate the relation between the Self and the Other. James's interest in the lie is a logical outgrowth of his fascination with other people.

"Mystification" was one of James's projected titles for The Golden Bowl. "The Marriages" was another.[16] Together, these two titles suggest the general thematic area that our analysis of the novel will cover as we attempt to explicate James's understanding of how such matters as lying and marriage display the epistemological and existential dilemmas involved in personal relations. First we shall examine how Adam and Maggie Verver's self-deceptive, almost solipsistic blindness about problems of personal relations helps to create a situation in which dilemmas and deceptions prevail. Then we shall see how Maggie comes to undertake reflections about herself and others that reveal difficulties in the relations between selves that had remained hidden from her before. Finally we shall learn how Maggie's strategies for saving her marriage and defeating Charlotte not only seek to create a sphere in which care can thrive but also prove that conflict is endemic to personal relations. James is neither sanguine nor skeptical about the problem of Self and Other, we shall find, but he understands that it is an aspect of experience full of paradoxes, perils, and challenges.

T W O

When they enter the novel, Adam and Maggie Verver are certain that they know each other through and through and care for each other with perfect felicity. But this conviction blinds them to the possibility that intimate personal relations could be less than straightforward and easy—that opacity could threaten transparency, for example, or that conflict could prevail over care. The Ververs show yet another side of what Matthiessen calls the "baffled and baffling innocence" of "the American character"[17] that so intrigued James—a naiveté about intersubjectivity and care that complements Isabel Archer's healthy-mindedness about freedom and Roderick Hudson's romantic extravagance of imagination. Their innocent faith in personal relations shows what the Prince calls "the follies of the romantic disposition" as applied to the problem of Self and Other. "You see too much—that's what may sometimes make you difficulties," he warns Maggie; "when you don't, at least, . . . see too little."[18] Isabel Archer's "romantic disposition" led her to see too much the possibility of freedom and too little the necessity of limitation, and Roderick Hudson's led him to see too much the imagination's wonders and too little its dangers. In the romanticism of Maggie's faith, however, she sees too much of the basis for rejoicing and too little of the reason for despairing about personal relations. Still, her history shows that blindness to the problem of Self and Other does not make it vanish but, quite the contrary, contributes to the development of crises in personal relations that can bring its dimensions to the attention of the naive with a terrible urgency.

The Prince discovers Maggie's blindness to the problematic nature of the relation between selves when he tries to assure her that he at least will not be a problematic Other. He asks, "You do believe I'm not a hypocrite? You recognize that I don't lie nor dissemble nor deceive?"

> The question, to which he had given a certain intensity, had made her, he remembered, stare an instant, her colour rising as if it had sounded to her still stranger than he had intended. He had perceived on the spot that any *serious* discussion of veracity, of loyalty, or rather of the want of them, practically took her unprepared, as if it were quite new to her. He had noticed it before; it was the English, the American sign that duplicity, like "love," had to be joked about. It could n't be "gone into."
> (1:15)

Ironically, perhaps, the Prince cannot tell Maggie that he deserves her confidence because his assurances presuppose the possibility of doubts about the trustworthiness of others—doubts that her faith will not allow her to entertain because they call that faith into question. To shun questions about "love" and lying means to avoid facing up to the existential and epistemological questions that bedevil relations between ourselves and others. To discuss "loyalty" would mean to raise conflict and care as an issue, while to examine "veracity" would mean to recognize that our inherent opacity to each other makes transparency a serious work that cannot be taken for granted. Maggie's innocent faith, however, simplifies the difficulties of personal relations self-deceptively—even if the need to "joke about" these matters may betray an anguished but still suppressed intuition of their potentially troublesome nature.

Adam Verver might seem an implausible innocent unless we join those readers who consider him evidence of James's ignorance about business. Actually, this enigmatic millionaire's apparent naiveté at the outset may be credible to the extent that others do not pose much of an epistemological or existential problem in the business world. Although financial negotiations may demand a sharp sense of the adversary's interests and a certain wariness of deception, a businessman can operate successfully on a limited notion of the Other. He need only assume that his competitor is the "rational economic man" who acts from the same motives, on the same principles, and with the same ends as he does. Similarly, business simplifies the existential problem of Self and Other by assuming that the conflict that reigns in the marketplace will take care of everyone's interests, desires, and needs. In any case, Adam certainly learns more about the difficulties of personal relations from his involvements with Charlotte and the Prince than anyone could from financial transactions. Adam's business experience need not make him immune to the deceptions and self-deceptions of someone inexperienced in personal relations.

Adam and Maggie Verver's self-deceptive blindness about the complicated matter of knowing and caring for others reveals itself clearly in their attitude toward the Prince as the novel opens. Although Maggie tells the Prince that he is "so curious and eminent that there are very few others like you," she also informs him that "you're not perhaps absolutely unique" and, even more, that "you belong to a class about which everything is known" (1:12). Knowing the Prince as an individual is no problem, Maggie thinks, because she knows everything about his type. A little earlier the Prince had warned Maggie that she and her father "really know nothing" about him because to know the public history of his ancestry is still not to know "my single self, the unknown, unimportant—unimportant save to *you*—personal quantity" (1:9). "Luckily, my dear," Maggie responds, "for what then would become, please, of the promised occupation of my future?" (1:9). Her insistence shortly thereafter that he is completely transparent does not indicate, though, at least at this early stage, that she thinks the occupation of penetrating his private opacity will keep her particularly busy. James believes—unlike Maggie here—that to know someone or something means to pay equal attention to both the individual and the type. To know the Prince's type is not to know his individuality because his past history may influence but cannot encompass the private self he is still always becoming. His type is nothing more than the ground on which his individual freedom is thrown.

Maggie considers the Prince transparent because she regards him as "what they call a *morceau de musée*"—"a rarity, an object of beauty, an object of price," and "a part of [her father's] collection" (1:12). As such a fine piece, he is all surface and no depth, all an object without any disturbing, volatile, and unfathomable subjectivity, and all his Self-for-Others inasmuch as his value is appreciated with a regard which renders irrelevant his Self-for-Himself. This is a misleading way of knowing the Prince, however. His true self is not contained in his properties but finds expression in his possibilities. As a great collector and in "the spirit of the connoisseur," however,

Adam Verver thinks he knows his son-in-law perfectly because, as a "representative precious object," the Prince shows "the great marks and signs" that indicate "the high authenticities" that the American millionaire "had learnt to look for in pieces of the first order" (1:140). Adam is even glad the Prince is a round and not "angular" object— that is, a compliantly simple member of their retinue and not a difficult because problematic and insistently singular Other. In one of his rare intrusions, though, the narrator observes that "nothing perhaps might affect us as queerer, had we time to look into it, than this application of the same measure of value to such different pieces of property as old Persian carpets, say, and new human acquisitions" (1:196) —the irony being, of course, that this is precisely a matter we are called upon "to look into."

To know the Prince falsely means to care for him wrongly. Maggie's mistaken epistemological certainty about him helps to blind her to the existential problems of "being-with" another in care, and her and her father's aesthetic attitude toward him abuses his freedom. Even an appropriate aesthetic appreciation of a work of art must evoke and cherish the subjectivity lodged in it. But in their aesthetic misappreciation of the Prince, Adam and Maggie care for him as an object pure and simple—as an object "present-at-hand" (*vorhanden*) for their pleasure, in Heideggerian terms, or at most as an instrument "ready-to-hand" (*zuhanden*) for their convenience.[19] Their attitude comes close to what Sartre calls the "infernal love that aims at subjugating a freedom" by making it "dependent, inessential."[20] Maggie thinks of Amerigo as a simple, transparent object for whom a reifying appreciation cares adequately and not as a mysterious, opaque Other whose freedom and subjectivity make it nearly impossible to know him completely and difficult indeed to share an intimacy with him based on a mutually liberating reciprocity.

Amerigo does not share Maggie's illusions about understanding and care in personal relations. He assures Maggie that he has "found out about" his benefactors "all there is to find," but he confesses more candidly to Charlotte later that "the difficulty is, and will always be, that I don't understand them" (1:8, 309). His dilemma is due in part to the difference between the American and European character. The gap between national identities, though, is both a manifestation of and a metaphor for the gap between the Self and the Other. The

Prince expresses his disturbing sense of the Ververs' unfathomable otherness with an image borrowed from a work by Edgar Allan Poe:

> the story of the ship-wrecked Gordon Pym who, drifting in a
> small boat further toward the North Pole—or was it the
> South?—than any one had ever done, found at a given moment
> before him a thickness of white air that was like a dazzling
> curtain of light, concealing as darkness conceals, yet of the
> colour of milk or of snow. There were moments when he felt his
> own boat move upon some such mystery. The state of mind of
> his new friends, including Mrs. Assingham herself, had resem-
> blances to a great white curtain. (1:22)

Here, as in its original context, the curtain suggests epistemological transcendence. In Poe's *Narrative of Arthur Gordon Pym*, however, the figure beyond the curtain seems to have an ontological or religious significance as either transcendent Being or God. But for James and the Prince, the image has become secular and existential; what is transcendent is simply the Other. Because the Ververs seem innocently, unwittingly opaque, the Prince envisions their curtain as white—unlike curtains he had known whose "purple even to blackness" had produced "a darkness intended and ominous" (1:22–23) that deviously disguised deceptions. Unwitting innocence is just as opaque, however, as lying that self-consciously takes advantage of the gap between the Self and the Other. It may even be more unfathomable because it is less able to explain itself if questioned. Amerigo finds himself separated epistemologically from the Ververs by "a great white curtain" because the being-for-others they present to him seems to disguise more than reveal their being-for-themselves. He does not assume as they do that to know someone's Self-for-Others is to know everything about him; for the Prince, this is where the Other's mystery begins, not where it ends.

Problems of knowing meet problems of caring here, since Amerigo wants to understand the Ververs in order to discover "what they expected him to do" (1:24) in return for all of their generosity toward him. He finds himself perplexed because Mr. Verver's "easy way with his millions had taxed to such small purpose . . . the principle of reciprocity" (1:5). Sartre calls generosity "the image of freedom"; through it, he argues, we can address each other's freedom in solicitude instead of insisting upon subservience.[21] In one sense, the Ververs' generosity leaves the Prince completely free inasmuch as it makes no demands on him. But the Ververs do not expect the Prince to make any return because they want him only to *be* the object they value and not to *do* anything as a subject in a reciprocal relation with themselves as other subjects. "In the absence of reciprocity," though, as Merleau-Ponty points out, "the world of the one then takes in completely that of the other, so that one feels disinherited in favour of the other."[22] The Prince has gained a fortune monetarily, then, but has been disinherited existentially since Maggie does not understand that only a relation of mutual recognition and reciprocal exchange would allow both her and her husband to be with each other in freedom. Charlotte and Amerigo express their dissatisfaction with this absence of mutuality when they complain that Maggie's "not selfish . . . enough"—"there's nothing, absolutely, that one *need* do for her" (1:101). The Prince "felt at moments as if there were never anything to do for the Ververs that was worthy—to call worthy—of the personal relation" (1:314). In a world where everything is taken care of for him, the Prince finds no room left for exercising care in return.

James himself would agree with the Prince that knowing and caring for others are problematic and not self-evident matters. Admittedly, his readers have found it difficult to determine where—if anywhere—James stands in *The Golden Bowl*. But the novel's famous ambiguity is due precisely to James's conviction that knowing and caring are prone to ambiguity because of the difficulties inherent in the relation between ourselves and others. James's well-known allegiance to "point of view"—his belief, as he explains in the preface to *The Golden Bowl*, that "the very straightest and closest possible" treatment demands rendering not "my own impersonal account of the affair in hand" but "my account of somebody's impression of it"[23]—this representational strategy acknowledges the epistemological dilemma that the Self and the Other present to each other and turns it to aesthetic advantage. According to James, as we have seen, and for his technique, the miracle of fiction lies in its ability to transport us into another's experience by giving us someone else's sense of the world. James's use of point of view miraculously transcends the gap between Self and Other by making accessible the otherwise inaccessible presence of another to himself. His intimately rendered "registers," in turn, are deeply enmeshed in the dilemmas involved in fathoming the unfathomable others around them. Like the Prince who wonders who the Ververs are and who he is for them, the Jamesian register struggles with the difficulties of understanding not only the presence of others to themselves but also the self he presents to the understanding of these others as his Self-for-Others. James positively revels in the complications that follow from the mysterious opacity of others; if others were completely transparent, much of the reason for finding them fascinating would be gone.

James's aesthetic manipulation of the gap between Self and Other presents the reader with complications just as great as—if not greater than—those that face the novel's characters. James's depiction of a character's consciousness may transport the reader, as I have suggested, into the world of another Self. But we overcome the barrier between selves in this way only to rediscover it because we find that the world opened up to us is closed to other worlds. We can only enter one character's consciousness by sacrificing immediate access to others. Furthermore, James's registers themselves become alternately transparent and opaque to us as they exchange the roles of Self and Other by alternately taking over and then ceding to someone else the novel's point of view. This alternation of perspectives gives the reader a better opportunity than any character within the novel enjoys to work toward intersubjectivity by comparing and contrasting different consciousnesses to achieve a unified, quasi-omniscient vision of the world they share. In conventional realism, such intersubjective omniscience is the privilege of the narrator. James's narrator may be all-knowing, but he leaves the achievement of a total vision as a challenge to the reader—a challenge for us to develop our imagination about the relations between worlds separated by their inwardness. Nevertheless, the refusal of all perspectives to harmonize (the divergence between what the Ververs think and what the adulterers understand, for example, or the irremediable antagonism later between Maggie and Charlotte), coupled with the irreducible opacity of some points of view (the enigma after Maggie's awakening of what her father knows)—these obstacles to the reader's quest for an all-encompassing unity serve as reminders of the ultimate impossibility of eradicating the gap between selves. By frustrating the reader's desire for a total vision, James calls our attention to the solipsistic dimension of personal relations. As an incitement to seek intersubjectivity and a reminder of the inevitability of solipsism, the experience of reading

James offers an education about the contradictions that complicate relations between the Self and others.[24]

James's epistemological and technical fascination with the problem of Self and Other also leads to his oft-noted confidantes and commentators like Fanny Assingham.[25] Her "irrepressible interest in other lives" is both stymied and inspired by her awareness that "one can never ideally be sure of anything" about the "relation, all round" that "we're mixed up" in inextricably (1:254, 86). Fanny herself is both clairvoyant and hopelessly, even comically, muddled about the others all around her—a testimony, in both her insight and blindness, to James's understanding of the importance and near impossibility of penetrating the mysterious opacity of others. Fanny's restless conscience, reminding her of the responsibilities she has incurred by meddling in the lives of others, also testifies to the limits to how well we can care for others that result from the restrictions on how well we can know them. "One was no doubt a meddlesome fool," she reflects; "one always *is*, to think one sees people's lives for them better than they see them for themselves" (1:388). Like the Prince's quandary over generosity and reciprocity, Fanny's somewhat tardy reflections about the wisdom of her overly zealous solicitude reveal James's concern with the way that difficulties in knowing and caring for others go hand in hand.

In their innocent blindness to any such difficulties, Adam and Maggie Verver share a communion so intimate and so independent of others as to border on solipsism. A number of readers have found incestuously Oedipal implications in what the *Notebooks* describe as the "intense and exceptional degree of attachment between the father and the daughter—he peculiarly paternal, she passionately filial."[26] If figuratively incestuous, their relationship shows why Freud describes the Oedipal situation as narcissistic and thus antisocial as well as why he finds its dissolution an important step toward integrating the child into the wider world beyond the family. Incestuous wishes are solipsistic so that overcoming them is necessary to prepare the child for a broader range of relations with others. "I don't think we lead, as regards other people, any life at all" (1:175), Maggie tells her father, although she does not understand the full significance of her statement because she is referring largely to their neglect of high society. But even Maggie's marriage to Amerigo does more to unite than to separate the father and the daughter—in part because her husband finds an answer to his questions about reciprocity by showing the consideration not to disturb their intimacy and in part, perhaps, because that marriage had been a joint project for the Ververs in which their subjectivities were mediated by the object (the Prince) of their mutual regard. In any case, their solipsistic communion is more fragile than they realize; it represents a self-deceptive blindness to the inescapable problems others pose for the Self.

Adam and Maggie begin to understand the fragility of their communion on that ominous Sunday morning at Fawns where the imperturbable Mrs. Rance boldly intrudes on Adam's solitude in the billiard-room. The matrimonially minded Mrs. Rance forces Adam to recognize the distinctly problematic character of the Other:

> For Maggie too at a stroke, almost beneficently, their visitor
> had, from being an inconvenience, become a sign. They had
> made vacant by their marriage his immediate foreground, his
> personal precinct—they being the Princess and the Prince.
> They had made room in it for others—so others had become
> aware. He became aware himself, for that matter, during the
> minute Maggie stood there before speaking; and with the sense
> moreover of what he saw her see he had the sense of what she
> saw *him*. (1:154)

Suddenly they "become aware" of their being-for-others by recognizing that their care for each other must face the prospect of conflict with others. More than a threat to Adam alone, Mrs. Rance represents a danger to the communal independence of the father and the daughter. Consequently, they react together with one of those communities of vision that mark them as a single Self separate from all others.

"There'll be others," Maggie realizes, because of her father's "unfortunate lack of a wife to whom applications could be referred" (1:168, 151)—a wife who would thus help preserve their private harmony from strife with others by excluding outsiders. As Maggie explains to her father:

> "It was as if you could n't be in the market when you were
> married to *me*. Or rather as if I kept people off, innocently, by
> being married to you. Now that I'm married to some one else
> you're, as in consequence, married to nobody. Therefore you
> may be married to anybody, to everybody. People don't see why
> you should n't be married to *them*." . . .

"So that you think," her father presently said, "that I had
better get married just in order to be as I was before?"
(1:172–73)

For Maggie and her father, her marriage to the Prince had changed
little or nothing in their relation to each other except, perhaps, to
make it even closer. Yet, to their surprise, others do not understand
their situation as they themselves see it, but instead regard it as less
intimate and thus more open to intrusion than before. Maggie wants
her father to marry in order to resolve some of the disharmony between their sense of themselves and their situation as others see it by
restoring some of their justification for remaining undisturbed in
peaceful, mutually caring isolation. With Mrs. Rance, for the first
time, others have become problematic for Maggie and her father because the two of them are compelled to recognize and struggle with
the difference between their being-for-themselves and their being-for-
others. The marriage that Maggie suggests would remedy the difficulties caused by this difference by bringing their being-for-others
more into line with their being-for-themselves.

Adam thinks through these difficulties with a line of argument not
quite the same as his daughter's, but similar at its foundations. Ini-
tially, Adam fears that to marry would mean to "reduce to definite
form the idea that he had lost her . . . by her own marriage" (1:206).
But he finally decides to marry as a way of "putting his child at peace"
by "so managing that Maggie would less and less appear to herself to
have forsaken him" (1:207–8). Concerned with consoling Maggie, he
will marry to show his care for her. His decision shares Maggie's fundamental concern with restoring the harmony between them that Mrs.
Rance's intrusion had threatened with presumptions that contested its
claims.

Both Maggie and Adam justify his marriage to Charlotte with logic
that is basically solipsistic insofar as it refers inward toward themselves more than outward toward others. Their reasoning aims more at
preserving their own communion than at building new connections
with different selves. It is not surprising, then, that Adam and Maggie
subsequently find themselves bound more closely together than ever
before. His marriage makes their solipsistic fortress against others
like Mrs. Rance more secure, and it is a simple extension of her protective role for Charlotte to join with the Prince to become the Ververs'

emissaries to the social world. Placed "definitely and by general ac-
clamation in charge of the 'social relations' of the family, literally of
those of the two households" (1:316), Charlotte takes care of others by
keeping them away from and thus unproblematic for the solipsistic
father and daughter. Where Mrs. Rance had created a crisis by rais-
ing disturbing questions about their being-for-others, Charlotte and
the Prince make these difficulties irrelevant by taking over the role of
being-for-others for Adam and Maggie. Ironically, though, as we shall
see, this self-deceptive scheme for making others unproblematic is
what eventually leads Maggie to realize how problematic others are.

Those who are self-deceived make themselves all the more vulnerable to deception. The most dangerous delusion in this respect is that
personal relations need involve no great epistemological dilemma; as
I have argued, lying itself is possible only because such a dilemma
exists. The adultery in *The Golden Bowl* is, in a certain sense, a
drama about the epistemological questions involved in deception and
self-deception. Accordingly, these issues take center stage in the pre-
paratory scenes in which Adam proposes to Charlotte and she accepts. Adam Verver might seem an unlikely victim of duplicity because "he cared that a work of art of price should 'look like' the
master to whom it might perhaps be deceitfully attributed; but he had
ceased on the whole to know any matter of the rest of life by its looks"
(1:146–47). Still, his solipsistic absorption with his plan for consoling Maggie blinds him more than he knows to the hidden sides behind
appearances. Enormous tension and suspense fill the scenes between
Adam and Charlotte at Brighton and then in Paris because of the difference between his reading of her feelings and of their situation (her
Self-for-Him) and her understanding of the problems posed by his
proposal (her Self-for-Herself). Adam envisions their marriage as a
generous act of kindness toward a childhood friend of Maggie's and as
a felicitous way of making his daughter "positively happy about me"
(he frankly confesses to Charlotte) by "effectually put[ting] out of her
mind that I feel she has abandoned me" (1:223). He fails to infer from
Charlotte's hesitancy and evident anxiety that she sees potential conflict where he sees only possibilities for care. But for Charlotte, of
course, the prospect of marrying him must raise the ghost of her past
relationship with the Prince—a secret that can only remain opaque to
Adam unless she renders it transparent. Adam does find Charlotte to
be behaving "a trifle inscrutably," and she even warns him that he

does not know her and that "when it's a question of learning" what one does not know "one learns sometimes too late" (1:231, 221). Nevertheless, blithely turning aside the hermeneutic challenge raised by the Other's inherent obscurities, Adam persistently misreads the depths beyond Charlotte's surface by assuming that her hesitancy and anxiety have an innocuous hidden side.

As the scene centering on the Prince's telegram shows, Adam is deceived by Charlotte only because he is so willing to delude himself by assuming naively that others are unproblematic and, consequently, that their mysteries need not disturb him. Both honorable and insidious motives seem to underlie Charlotte's offer to show him her former lover's telegram—an offer that, she realizes, "would in all probability at once have dished her marriage" (1:291) had Adam accepted it. Her offer is an act of conscience that would give him the chance to make her opacity transparent by uncovering her secret. With this honorable gesture, she reflects later, "her position in the matter of responsibility was . . . inattackably straight" (1:291). Hardly beyond reproach, however, she would surely have acted more "responsibly" by giving Adam a full confession and not just the possibility of one. But such a transparent course would have interfered with her more obscure and insidious motives—not just her desire to secure financial means and regain access to the Prince but even more, perhaps, her wish to test Adam to discover how much she can depend on him to turn a blind eye to secrets. His refusal to examine the telegram represents an honorable trust in and a deplorable shyness about the hidden sides of others. When he declines to look at the telegram because it's not "funny" but "grave . . . very grave" (1:240–41), he joins Maggie in declaring that matters of "loyalty" and "veracity" are best not "gone into." His refusal sets the stage for the adultery by giving positive proof of Adam's and Maggie's reluctance to wonder about the opacity of others and thus by establishing their vulnerability to lying.

Charlotte and Amerigo need to practice extraordinarily little overt duplicity to protect from their spouses the secret of their adulterous relationship. The Prince marvels at how "the magic web had spun itself without their toil, almost without their touch" (1:298). Since Maggie and Adam seem so willing to disregard the dilemmas created by the Other's mysterious depths, it is almost as if the truth itself is sufficient for lying to the blind. Charlotte and Amerigo need only let their spouses remain blissfully ignorant about the many-sidedness of "truth" given the complication that the same state of affairs may have different meanings for different subjects. And this is precisely the strategy they decide on during the scene that leads up to their first adulterous kiss. The Prince asks Charlotte:

> "What, at any rate, when you get home . . . shall you say that you've been doing?"
> "I shall say, beautifully, that I've been here."
> "All day?"
> "Yes—all day. Keeping you company in your solitude. How can we understand anything," she went on, "without really seeing that this is what they must like to think I do for you?— just as, quite as comfortably, you do it for me." (1:306–7)

Charlotte trusts Maggie and Adam not to suspect that what they "like to think" about a situation might differ from what others think about it—that such "keeping each other company" might have an adulterous rather than innocuous meaning. Inclined to behave honorably toward his benefactors, the Prince might not have consented to conspire with Charlotte to deceive them if their epistemological naiveté had not enabled him to act so openhandedly and thus to "keep moving, and be able to show . . . that he moved, on the firm ground of the truth" (1:269). More aggressive and self-seeking than her lover, Charlotte feels a positive "eagerness, really, to *be* suspected, sounded, veritably arraigned" (1:249) by Fanny at the embassy ball in order to triumph by refuting all accusations. But she cannot expect a similar opportunity with her stepdaughter until Maggie's awakening makes her understand as Fanny does that the opacity of others can disguise accusable secrets.

The Prince summarizes the epistemological naiveté that allows the adultery to go undetected when he observes of the Ververs "that knowledge was n't one of their needs and that they were in fact constitutionally inaccessible to it"—that Maggie "in particular" is too "placid" because "her imagination was clearly never ruffled by the sense of any anomaly" (1:333–34). Indifference to anomaly is particularly ominous because, as we saw with Isabel Archer, the incongruities on the visible sides of an object contain suggestions about its hidden sides that should make us suspect our assumptions about them.

Maggie offers herself as an easy victim of deception and thus of adultery because she does not understand that the opacity of others makes their anomalies especially worthy of attention.

Maggie and Adam trust their spouses—but with a confidence that overlooks how the unfathomable, unpredictable subjectivity of the Other makes trusting potentially dangerous. They do not think of Charlotte and the Prince as "Other," however, because they do not think of them as independent selves. Only an independent subjectivity can lie, keep secrets, or commit adultery. We have already seen how Maggie and Adam reify the Prince. Similarly, they regard Charlotte not as a "person" with a private world but as a "Personage"—a functionary whose being is described completely by her social role. She is one of those who "live in state and under constant consideration; they have n't latch-keys, but drums and trumpets announce them" (1:306). She is a public dignitary without any personal life. It may be that Charlotte and the Prince take over responsibility for the problem of the Other for Maggie and Adam by becoming their representatives to the outside world; but the innocent pair fail to recognize that they have not removed but only displaced the problem of the Other, since their spouses are still others to them too.

Considered existentially, the adultery's frame of reference expands from questions of blindness and insight to include issues of conflict and care and also of freedom and bondage. The adultery involves these matters because of all it has to do with the exercise of solicitude. According to Heidegger, solicitude for another's welfare may have a liberating effect by enhancing that person's possibilities, but it may also go wrong by dominating the other in a way that takes his freedom away from him. Solicitude under the sign of care advances another's freedom, then, where solicitude under the sign of conflict seeks to put him into bondage.[27] As we have seen, Maggie and Adam Verver believe that, through their bountiful generosity, they are exercising a liberating solicitude for their spouses' welfare when they are, actually if unwittingly, taking Charlotte's and Amerigo's freedom away from them by reifying them (her as a "Personage" and him as a "*morceau de musée*") and by denying them reciprocity because that very generosity is so overwhelming. As we shall see, though, the contradiction here between what the Ververs think and what they do leads the Prince and Charlotte to respond with a contradictory strategy of their own—acting to regain their liberty but justifying themselves on grounds that disguise their conflict with the Ververs in terms of care.

The Ververs leave Charlotte and the Prince perfectly free, but at the same time they leave them unfree by their expectations. The Prince resents "being thrust, systematically, with another woman, and a woman one happened, by the same token, exceedingly to like, and being so thrust that the theory of it seemed to publish one as idiotic or incapable" (1:335). That is, he resents "the grotesque theory" that fails to comprehend that one could hardly "do anything *but* blush to 'go about' at such a rate with such a person as Mrs. Verver in a state of childlike innocence, the state of our primitive parents before the Fall" (1:335). To seem "idiotic or incapable" is to seem less than the person one is—in this case less than the "galantuomo" the Prince understands himself to be. More than American Puritanical ethics at odds with European worldly wisdom, though, the Ververs' attitude follows from their failure to understand the Prince as a free subjectivity—an independent self who, in his hidden depths, might think about betraying their trust or who, even more fundamentally, might enjoy the power to think differently about something than they do. Further, in their blindness to others, they do not understand that Amerigo might have a different being-for-others than he has for themselves. It never occurs to them that the interpretation that others might give to his situation with Charlotte could differ from their own, thereby throwing the Prince into a crisis because of the conflict between what they and others demand of him. Their "grotesque theory" makes him "blush," and this sign of his shame shows that the Ververs endanger his identity by misunderstanding him.

By committing adultery, though, Amerigo reasserts his freedom while rescuing his identity. He acts when he had been assumed passive. He shows himself an uncontainable subjectivity by defying the Ververs' expectations. The tables turned, the Ververs are then trapped by the misconceptions that had imprisoned the Prince. After the adultery, they are more acted upon than acting, more known than knowing, more object than subject. All this is involved in the Prince's choice to act the "galantuomo" with Charlotte instead of playing an innocent before the Fall—a choice that rejects the awkward Self-for-Others that the Ververs would impose on him in favor of the more worldly-wise being-for-others that he feels more in line with his

being-for-himself. In Sartrean terms, then, Amerigo's adulterous relation with Charlotte enables him to reassert his subjectivity by transforming a situation in which he had been objectified; it redefines the
situation the Ververs had defined for him. The Prince thus transcends
the maddening misunderstanding of those who had bound him by the
way they regarded him.

Eschewing the language of conflict, however, the Prince and Charlotte begin their adultery by dedicating themselves to "a conscious
care" (1:312) for Maggie and Adam. Not simply a rationalization for
the Prince, this declaration contributes to his freedom by making reciprocal a situation that had seemed to him to preclude mutuality. By
regarding the adultery as an "intimacy of which the sovereign law
would be the vigilance of 'care'" (1:325), he joins with Charlotte to
make the millionaire and his daughter the objects of their solicitude
when heretofore he had seen himself only as the recipient of a one-
way generosity. As the Prince explains to Charlotte, "all we can desire
is to give them the life they prefer, to surround them with the peace
and quiet, and above all with the sense of security, most favourable to
it" (1:338). Nevertheless, the adulterers exercise a solicitude which,
like the Ververs' for them, dominates more than it liberates because it
preserves the debilitating, solipsistic ignorance of their spouses. Beyond their relation to their spouses, of course, Charlotte and Amerigo
claim to enjoy a mutually caring, liberating reciprocity with each
other that neither finds in marriage to the self-consumed Ververs.
What the Prince calls his and Charlotte's "exquisite sense of complicity" extends from the sessions of analysis and criticism that they
devote to their spouses to those "identities of impulse" that convince
him that "no union in the world had ever been more sweetened with
rightness" (1:335, 356). The Prince thinks that he and Charlotte
share understanding and care that are impossible for him and Maggie.

Actually, in one final complicating twist, Amerigo may not understand Charlotte as well as he believes, and she may dominate him
more than he knows in her solicitous concern for helping him find
freedom and care through adultery. Charlotte does not seem completely candid when, proposing that they resolve their mutual dilemma by rekindling their former relationship, she asks Amerigo:
"What else can we do, what in all the world else?" (1:303). "Have n't
we therefore to take things as we find them" (1:303), she adds—ignoring how she has helped shape those "things" by reappearing just be-

fore his marriage, winning Adam over with her charms, accepting his proposal under dubious circumstances, and orchestrating the two households' social affairs so efficiently as to shelter the Ververs in even greater privacy than they expected. She is certainly the victim of the Ververs' misunderstandings, but she finds these misconceptions more liberating and less frustrating than the Prince does because they provide a screen behind which she can operate, moving all the time "in the direction . . . of her greater freedom—which was all in the world she had in mind" (1:235). Throughout their adulterous affair, she seems the agent of their destiny and he the victim of his fate; she proposes and leads, he accepts and follows. At Matcham, for example, she plays the active and he the passive role—she making arrangements for the Gloucester outing and he only fantasizing about it but acquiescing gratefully. Their care for each other, then, may itself contain the seeds of conflict. In any case, with all its contradictory causes and consequences, motivations and justifications, the adultery demonstrates that personal relations involve both conflict and care and cannot be adequately described if either is neglected.

All of these complications flourish, then, because Maggie's and Adam's simplicity about others prevents them from suspecting the complexities of personal relations. "They feel a confidence," as the Prince observes; "they're extraordinarily happy" (1:305, 310). The Ververs enjoy untroubled bliss because everything seems to them felicitously, even perfectly, "arranged" to the advantage of everyone's well-being. The words "arrange," "arranged," and "arrangement" appear in the novel in a greater variety of contexts than I can conveniently illustrate by quotation.[28] The point, however, is that Maggie and Adam do not see the flaws in the foursome's "arrangement" because they fail to understand that nothing is ever "perfectly arranged" in personal relations. The relation between Self and Other is in constant disequilibrium—epistemologically out of balance because of the difference between my transparency and the Other's opacity, existentially in danger because of the upper hand conflict seems to enjoy over care.[29] Much of James's own fascination with personal relations has to do with the way they are forever arranging and rearranging themselves, defying the containment of any definitive equilibrium.

In the second volume of the novel, Maggie herself discovers how difficult it is to maintain even the appearance of such an equilibrium because of the forces that threaten to upset it. As the first part of her story closes, however, she does not understand how the spectacle of a perfectly arranged peace can hide a potentially volatile crisis—how conflict can lurk behind the facade of an apparently all-embracing care. As Maggie is about to learn, however, any attempt to make harmony prevail over strife must preface itself on an understanding that the dilemmas of Self and Other are not easily arranged away but, rather, must be confronted boldly in all the inherent difficulty that makes them seem to defy resolution.

THREE

Fanny identifies the dawn of Maggie's awakening as "her beginning to doubt. To doubt for the first time, . . . of her wonderful little judgement of her wonderful little world"—which means, according to this observer's sometimes skeptical but here sympathetic husband, "to doubt of fidelity—to doubt of friendship" (1:380). To them, Maggie seems about to embark on a voyage of discovery that will take her into matters concerning "veracity" and "loyalty" that, as we saw earlier, she had shunned with the Prince because of her innocent reluctance to "go into" the troubles bedeviling personal relations.

James describes this turning point in Maggie's history by invoking the well-known symbolic pagoda—an image containing references to some of the most significant dilemmas of Self and Other that have contributed to the crisis Maggie's awakening will uncover. Maggie compares the foursome's situation to

> some strange tall tower of ivory, or perhaps rather some wonderful beautiful but outlandish pagoda, a structure plated with hard bright porcelain, coloured and figured and adorned at the overhanging eaves with silver bells that tinkled ever so charmingly when stirred by chance airs. . . . The great decorated surface had remained consistently impenetrable and inscrutable. At present, however, to her considering mind, it was as if she had ceased merely to circle and to scan the elevation, ceased so vaguely, so quite helplessly to stare and wonder: she had caught herself distinctly in the act of pausing, then in that of lingering, and finally in that of stepping unprecedentedly near. . . . The pagoda in her blooming garden figured the ar-

rangement—how otherwise was it to be named?—by which, so
strikingly, she had been able to marry without breaking, as she
liked to put it, with her past. . . . That it was remarkable they
should have been able at once so to separate and so to keep
together had never for a moment, from however far back, been
equivocal to her. . . . So it was that their felicity had fructified;
so it was that the ivory tower, visible and admirable doubtless
from any point of the social field, had risen stage by stage.
Maggie's actual reluctance to ask herself with proportionate
sharpness why she had ceased to take comfort in the sight of it
represented accordingly a lapse from that ideal consistency on
which her moral comfort almost at any time depended. . . .
Moving for the first time in her life as in the darkening shadow
of a false position, she reflected that she should either not have
ceased to be right—that is to be confident—or have recognized
that she was wrong. (2:3–6)

By questioning the meaning and value of the "pagoda," if as yet un-
easily and vaguely, Maggie begins to doubt the apparent beauty of the
foursome's perfect "arrangement." She thus opens herself to the multitude of dilemmas about personal relations that that arrangement had
covered up with its brilliant surface and cheerful sounds. She may not
understand the conflicts that divide them behind their facade of unity,
and she does not suspect her and her father's guilt or her husband's
and Charlotte's affair. But she at least feels "equivocal" rather than
"confident" about the "felicity" of the care that they have all exer-
cised toward each other.

The pagoda's "great decorated surface," reassuring to the Ververs
in their solipsistic phase, now seems to hide some inaccessible mystery where Maggie had not suspected previously that the opacity of
others could cloak secrets. No longer indifferent to "anomaly," Maggie
now finds the very perfection of the pagoda less normal and natural
than strange and perhaps artificial. Her own change in attitude—
along with the danger of finding herself in a "false position" because
of her inconsistency—is to her a thought-provoking anomaly in itself.
When "the thick air" clears "that had begun more and more to hang,
for our young woman, over her accumulations of the unanswered"
(2:14), Maggie will discover "the horror of the thing hideously *behind*,
behind so much trusted, so much pretended, nobleness, cleverness,

tenderness" (2:237)—behind the wonderful and beautiful facade of the pagoda. The reflections that open the novel's second volume mark Maggie's first faltering steps toward this discovery that conflict can disguise itself as care because the opacity of others makes their hidden sides ultimately unfathomable.

The experiences that lead to Maggie's awakening differ somewhat from those through which we saw Isabel Archer come to self-consciousness. Like Maggie, Isabel begins to reflect on her situation after noticing something anomalous about an arrangement—in her case the peculiar way Osmond and Madame Merle have arranged themselves when she accidentally discovers them, him seated and her standing. Beyond this point of departure, however, Isabel accomplishes the most important part of her reflective work during a solitary night-long vigil of reveries and memories. Maggie's process of awakening does involve solitary reverie, but it depends more on another facet of reflexivity. She comes to a more satisfactory awareness of her situation by conversing with others and interpreting the text of what they say and do not say. Her awakening shows how reflection may involve relations between ourselves and others not only as its object of knowledge but also as its way of seeking to know that object. Maggie's awakening is an intersubjective and hermeneutic experience.

This facet of reflexivity shows itself most clearly and crucially, I think, in the pivotal scenes in which Maggie, talking to Fanny and the Prince after her conversation with the Bloomsbury shopkeeper, shows she has learned the secrets of the golden bowl. Although this highly significant object has received as much attention as almost any symbol in modern literature, most critics have asked primarily *what* the bowl signifies—what meanings and references it holds. We shall ask *how* it signifies, how Maggie interprets its significance, and how its signifying power and her interpretive experience contribute to her awakening.[30] We shall also ask what her awakening shows about the limits of reflection. To ask how the bowl signifies is to ask how Maggie, after her uneasiness about the pagoda, awakens to the problems involved in the relation between the Self and the Other.

"That cup there has turned witness" (2:163), Maggie tells Fanny while explaining that the golden bowl has revealed to her the secret of her husband's and Charlotte's past and present intimacy. Gazing at the bowl in astonishment at its revelatory power, Fanny finds it "inscrutable in its rather stupid elegance, and yet" expressive "as a 'document,' somehow" (2:165). Taking up Fanny's wonder, we should ask: How can an object like the golden bowl offer revelations—and particularly revelations about subjectivities? According to William James, "our minds meet in a world of objects which they share in common" and which thus offer themselves as intersubjective mediators between ourselves and others. Or, as Merleau-Ponty notes, "in the cultural object, I feel the close presence of others beneath a veil of anonymity. *Someone* uses the pipe for smoking, the spoon for eating, the bell for summoning."[31] Others are anonymously and thus inscrutably present through the bowl—but present with an opacity that can be rendered more transparent. To begin with, then, the bowl contributes to Maggie's growing insight into the problem of other minds because it testifies to that otherness at the same time that it offers access to it through interpretation. The bowl owes whatever aesthetic meaning and value it may enjoy to the past participation of other subjects in its creation and appreciation. More importantly to Maggie, it also holds meanings that adhere to it as the residue of Charlotte's and the Prince's involvement with it during their outing before his wedding. They have contributed to the bowl's history, just as those who handle an object or a tool may leave their mark on it, perhaps invisible but still signifying their one-time presence—or, in a related analogy, just as those who appreciate a work of art may contribute to its significance and its life by virtue of their engagement with it.[32] Charlotte and the Prince have left their mark on the bowl as much as those responsible for its flaw. But the adulterous pair's encounter with the bowl has changed the meaning of the crack. They have endowed it with a multiplicity of significance both for Maggie and for us that it would otherwise lack.

More than an ordinary object, the bowl acts as a symbol both for Maggie and for us because it resonates with a plurality of meanings. It functions symbolically within the context of the novel itself and not just in its reference to *Ecclesiastes* and other literary contexts where the image of the golden bowl has accumulated a cultural history laden with multiple meanings. As we learned in our discussion of James's aesthetics, Ricoeur describes a symbol as a two-tiered structure that calls for interpretation because its direct meaning both disguises and reveals an indirect meaning.[33] The bowl has this structure and functions in this manner inasmuch as its gilt surface demands deciphering to reveal its crystal interior and disguised flaw. Whatever further interpretation we or Maggie give to the bowl and its parts—reading its hidden crack, for example, as a comment on the flaw in the foursome's arrangement—is made possible by and will consequently recapitulate the structural division that constitutes the object as a symbol. In turn, the bowl's symbolic function duplicates the epistemological problem of others whose surfaces also require interpretation to disclose their depths. The bowl "turns witness" for Maggie by calling her attention to the disparity between the adulterers' outward demeanor and hidden inwardness thanks to the difference between its own exterior and interior.

As we also learned earlier, Ricoeur contends that interpreting symbols can be an act of reflection. By deciphering the meanings that others have deposited in symbols, he argues, man finds himself revealed to himself; the growth of "his understanding of the other" adds to "the growth of his own understanding of himself. . . . Every hermeneutics is thus, explicitly or implicitly, self-understanding by means of understanding others."[34] James makes this reflective aspect of interpretation quite explicit in Maggie's encounter with the bowl. That symbolic object has revelatory power because it offers Maggie an opportunity to increase her understanding of her own world by adding to her knowledge about the worlds of others. The bowl holds up a mirror that reflects her situation and calls for her to reflect about herself and her involvements. Maggie's hermeneutic trials also contribute to her self-awareness because she must often examine herself and her past in order to fill out sides hidden from her perspective. In unraveling the secrets of the bowl, for example, Maggie must ponder anew her jealousy of Charlotte, her love for the Prince, her worries about her marriage, her suspicions about anomalies in the foursome's arrangement, and much more. The opacity of others compels her to turn inward and probe her own consciousness to discover grounds for the hypotheses she must generate to make them more transparent.

The very disparity between herself and others is a further source of self-consciousness. Maggie's sense of her similarities with and differences from other selves in her world allows her to thematize her own identity more explicitly. After her awakening Maggie develops a firmer, more articulated sense of who she is and what she wants than she had before she became aware of her opposition to Charlotte or before she saw cause for concern about her allegiance to her father. Her heightened sense of antagonisms and communities reveals to her more clearly and precisely than ever before the oppositions and affinities that define the boundaries of her world and its relations to other worlds. In all of these ways, the duplication of consciousnesses that occurs when the Self meets the Other can lead to the internal reduplication of consciousness that is the essence of self-reflection. Maggie's encounter with the others absent from the bowl but present through its signifying power is a challenge to the development of her consciousness about her history and identity.

My explanation of the golden bowl's revelatory power should suggest that this object of Maggie's interpretive attention matters less than the hermeneutic activity it evokes. The gilt cup remains mute until Maggie, with the shopkeeper's help, makes it speak. The bowl does not liberate Maggie from delusion; rather, she liberates herself by deciphering its meaning and by unfolding the significance of that meaning for her situation with the Prince, Charlotte, and Adam. This is one of the things Fanny Assingham inadvertently demonstrates by breaking the bowl. Fanny explains that she destroyed the bowl in order to do away with her friend's interpretation of it. "Whatever you meant by it," she tells Maggie, "has ceased to exist" (2:179). Ironically, however, what Maggie "meant" not only survives the breakage but stands out all the more strikingly because it endures. Although the bowl's material value has changed, as Maggie explains to the Prince, "its other value is just the same—I mean that of its having given me so much of the truth about you" (2:189). Actually, Fanny's act of destruction is gratuitous because Maggie herself has already broken open the bowl by her interpretation. The broken bowl presents itself as the interpretation of the unbroken bowl, with its structure revealed and its secret unraveled. The difference between the bowl before and after is like the difference between a work of art and the reading we give it, aiming not to reproduce the work again but to make available the meanings and values it offers. In any case, Maggie achieves a greater effect on the Prince by exhibiting the bowl in pieces rather than whole. When she displays its fragments on the mantelpiece, she presents to him not the object itself but the object acted upon, interpreted, and understood—her reading that declares that "he should have no doubt of it whatever: she *knew*, and her broken bowl was proof that she knew" (2:183).

Still, it might seem that Maggie does not interpret the bowl so much as the mysterious shopkeeper deciphers it for her by remembering

Charlotte's and the Prince's visit to his store after identifying their photographs. But he only provides Maggie with a point of entry into the hermeneutic circle. He unwittingly reveals a hidden side of Charlotte's and Amerigo's relationship that surprises Maggie—and she makes "no secret of the shock, for herself, so suddenly and violently received" (2:225) through his disclosure. Then, in the manner of surprising hidden sides we have seen before, his revelation prompts her to revise her assumptions about a plethora of related matters. The shopkeeper represents more than a deus ex machina, then, inasmuch as the unexpected and radically unsettling character of his disclosure emphasizes the suddenness with which unforeseen aspects can emerge and the global ramifications that their discovery can have.

After her talk with the shopkeeper, Maggie's conversations with Fanny and Amerigo about the bowl's significance are not only the result of her hermeneutic adventure but also a continuation of it. Although Maggie presents her findings to them in a largely declarative manner that makes her interpretation seem like finished business, both conversations seem to take place in an interrogative mode that indicates that it is still a work in progress. Not only do Fanny and the Prince question and wonder what Maggie knows and how they should respond, but she herself seems to observe their reactions inquisitively to check the validity of her interpretation, to gauge its consequences, and to add to the understanding she has begun to achieve with the bowl.

As they begin their conversation, Maggie tells Fanny that everything is "explained: fully, intensely, admirably explained, with nothing really to add" (2:166). But later she informs the Prince that Fanny "has really been a help" by assisting her to "know more about what I had learned . . . than I could make out for myself. I made out as much as I could for myself—that I also wanted to have done; but it did n't in spite of everything take me very far" (2:190). Fanny does not tell Maggie much of anything new, though, except that "your husband has never, never, never . . . been half so interested in you as now" (2:178)—an ambiguous assertion whose meaning and validity remain to be explored during Maggie's subsequent talk with Amerigo. But Fanny is still a "help" to Maggie in at least two senses. First, the act of explaining her interpretation to Fanny seems also to clarify it for Maggie herself. It is as if Maggie does not know precisely and completely what she thinks until she objectifies and refines her thoughts by presenting them to another. Second, in line with Peirce's argument that the meaning and validity of any interpretation lie in its "practical bearings" and consequences,[35] her conversation with Fanny tests Maggie's reading of the bowl to determine its efficacy. Her reading proves its worth pragmatically by demonstrating its ability to break down the baffling opacity of others. Fanny can no longer take advantage of her opacity to Maggie as she once did by lying boldly to deny any intrigue between Charlotte and the Prince. Reserved and hesitant if no longer ready with refutations, Fanny remains opaque to her friend during their conversation about the bowl—but with the difference that Maggie has become able to read her interlocutor's uneasy surface as a confirmation that the full exposure of her depths would not contradict.

Similarly, with Amerigo, who is also reserved and cautious if undenying, Maggie's interpretation proves itself and expands the territory it commands by demonstrating its usefulness. It guides her in developing her conversational strategy toward him by helping her read the inner turbulence inadequately disguised by the calm facade he affects. Fanny's and Amerigo's reserve would seem to deprive Maggie of the validation that, as we have seen, intersubjective agreement can provide. But through her interpretation of the bowl, Maggie has developed her hermeneutic abilities to the point where she can achieve that validation anyway by penetrating their reserve and discovering the implicit agreement it veils. Maggie has come so far as a reader of depths from surfaces that she is even prepared to find meaning in the Prince's silence if he avoids her in order to avoid questions about the bowl: "[H]is keeping away from me because of that," she asks Fanny, "what will that *be* but to speak?" (2:167). Maggie's interpretation of the bowl's opacity has transformed her into an interpreter of the opacity of others.[36]

This transformation can take place only because the activity of interpreting texts, symbols, and cultural objects is intimately related to other modes of understanding in other realms of existence. Many students of hermeneutics have argued that "interpretation is more encompassing than the linguistic world in which man lives" and that, "indeed, existing itself may be said to be a constant process of interpretation." In particular, as Peirce points out, "perception is interpretative."[37] Maggie's history shows how much James would agree with these observations. Commenting on her interpretation of the

golden bowl, the Prince observes to Maggie: "You're apparently drawing immense conclusions from very small matters" (2:193). But this
description of Maggie's hermeneutic activity would also apply to Anne
Thackeray Ritchie's "impression" and to how her brief glimpse of a
pastor's household allows her to draw "immense conclusions" about
French Protestant youth. In much the same manner as Ritchie's impression, Maggie's interpretation of the bowl allows her to learn a lot
from a little by taking one "aspect" of a state of affairs (in Husserl's
terminology) and then spinning out a wide range of other aspects that
harmonize and agree with it—that is, by taking the shopkeeper's disclosure about her husband's outing with Charlotte and spinning out its
implications for their past and present intimacy.

"If there was so much between them before," Maggie tells Fanny,
"there can't—with all the other appearances—not be a great deal
more now" (2:167–68). As in Ritchie's case, Maggie's truth is a tissue
of hypotheses—a series of inferences that explicate the horizons of
the perspective given to her by her brief glimpse of Charlotte's and
Amerigo's intimacy during their outing before his wedding. Maggie's
double negative suggests how tenuous her construction is, but her
confidence in her suppositions grows as they complement and complete each other: "[T]here was support, and thereby an awful harmony, but which meant a further guidance, in the facts she could add
together" (2:164). As we first saw with Maisie, to know for James is to
believe, and the validity of a hypothesis is provisionally established
by its ability to fit parts together into a coherent whole. (Conversely,
as Maisie's "career of unsuccessful experiments" also suggested, a
part that refuses to fit is a falsifying anomaly.) Maggie's "facts" are not
independent givens. They take on meaning for her only as she manages to align them in a coherent interpretive scheme. Maggie's reasoning is circular; her belief about the whole (the adulterous relation)
is necessary to make sense of the parts (the Bloomsbury outing and
her other suspicions), but her assumption about the whole is an infer-
ence from those parts. The circle here is inescapable, however. It
is the hermeneutic circle that characterizes all understanding. Ritchie's impression is similarly a hypothesis about the entirety of French
Protestant youth that is based upon one element (her view from the
staircase), which it in turn makes sense of. The teleology of the
Jamesian impression is a manifestation of the inherent circularity of
understanding.

Maggie's interpretation has the same structure as the impression, then, but it is also prepared for and followed by impressions in the perceptual realm. Long before the bowl's revelations, Maggie ponders "two strangely unobliterated impressions" she received after deciding to act on her dissatisfaction with the foursome's arrangement by waiting alone (and not, as usual, with her father) for her husband's return home from his long weekend with Charlotte. These two "impressions" are:

> the physiognomic light that had played out in her husband at the shock—she had come at last to talk to herself of the "shock"—of his first vision of her on his return from Matcham and Gloucester, and the wonder of Charlotte's beautiful bold wavering glance when, the next morning in Eaton Square, this old friend had turned from the window and begun to deal with her. (2:103)

The Prince's surprise at finding her home alone, Charlotte's "prompt uncertainty" about the meaning of Maggie's act, combined with the "kinship of expression in [their] two faces"—these are small matters with large suggestive power for Maggie because they seem to indicate some "inscrutable comradeship" between the adulterers "against which the young woman's imagination broke in a small vain wave" (2:35, 49). Although as yet obscure in themselves, these impressions of Amerigo and Charlotte give Maggie an anticipatory understanding of their secret communion that prepares her for interpreting the bowl; they give her that foreknowledge that is essential for all interpretation because the hermeneutic circle only allows us to explicate what we already understand in advance.[38] These perceptions also show how the impression can act to bridge the epistemological gap between ourselves and others by allowing us to take hints from their being-for-us (Charlotte's and Amerigo's surprised expressions) in order to draw conclusions about their being-for-themselves (the pair's apparent liaison behind the scenes). Maggie learns from her awakening that "one must always . . . have some imagination of the states of others" (2:258). She also learns—and better than she knew before her hermeneutic encounter with the bowl—how to generate the impressions and make the interpretations necessary to discover those "states." Her perceptual activity benefits markedly from her sudden increase in hermeneutic mastery thanks to a kind of transference effect made possible by the relationship between interpretation and perception.

Maggie makes a great leap forward in her awakening, then, but she hardly attains a perfect understanding either of others or of herself. She has overcome her self-deceptive solipsistic attitude; she has come to realize that others are more problematic than she had imagined. But this very realization makes Maggie aware of how "there are many things . . . that we shall never know" (2:175). She understands, for one thing, that she can never make others completely transparent— that, in particular, what Charlotte thinks must always remain some- what a mystery but also that the Prince and even Adam can have more opacity about them than she suspected. But Maggie does not realize that she can never even make herself completely transparent to her own understanding. To recall a point first introduced in our analysis of Maisie's epistemological trials, Merleau-Ponty contends that a certain ambiguity or obscurity always haunts us because our reflections can never catch up with our unreflective experience. The unreflected al- ways enjoys a surplus over the reflected from the moment we attempt to appropriate our lived experience into understanding. And "since the lived is thus never entirely comprehensible, what I understand never quite tallies with my living experience," he argues; "in short, I am never quite at one with myself."[39] Maggie is never quite at one with herself in this manner. Even after her awakening, the gap be- tween the unreflected and the reflected leaves the "recesses of her imagination" dusky—although before "they had been duskier still"— and shrouded "by mysteries she was not to sound" (2:218–19), often because she refuses to examine them. Maggie does confess to herself that "knowledge, knowledge, was a fascination as well as a fear" (2:140). More than she realizes, however, she seems neither fasci- nated nor fearful but simply obtuse about certain areas of her experi- ence—such as, for example, her own and her father's role in creating their dilemma because of their manipulative disregard of Charlotte's and Amerigo's integrity.[40] Here and elsewhere Maggie still shows a tendency that her awakening should perhaps have eliminated—a ten- dency, namely, to prefer the security of blindness to the risks of in- sight. It sometimes seems as if, perhaps understandably, she requires the safety of ignorance about some matters in order to sustain her as she challenges other matters with reflection.

The unreflected can also be dangerous, though, because it threat- ens to control us if we fail to master it. Much of the drama in Maggie's attempt to resolve her dilemma with Charlotte, the Prince, and Adam derives from her struggle to narrow the gap between the reflected and the unreflected, just as many of the troublesome aspects of her behavior are ultimately due to her failure to close it adequately. Consider, for example, her "terror of the weakness . . . produced in her" by Amerigo's embraces and her resistance to his sexual power because she believes "that she had positively something to do, and that she must n't be weak for this, must much rather be strong" (2:29). Like Isabel Archer's fascination and fear in the face of Caspar Goodwood's lightning-like kiss, Maggie's ambivalent reaction to the call of desire betrays an anxiety that reveals that she has not adequately examined or understood her own sexuality. Her experience thus provides an image of how the unreflected threatens to overwhelm the reflected, how the lived threatens to drown the understood. For Freud, the power of the unconscious to tyrannize and terrorize results because its dark forces have not yet been brought into the light of meaning through reflection. If Maggie succumbed to the force of desire with her husband, she would risk losing self-conscious mastery of her situation. In this particular instance, then, the limits to her sexual self-understanding present Maggie with a restricted choice in deciding how to respond to the Prince: either total surrender or complete resistance. Overall, however, the limits to Maggie's understanding of herself and others impose constraints on the kind of resolution she can seek for the dilemma her awakening has uncovered—limits, that is, to how well she can restore care to a situation where she has discovered conflict.

FOUR

Unequivocally destroying her innocence about personal relations, Maggie's awakening reveals to her a complicated situation that displays the opposition between conflict and care in an awesome variety of forms. She seems called upon to respond to the contradictions she faces with an equally contradictory strategy—one that seeks to combine a struggle for power with the exercise of a genuine solicitude. As we shall see, she cares deeply for Adam and Amerigo, but the solicitude she exercises toward both of them includes an element of domination that indicates that she is also at odds with them. She regards Charlotte as her enemy, but she engages in battle with this foe in the hope of preserving the care that she and her father have for each other while establishing a loving relationship with her husband—not to mention the further complication that she seems sincerely concerned about the suffering her stepmother undergoes. Maggie wants to restore "the golden bowl—as it *was* to have been. . . . The bowl with all our happiness in it. The bowl without the crack" (2:216–17). But this desire for the felicitous reign of an all-encompassing harmony is accompanied in Maggie by an acute sense of the pervasiveness of strife in her world. For Maggie, then, to confront the dilemma that her awakening has exposed means to become profoundly involved in the contradictions bedeviling personal relations because of the contradiction between conflict and care.

Maggie understands the consequences of the liaison between Charlotte and Amerigo in terms that combine power and solicitude. She feels overwhelmed by the care with which the adulterers strive to maintain the foursome's arrangement:

> . . . she sat there in the solid chamber of her helplessness as in a bath of benevolence artfully prepared for her, over the brim of which she could but just manage to see by stretching her neck. Baths of benevolence were very well, but at least, unless one were a patient of some sort, a nervous eccentric or a lost child, one usually was n't so immersed save by one's request. It was n't in the least what *she* had requested. (2:44)

Not understanding how she and her father have contributed to their own fate, Maggie does not recognize how they are in fact at least partially responsible for the treatment they receive; according to the Ververs' plans, Charlotte and Amerigo were supposed to be bathed in benevolence without returning the favor by bathing their benefactors. But Maggie does begin to sense how solicitude can disguise the exercise of power. She suffers the same lack of reciprocity that disturbed the Prince and that imprisons her as it paralyzed him. As he did earlier, she feels here that the solicitude of others deprives her of her liberty. It is a sign of how personal relations have become problematic for Maggie that benevolence, once the simplest matter in the world, now seems a most difficult dilemma. By resisting the stifling consideration with which Charlotte and the Prince treat her, Maggie protests against the reifying effects of the Sartrean policy of transcending the Other's transcendence that lies behind the adultery. Their benevolence disturbs her because it is a disguise that cloaks the conflicts dividing the foursome in a deceptive language of care.

In this battle between the Self and the Other where the stakes are freedom or bondage, Maggie transcends the transcendence of her existential captors—objectifying the subjectivities that had objectified her—in the very act of discovering their secret liaison. As she explains later: "They thought of everything but that I might think" (2:332). Maggie offered herself as an easy target for objectification because she did not think much about others during her solipsistic innocence. But by thinking—by undertaking the interpretations and reflections that make up her awakening—Maggie reasserts the subjectivity and thus the freedom and power that the dominating solicitude of the adulterers had denied her. This step is just the beginning of Maggie's struggles, however, not only because the conflict that she discovers beneath an elaborate facade of care is not extinguished simply by her awareness of it but also because, as I have indicated, she wants to make love rather than power her guiding principle and her ultimate goal. The contradictory question she must answer is: How can she preserve and strengthen her freedom without sacrificing the ideal of care, inasmuch as the former seems to demand that she involve herself with power, strife, and manipulation while the latter calls for reciprocity, trust, and sympathetic understanding?

Maggie attempts to answer this question with a paradoxical, problematic strategy—an elaborate strategy of deception whereby she lies not only to triumph in combat but also, and at the same time, to exercise care. Let us look for the moment at the general outlines of her complicated, duplicitous policy. Then we shall examine in detail the role that lying plays in Maggie's relations first with Amerigo, then with Adam, and finally with Charlotte.

Maggie's basic tactic is to deny to Charlotte and Adam that she knows of anything amiss in the foursome's arrangement or that she herself has any covert designs. She enlists the Prince as a co-conspirator who lies with and for her by making similar denials. Maggie hopes this tactic will serve the causes of both conflict and care by defeating Charlotte's challenge in their battle for power and by reuniting her with the Prince, all the while sparing her father any hurt and salvaging as much of their cherished communion as possible. In "this extraordinary form of humbugging, as she had called it," everything depends

for Maggie on "her need not to be penetrable": "It was only a question
of not by a hair's breadth deflecting into the truth" (2:226, 250–51).
Maggie has transformed herself from the deceived into the deceiver
thanks to the power that her awakening has given her not only to penetrate the mysteries of others but also to manipulate her own opacity
in the eyes of others. Once innocent about the complications that
result from the gap between our being-for-others and our being-for-
ourselves, Maggie now relies on this gap for the success of her strategy; only because of it can she disguise her private inwardness behind
a misleading, impenetrable facade. Undaunted by "the difficulties of
duplicity" but without any illusions about them, Maggie shows an
"ability to preserve an appearance" and to avoid "exposing herself"
(2:207, 209) that provides an index of the growth in her mastery of the
problem of Self and Other since the time before her wedding when she
had refused to discuss the troublesome aspects of personal relations
with the Prince.

It is a further index of her newfound sophistication about relations
with others that she can pursue goals based on contradictory principles through one and the same strategy of deception. Under the sign of
conflict, as we shall see more fully when we study her two major confrontations with Charlotte, lying enables Maggie to transcend the transcendence of those around her while nullifying the possibility of re-
taliation. Offensively, lying gives Maggie control over the foursome's
situation because she is more knowing than known while they (including Adam and the Prince, but to a lesser extent than Charlotte) are
more known than knowing. Defensively, her deceptions protect her
against challenges that might jeopardize her plans by forcing her to
justify her motives and aspirations—thereby making her more known
than knowing. Under the sign of care, in addition to her solicitude for
Adam and her hopes for revitalizing her marriage, Maggie's lies serve
to maintain the "precious equilibrium" that keeps their collective
world from collapsing: "*That* was at the bottom of her mind, that their
equilibrium was everything, and that it was practically precarious, a
matter of a hair's breadth for the loss of the balance" (2:17). Maggie's
preoccupation with "the constant care that the equilibrium involved"
(2:21) differs from her earlier confidence in the foursome's felicitous
arrangement. No longer blind to the hazards of personal relations,
Maggie struggles valiantly to preserve a delicate harmony among the

foursome against the constant threat of an almost Hobbesian war of all against all that seems ready to break out at her least lapse.

The contradictory aspects of Maggie's strategy display themselves clearly in her relationship with the Prince. She exercises toward him a solicitude at once liberating and dominating as she seeks to build on the consequences of her awakening. Let us consider again her conversation with him about the golden bowl. This turning point in their relationship leads to a deeper communion between them as he changes sides and joins Maggie in her battle with Charlotte. To the extent that Maggie acts here with a liberating purpose toward her husband, she dramatizes what Binswanger claims when he observes that "the founding of a union" depends on the reciprocity between one partner's call and the other's response.[41] Maggie testifies to her love for Amerigo by announcing her desire for a revitalized union between them—a desire heightened rather than dimmed by the bowl's revelations—and by restraining the attack on him that her new knowledge would allow. His response bears out her belief that this testimony "had laid a basis not merely momentary on which he could meet her" (2:189). Seeking a reciprocal care with her husband, Maggie hopes "that by her helping him, helping him to help himself, as it were, she should help him to help *her*" (2:187). Responding to her solicitude for him by acting solicitously toward her, the Prince answers her call by testifying himself in the attitude he takes toward Charlotte after this conversation.

Maggie and the Prince do not speak openly to each other with the mutual transparency of true dialogue, but their reserve helps more than hurts their efforts to found a new union. In the absence of trust, it enables them to work gradually toward reciprocity; even more, though, by respecting her husband's reserve, Maggie shows him that she cares about his integrity and thus his freedom to decide his own destiny. As she explains later to Fanny, "I made sure he understood— then I let him alone" (2:215). It is this liberating concern for allowing the Prince here and elsewhere to choose his response on his own, apparently without coercion, that leads Crews, among others, to argue that "significantly, the final step in his salvation depends only on himself; Maggie 'had thrown the dice, but his hand was over her cast.'"[42]

This metaphor is more misleading than Crews suggests, however, because the liberating appearance of Maggie's behavior disguises a dominating design. Calculating and controlling her every move and hardly leaving the throw of her dice to chance, Maggie presents the Prince with a severely limited choice that she has carefully orchestrated. She may feel compassion for him, but "she felt with her sharpest thrill how he was straitened and tied" (2:192). After all, if she had felt robbed of freedom and power because he and Charlotte had joined in adultery to transcend her transcendence, the tables are turned now and "her superior lucidity" (2:189) gives Maggie the advantage in their battle—an advantage she will not readily sacrifice. Her ascendancy is confirmed by the agitation that the Prince "could n't help betraying if only as a consequence of the effect of the word itself, her repeated distinct 'know, know,' on his nerves" (2:200)—the word by which she asserts the superior claims of her subjectivity because she is now more knowing than known. Acting as much in obedience as in reciprocity, then, the Prince acknowledges Maggie's ascendancy when he agrees "to abide without question by whatever she should be able to achieve or think fit to prescribe" (2:228). Although, as we have seen, all freedom must consent to the necessity of bondage, Maggie sets particularly narrow limits on Amerigo's possibilities because she needs to dominate and manipulate him to secure victory in her battle with Charlotte. Maggie's and Amerigo's marriage may receive new life thanks to the pact they agree on after her awakening. But their relationship is fraught with uneasiness until the novel ends because of the tension between care and domination, reciprocity and manipulation, that results from the contradictory impulses of Maggie's strategy.

Maggie's relationship with her father—an uncomplicated, unquestioned article of faith in simpler times—becomes, after her awakening, no more easy or straightforward than her relationship with the Prince. Most of the attention that Adam Verver has received from readers of the novel centers on the question: Does he know about Charlotte's and Amerigo's intimacy and about his daughter's travails despite her efforts to keep him in ignorance? Of greater significance, though, is the very fact that this is a question at all—that whether he knows has become an issue for Maggie. It shows how far she has passed beyond her original innocence about others that she can ask about her former partner in solipsism: "[W]ho but himself really knew what *he*, after all, had n't, or even had, gained?" (2:263). Early in her awakening, Maggie realizes that her father's perceptions and understandings, "which she had so long regarded as of the same quality with her own," can have an inscrutable quality "which, so distinctly now, she should have the complication of being obliged to deal with separately" (2:31). Adam has taken on the character of an opaque, problematic Other for Maggie, and the mutual transparency of their solipsistic communion has lapsed.

Her attitude toward him may still seem somewhat narcissistic. After all, she makes his welfare one of the foremost concerns of her strategy, and she struggles to preserve as much as she can of their former intimacy. But she demonstrates her concern for him and for their relationship by lying—an activity that depends on the gap between the Self and the Other that their earlier union had denied, a strategy that compels her to make herself an opaque Other to him by disguising her Self-for-Herself behind the facade of her Self-for-Him. Moreover, she lies to him not only to protect him from disillusionment about what they have wrought but also to preserve the precarious equilibrium that keeps the foursome in balance despite their hidden conflicts. If she fears that he might act vengefully or at least unpredictably if enlightened, then she shows further that she considers him a separate, volatile subjectivity whom she cannot perfectly trust or absolutely control.

Maggie does seek to control him, however. Her solicitude for Adam's well-being is both dominating and liberating in much the same contradictory manner we have seen before. She may lie to her father in order to keep from hurting him, but her strategy of deception bathes him in a benevolence that he never requests and that he therefore has as much right to resent as Maggie did to protest against the similarly oppressive attention of the adulterers. Maggie needs to dominate him to the extent that he is a pawn in her battle for power with Charlotte. She fears that her father's wife might "take him into her confidence" and "prepare for him a statement of her wrong, . . . lay before him the infamy of what she was apparently suspected of" (2:239), in order to triumph over Maggie by forcing her to deny everything in the interests of protecting Adam and the foursome's facade of harmony. (As we shall see, though, Maggie's eventual denials give victory to her and not to Charlotte.) To counter Charlotte's threat, Maggie needs to enlist Adam as a co-conspirator—but by manipulating him into position rather than by openly soliciting his assistance. An open request could jeopardize the fiction of felicity all around that keeps everyone from falling out of harmony. It might ask more of him than he is able to give because she can no longer depend on understanding completely what he knows and feels.

Now Adam does seem to know his daughter's secret, and she seems to know that he knows. No more than Maggie can we be sure, of course, about what her father understands. But a less suspicious, more complacent Adam Verver refuses to read Amerigo's telegram to Charlotte, I think, than the Adam Verver who holds "in one of his pocketed hands the end of a long silken halter looped around her beautiful neck" and who seems to Maggie to betray to her by "two or three mute facial intimations" (2:287) that he acts knowingly on her behalf. Maggie's manipulations succeed only because Adam tacitly consents to them and supports them by joining his daughter in maintaining the silence on which her deceptions and everyone's harmony depend. He transforms her one-sided benevolence into a reciprocal care when he responds by "practically *offering* himself, pressing himself upon her, as a sacrifice" (2:269). Contradictorily, perhaps, his "sacrifice" keeps up their mutual communion even as it separates them; it testifies to his care for her while agreeing to widen the distance between them—all in the act of helping her regain the Prince and vanquish Charlotte by leaving and taking his wife with him. But if Maggie and Adam do still understand each other intimately at the end, they do so less by the immediate mutual intuition that their earlier transparency to each other had allowed than by the more arduous, more uncertain process of interpreting each other's opacity. Still united after the conversation at Fawns where Adam decides at Maggie's subtle urging to depart for American City, "nothing truly *was* at present between them save that they were looking at each other in infinite trust" (2:285). But their "trust" here and later, even if it harks back nostalgically to their earlier solipsistic communion, has a radically different significance because it has weathered the possibility of mistrust and misunderstanding. Although they are hardly "lost to each other" (2:333) as Maggie protests just before her father's departure, whatever remains of their union has consented to the necessity of separation—to the inevitability of difference between their worlds where before identity had seemed secure.

Maggie's relation with Charlotte is at once simpler and more complicated than her relations with her father and her husband. It is simpler because it unfolds almost exclusively under the sign of conflict.

But it is also more complicated, not so much because of the lingering role of care in it as because of the elaborate counterpoint of strategies on both sides through which these antagonists fight their battle for freedom and power. Maggie regards her stepmother as a dangerous enemy because Charlotte challenges her stepdaughter's hegemony in several ways: as a rival for control over the Prince and even Adam, as a threat to the equilibrium that Maggie's manipulations seek to maintain, and as a free and powerful subjectivity in herself who, in the adultery, has proven her ability to bind Maggie by transcending her transcendence. Their two confrontations at Fawns—the first, which moves from the terrace to the drawing-room, and the second, which takes place in an arbor in the garden—show Maggie and Charlotte engaged in a struggle that embodies almost purely the Sartrean paradigm of conflict between the Self and the Other.

Their first confrontation begins with Maggie standing alone on the terrace, watching the others play bridge and enjoying the sense of power that, according to Sartre, comes from looking without the disturbance of being looked at. From her superior vantage point, Maggie feels herself "consciously, as might be said, holding them in her hand" (2:232)—ascendant over them because her gaze is commanding just as her strategy of deceptions has granted her control over their destinies. When Charlotte appears, however, her gaze challenges the rights of Maggie's, and "the intensity of their mutual look might have pierced the night" (2:241). This "mutual look" announces the battle that will follow, where victory will go to whoever can assert the ultimate superiority of her subjectivity by looking at the other with greater penetration than she allows herself to be looked at in return. The goal for each of them is to transcend the other's transcendence by controlling the final meaning of their encounter. Maggie seems to concede defeat before the battle even begins. Filled "with a definite prevision, throbbing like the tick of a watch, of a doom impossibly sharp and hard," she submissively "bowed her head" and "came on with her heart in her hands" (2:242). Together they look at the scene that Maggie had observed unchallenged just before, "but now it was she who was being shown it, and being shown it by Charlotte, and she saw quickly enough that as Charlotte showed it so she must at present submissively seem to take it" (2:244). Charlotte's epistemological and thus existential power extends so far that Maggie feels "as if the particular way she should look at" even her father "were prescribed to

her; quite even as if she had been defied to look at him in any other"
(2:244).

But Maggie's submissive attitude eventually becomes a major point
of strength in their struggle, and her capitulation when Charlotte demands unconditional exoneration from any charges gives her a victory
disguised as a defeat. As a refusal to render herself transparent to
Charlotte's understanding, Maggie's denial of any secret knowledge or
covert designs "positively helped her to build up her falsehood"
(2:249) and thereby to strengthen the opacity to which she owes her
strategic ascendancy. By lying, Maggie exercises a subjectivity superior to because it is more knowing, acting, and controlling than the
subjectivity of the woman she deceives; she reasserts the liberty and
power that her strategy of deceptions had granted her but that Charlotte's challenge had endangered. This is a case in which, in Hegelian
terms, the apparent slave is more free because she is more self-
conscious than the master inasmuch as Maggie's greater self-
consciousness about their confrontation's meaning ultimately controls
their encounter. Maggie's understanding here encompasses and thus
objectifies Charlotte's knowledge.

Consider, for example, "the prodigious kiss" that announces with
"a high publicity" to the others who watch from the doorway that Maggie and Charlotte are reconciled (2:251–52). To Charlotte's understanding, the kiss seals her victory over Maggie and proves to everyone that her honor remains triumphantly unimpugned. But on a
higher, more encompassing level of interpretation, Maggie's understanding of the kiss not only takes in Charlotte's reading but also recognizes that "the message of the little scene had been different for
each" (2:277) of the observers as well. Furthermore, with a superiority of vantage point if anything more secure than before their encounter, Maggie's understanding of everyone's reaction, including
Charlotte's false self-confidence, contributes to her sense of how her
denial had helped keep up the foursome's precarious equilibrium—
how "it re-enforced—re-enforced even immensely—the general
effort, carried on from week to week and of late distinctly more successful, to look and talk and move as if nothing in life were the matter" (2:277). Although this first confrontation moves from Maggie
watching the others to her being observed by them, she is still stu-
diously viewing them at the end—and with greater freedom, power,
and penetration than they watch her.

Maggie asserts her ascendancy here and elsewhere by acting. Variously called an "overworked little trapezist girl" or "a tired actress" worn out with the strain "of quite remarkably, of quite heroically improvising" (2:302, 231, 33), Maggie depends for the success of her strategies on the relationship between play and freedom. As Sartre suggests in his well-known example of the waiter who cannot *be* a waiter but only *acts* his part, we are always performing roles; we cannot be those roles because "we can be nothing without playing at being."[43] A role is something object-like and in-itself, he argues, whereas we are riven with the nothingness of the for-itself because we are condemned to freedom. When we undertake deliberately and self-consciously to act or to play, however, we assert our liberty by widening the gap between the for-itself of existence and the in-itself of being. Playing emphasizes that we are not what we are inasmuch as our freedom defines us as nothing rather than something. Maggie asserts her freedom, then, when she pretends to be what she is not and not to be what she is.

Maggie "acts" in this manner even more demonstratively in her second confrontation with Charlotte than in the encounter that ends with their dramatic kiss. The scene begins with Maggie, her superior vantage point guaranteed by their last confrontation, standing at her bedroom window and watching the garden from a "seemingly perched position—as if her outlook, from above the high terraces, was that of some castle-tower mounted on a rock" (2:306). Her epistemological ascendancy is never threatened by Charlotte in their second encounter as it was in their first. Noticing Charlotte and pursuing her into the garden just as her enemy had formerly pursued her on the terrace, Maggie proceeds to put on an elaborate act of submission that is voluntary from the beginning and calculated to guarantee her liberty by sealing Charlotte's bondage. Inspired by a "consciousness of turning the tables on her friend," Maggie actively seeks a confrontation that she envisions as "a repetition . . . of the evening on the terrace" (2:308–9). This self-conscious quest to repeat the past in the present is itself a sign of Maggie's freedom because repeating an event means to "play" it at a distance that enables greater mastery.

Apparently generous almost to a fault, Maggie wants "above all to make it as easy for [Charlotte] as the case permitted"—to allow her enemy the freedom to make the outcome of their encounter "whatever she would, whatever she could" (2:309). But this benevolent attitude of the victor toward the vanquished is actually an insidious solicitude that dominates in the guise of liberating. Maggie feels that "the great thing was to allow her, was fairly to produce in her, the sense of highly choosing" (2:310) her destiny—namely the exile to American City that Adam and his daughter agreed upon earlier. Maggie allows Charlotte nothing more than the false sense of choosing a fate already decided for her. Maggie is still lying and acting, then, when she pretends solicitude for Charlotte's power of self-determination by feigning "supreme abjection" at her enemy's hands, by acting as if "she had presented herself once more to (as they said) grovel" (2:313). Secure in "the felicity of her deceit" (2:316), Maggie once again enjoys the defining, controlling upper hand in their encounter because her understanding outstrips and encompasses Charlotte's sense of what their confrontation means. If their first encounter showed Maggie on the defensive to protect her opacity against the threat of her antagonist's penetrating gaze, then she takes the offensive in their second confrontation by using that opacity to put on a performance that demonstrates her freedom and power conclusively; and she does so by "playing" in a Sartrean manner—that is, by creating a situation that does not mean what it seems to mean because she is not what she seems to be.

Some critics, though, find in this second confrontation a disturbing "suggestion of obscure and perverse self-gratification" on Maggie's part that betrays a combination of "masochistic self-manipulation and disguised sadism."[44] Now Maggie's strategy is cruel, and her encounter with Charlotte does gratify her because it confirms and strengthens her ascendancy over her foe. Furthermore, the limits to her self-understanding that we examined earlier blind Maggie to the extent—and it is still only a certain extent—to which she should feel genuine contrition toward Charlotte because of her own and her father's part in contributing to their dilemma all around. Nevertheless, neither neurotically driven nor perversely gratuitous in the manner of sadomasochism, her performance is both self-consciously controlled and intensely purposive in the manner of a Sartrean strategy for vanquishing the enemy in a conflict for freedom and power.

Actually, Charlotte functions not only as Maggie's enemy but also as her ally. Charlotte's efforts at self-deception are a great help to Maggie's strategy of deception. If Charlotte finds herself trapped on all sides after Maggie's awakening, then "the cage was the deluded condition" (2:229), and she traps herself with her own misapprehensions as much as her stepdaughter binds her with deceptions. Dupee may overstate the case when he calls Charlotte "an unconscious opportunist" whose "prodigious egotistical unawareness" brings her own downfall.[45] But when Charlotte eagerly takes up Maggie's gambit in the garden at Fawns in order to save face, she demonstrates what a radical turnabout has taken place since the days when she could count on the Ververs' penchant for self-deception to help her deceive them about her adultery with the Prince.

Charlotte does seem to know that she is vanquished rather than victor—at least Maggie insists, "She knows, she knows!" (2:348). But her knowledge only makes her effort to seem unknowing seem more pathetic and debilitating. Maggie feels compassion for her rival because "Charlotte was hiding neither pride nor joy—she was hiding humiliation" (2:329)—and hiding it not only from others but, desperately, from herself. Charlotte seeks to cover up her "humiliation" and to deny any diminution of her liberty or power by going boldly "on the swagger" (2:292), by engaging herself almost frenetically with the duties of gallery keeper and tour guide at Fawns and then with the chores of readying her husband's collection of precious pieces for transport to American City. Attempting to dull her senses by keeping busy, she displays dramatically what Heidegger means when he argues that losing oneself in what is near at hand provides an alienating way of fleeing and covering up anguishing dilemmas.[46] At most we might argue that Charlotte's struggle to save face represents an attempt to maintain her dignity even if Maggie has taken away her freedom. Then, with Sartre, we might argue that such dignity can represent a passive rebellion by the oppressed who "oppose their oppressors without having the means of imposing a change in their status."[47] But even this silent assertion of dignity advances rather than undermines Maggie's cause, inasmuch as it fortifies rather than challenges the "marked reserves of reference" (2:297) on which the foursome's equilibrium depends. Such dignity is not far from self-deception. In either case, through delusion or dignity, the false front with which Charlotte seeks to disguise her suffering contributes to the atmosphere of opacity that is necessary for the success of Maggie's designs.

Although conflict reigns supreme in her relation with Charlotte, as we have just seen at length, their struggle still contributes most to Maggie's designs by the service it renders to care. Maggie's victory in their battle provides a foundation for care in her marriage with Amerigo and her communion with Adam because, in her defeat, Charlotte acts as a "scapegoat" whose exclusion unites the others. Now Krook calls Maggie and not Charlotte the "scapegoat" in the novel.[48] And even Maggie identifies herself with this role, inasmuch as she feels called upon by the others to accept responsibility for

> the whole complexity of their peril, and she promptly saw why: because she was there, and there just *as* she was, to lift it off them and take it; to charge herself with it as the scapegoat of old, of whom she had once seen a terrible picture, had been charged with the sins of the people and had gone forth into the desert to sink under his burden and die. (2:234)

But the role Maggie describes here is the role she forces Charlotte to carry out. A dignified and impenitent scapegoat, Charlotte will probably not "sink under her burden and die" in the cultural "desert" of American City. But her suffering does seem to free the others from the burden of many of the complexities in their relationships that threatened to divide them. As Maggie herself admits, "It's as if her unhappiness had been necessary to us—as if we had needed her, at her own cost, to build us up and start us" (2:346).

Charlotte acts as the foursome's scapegoat in much the same way that, according to Sartre and Michel Foucault, the criminal and the insane can act for society as a whole. In his study of how madness became an institution during the Enlightenment, Foucault argues that the "sane" and the "reasonable" define themselves by excluding the "mad." As an outsider, the "madman" establishes the identity and guarantees the unity of the insiders.[49] Or, as Sartre contends, bourgeois society solidifies itself and secures its virtue by identifying certain others as criminals and by projecting evil onto them.[50] Charlotte is sent into exile—at first figuratively, by her exclusion from the conspiracy that joins the other three, and then literally, with Adam as her keeper—in a similar manner and to the same ends as the madman is sent to the asylum or the criminal to prison. Although not labeled "mad," Charlotte is made an outsider as Foucault describes and thus unifies the others because she is excluded. Charlotte may not be legally a "criminal," but Maggie, in the manner Sartre outlines, simplifies the complex problem of evil and continues to blind herself to her own culpability by projecting guilt almost exclusively onto her banished foe. As René Girard explains, "the sacrifice" of a scapegoat like Charlotte serves "to restore harmony to the community, to reinforce the social fabric"; the scapegoat "protect[s] the entire community from its own violence" by allowing the group to channel off "all the dissensions, rivalries, jealousies, and quarrels" that might otherwise tear it apart.[51]

Her role as the group's scapegoat defines Charlotte as the "Other" with the largest of capital letters against whom the remaining three can define themselves as a more than less united "Self." By shunting most of her animosity onto a single scapegoat and by concentrating most of her drive for power on her antagonism with Charlotte, Maggie frees herself, Adam, and Amerigo to show more care toward one another than they might otherwise have found possible. Charlotte mediates the subjectivities of the other three as the object that cements their complicity. In her deceived and self-deceived state, her transcendence is unanimously transcended by the other three who, together, are more knowing than known. When Adam takes his wife into exile, he continues to act on Maggie's behalf and thus remains with her even as they separate just as a guard in a prison or an attendant in an asylum remains with society against the criminal and the insane whose status as scapegoats he safeguards.

Similarly, Maggie and Amerigo come together in care for each other by placing Charlotte apart as the object of their mutual, mediated regard. "They were together thus, he and she, close, close together," Maggie feels, "whereas Charlotte, though rising there radiantly before her, was really off in some darkness of space that would steep her in solitude and harass her with care" (2:250). The distance between Maggie and the Prince seems inversely related to the distance between themselves and Charlotte. By lying for Maggie and sharing the secret of her awakening, the Prince joins her in a collaboration of subjectivities who become relatively transparent to each other by making themselves mutually opaque to Charlotte and who are thus united in care by their dispute with another. Whatever reciprocity they enjoy with each other seems to depend on their lack of reciprocity with Charlotte. As Philip Weinstein observes, "it is a curious intimacy Maggie exults in, one which consists more in the exclusion of Charlotte than closeness with the Prince."[52] Scapegoating is indeed an uneasy, hardly felicitous compromise between conflict and care. It enables a certain intersubjectivity only by sentencing the scapegoat to

solipsism. As an attempt to build harmony on a foundation of antagonism, it announces that people can be with one another in reciprocity
only by joining in opposition to someone else. The inadequacies of
scapegoating as a resolution to the problem of Self and Other testify to
the difficulties of personal relations by showing them to be, if anything, as prevalent and disturbing as ever.

The contradiction between conflict and care remains unresolved,
then, as the novel closes. In fact, contesting each other's claims up to
the very end, both terms of this contradiction express themselves in
the final embrace on which the curtain falls. With "his hands holding
her shoulders, his whole act enclosing her," Amerigo tells Maggie: "I
see nothing but *you*" (2:369). This declaration may seem to express
the fullness of a caring devotion—to testify to a trusting openness toward Maggie that looks forward to a strengthening of their union. Still,
it also shows the Prince enthralled by his wife. As before, "she mystified him" (2:344), and she fascinates him because he does not understand her. Their relative transparency toward each other as co-
conspirators against Charlotte has been limited by Maggie's need to
remain somewhat opaque toward him, as we saw, to assure her control
over him for the sake of her overall strategy. She retains her ascendancy even at the end; as yet unready to seek greater transparency,
she continues to baffle and enthrall him.

On her side, Maggie feels "pity and dread" (2:369) at the Prince's
declaration. Her "pity" may indicate a solicitous compassion for her
helpless, mystified husband because of the ordeal of constraint and
obedience she has put him through. A little earlier, she had found that
"he struck her as caged" even if largely "by his own act and his own
choice" (2:338) because he, unlike Charlotte, at least consented to
her regime. Her sympathy for him then and now may look forward to
the possibility of liberating him with care instead of dominating him
in conflict. Her "dread," however, may betray a fear of his own power
to dominate her as well as "a terror of her endless power of surrender"
(2:352). But it may also reveal an understandable anguish about all of
the responsibility she has accepted for the foursome's destiny and
about all of the responsibility that lies ahead for her in her relationship with Amerigo. Just before their embrace, Maggie had reflected
that "their freedom to be together there always" was "her reason for
what she had done" (2:367). Her goal, then, may be to make a
Heideggerian care the ultimate principle of their relationship, so that

she and Amerigo can "be with" each other in a mutually liberating reciprocity, united in peace rather than divided in strife. At the end, though, the question remains whether a fulfilling care can grow up between Maggie and Amerigo on foundations prepared by manipulation, deception, and scapegoating or whether the legacy of conflict behind them will always contaminate their relationship.

In one of his prefaces, James declares that "the personal drama of the future" lies "in the dauntless fusions to come"—"intellectual, moral, emotional, sensual, social, political"—which will "abridge old rigours of separation." [53] He seems to agree with his brother William that "our world is incompletely unified teleologically and is still trying to get its unification better organized." [54] Both brothers hope for the victory of union over separation that will not come in personal relations until care has triumphed over conflict. The ending of *The Golden Bowl* is at most teleological in this manner, with the hope that Maggie and Amerigo may work toward a fulfilling communion but with the threat that opposition and antagonism may never be transcended. Maggie and Amerigo have overcome many of the obstacles that separated them in the days of Maggie's absolute innocence about the epistemological and existential dangers dividing the Self and the Other. As they embrace, however, the further development of their union looms as an unfinished task shrouded in the uncertainty that plagues personal relations because neither the hope of care nor the despair of conflict has yet to prevail.

FIVE

Having finished our reading of *The Golden Bowl*, we have almost completed the work we set out to do of surveying James's understanding of the various aspects of experience. As before, our study of this last area—of how personal relations involve opacity and transparency, conflict and care—has shown us the fundamental unity of all the intentional foundations on which James built his house of fiction. We have seen again the inherent relatedness that James's works attribute to all aspects of experience. Examining the meaning of personal relations for James has brought us to explore anew, in a different context, familiar questions about freedom, the imagination, and the impression.

As we saw in Maggie's struggle with Charlotte and in the policy behind the adultery, the Self and the Other engage in conflict to decide the fate of their freedom. Care, too, involves issues of freedom and bondage. Either liberation or domination can follow from a concern with another's welfare; we saw this again and again whenever the novel's characters exercise solicitude toward one another, from the Ververs' generosity toward the Prince to Maggie's double-edged care for her husband and her father in her strategies of deception. When the novel ends, the reciprocity that Amerigo and Maggie have yet to find is the grace of being with each other in freedom. Moving back from freedom to the next of James's foundations, Maggie's awakening from ignorance about personal relations requires the development of her imagination—of her ability first to project imaginatively the hidden, sometimes disguised states of others and then to construct with resourceful ingenuity duplicitous tactics based on her newfound insight. Similarly, moving from the imagination to epistemology, the hermeneutic activity that contributes to Maggie's awakening leads her to develop the perceptual ability to unmask the opacity of others by spinning out the hidden sides implied by her impressions. Once again, then, as I argued at the beginning and as we have seen throughout, Maggie's story shows that there is a fundamental unity of knowing and doing in James, based both on the unity of his intentional foundations and on the unity of the aspects of experience to which these foundations correspond.

We have not quite finished our work, however, because our study of personal relations in James has raised questions about his attitude toward society, politics, and history. For example, as Sartre and Foucault describe it, scapegoating is not just an interpersonal process but a social and political procedure whereby some groups appropriate power for themselves at the expense of others. Furthermore, the "fusion" that James envisions to "abridge old rigours of separation" is a prediction about the course of history that extends from the realm of personal relations to the wider spheres of society and politics. What place do society, politics, and history occupy in James's world, then, and how do they bear on his understanding of personal relations, freedom, the imagination, and the impression?

SOCIETY AND HISTORY:

THE POLITICS OF

EXPERIENCE AND

THE SPOILS OF POYNTON

ONE

Henry James claims in "The Art of Fiction" that the duties of the novelist and the historian are essentially the same.[1] But James himself has often been berated for neglecting social and political matters in his fictions. Apparently thinking of the international theme, Ford Madox Ford calls James "the historian of one, of two, and possibly of three or more, civilisations."[2] James defines his own artistic program in social and historical, if not political, terms when he declares: "I want to leave a multitude of pictures of my time."[3] But many of his critics reply that James "knew nothing at all about the life of his time."[4] Following the argument laid out by Van Wyck Brooks, they call James "a stranger in a strange land" whose self-imposed exile from America left him forever an alien in his adopted country—a "homeless man" locked almost solipsistically in the private world of his art but unfortunately out of touch with the wider world.[5] Brooks and others blame this isolation for the excesses and eccentricities of James's late style. They also fault it for James's narrow concentration on the drama of the private life—a concentration that "implies an antihistorical attitude," according to Philip Rahv, because it turns its back on the larger drama of social and political change.[6]

Still, James values private experience for political reasons that respond to social history as he understands it. Expressing sentiments that James often repeats, one of his characters explains that "it was the inner life, for people of his generation, victims of the modern madness, mere maniacal extension and motion, that was returning health."[7] But this justification nevertheless depicts private experience as a withdrawal from social storm and stress. It leaves open the question of whether a preoccupation with private experience—with the intimate realm of consciousness, for example, or with personal dramas of imagination, freedom, and care—compels James to neglect matters relevant to the politics of social reality and decisive for the course of history. History, society, and politics do not make up the strongest of James's intentional foundations. His stance toward them does deserve scrutiny, though, because we are all in history and because, even when we abstain from political activity, we help to define ourselves by the attitude we take toward our social situation.

Like James, phenomenology has also been accused of emphasizing the private and the personal at the expense of the social and the political. Herbert Marcuse and other Marxist critics of phenomenology complain that, in giving primacy to the experience of the thinking subject, Husserl overlooks man's fundamental social being. Husserl ignores history, Marcuse argues, because he grants the status of an eternal, universal absolute to the isolated self of bourgeois individualism.[8] Phenomenology replies that man is indeed a political animal, as Marx and Aristotle contend, and that Husserl's work helps to explain the lived experience of our social being as participants in history. According to Mikel Dufrenne, and as we saw in the last chapter's study of personal relations, the subject is never an isolated individual but is always "social, that is, living among other subjects and participating with them in a certain style of life."[9] Social reality as a whole lies on the horizon of my day-to-day experience with groups in which I am involved in particular, historically significant ways. We participate in history through the temporal horizon of our experiences with groups—the horizon that joins the past, present, and future of individuals to the past, present, and future of their social world. Politics similarly goes back to our lived experience with others. As Ricoeur explains, "politics is the sum total of activities which have for their object the exercise of power."[10] There is a continuity between the politics of power on the vast stage of social history and the struggles for ascendancy that, as we have seen, decide the fate of freedom and care in personal relations.

As Marx describes it, for example, the politics of the class struggle is an abstraction from the concrete experience of workers who find their labor-power alienated from them at the hands of capitalists. Sartre, Merleau-Ponty, Ricoeur, and others have in fact argued that Marx and phenomenology have much in common, including this insistence on grounding abstract concepts in concrete experience. The argument of some Marxists that economic conditions are all-determining might seem incompatible with phenomenology's emphasis on freedom. But Marx himself argued that "men make their history upon the basis of prior conditions."[11] In phenomenological terms, this means that economic circumstances contribute to the historical, social situation that people must accept as a ground for their freedom; but although these "prior conditions" set limits to our possibilities, our circumstances do not deprive us of the choice of how to respond to them, and we may decide to seek to transform them. Marx is not the rigid determinist he is sometimes made out to be. His work need not compete with phenomenology, then, but can instead help with its sociology.

It is not immediately obvious, though, how a reconciliation between Marx and phenomenology can help clarify the place of history, society, and politics in James's world. As many have noted, James is deeply conservative—even at times antidemocratic—in his explicit pronouncements about politics and society. In *The American Scene*, for example, James speaks his views clearly—criticizing the leveling effects of democracy as opposed to the value of aristocratic discriminations, bemoaning his country's lack of traditions to defend against "the dreadful chill of change," and declaring his preference for a community of "organic social relations" of a quasi-feudal kind sustained by "the squire and the parson" and unified by a national church.[12] What matters, though, is the relevance of James's political statements to his art. Here a curious contradiction seems to emerge. James's aristocratic feudalism and disdain for change seem to contradict the allegiance to transcendence that, as we have seen, informs his epistemology and his moral vision. James's wish to freeze the flow of history, for example, seems at odds with his delight in the process of "going-beyond"—the teleological process that lends power to the impression and that makes the imagination wonderful. His preference for aristocratic social differences seems incompatible with his joy in freedom's possibility and his awareness of the dangers in personal relations when distances between people allow opacity to prevail over mutual transparency.[13] This divergence between James the artist and

James the social commentator suggests that his statements of political conviction may diverge from the kind of social criticism implicit in his art. [14]

A major obstacle to understanding the implied social criticism in James's art has been the tendency to limit study of the politics of his fiction to works with overtly political subject matter. When critics like Lionel Trilling and Irving Howe ask about James's attitude toward social issues, for example, they turn immediately to *The Princess Casamassima* and *The Bostonians*, the two works in his canon with the most explicitly political themes. [15] Recent theorists of literary history like Goldmann, Jauss, and Weimann have suggested, however, that a literary work's themes are not the only or even the best indication of its social, historical significance. Even a more traditional sociologist of literature like Ian Watt does not limit himself to political or commercial subjects when he elucidates the importance of free-market individualism for the rise of the novel as a literary form. [16] We need not accept the thematic limits that Trilling and Howe impose on themselves. Instead, since phenomenology argues that social reality as a whole is an extrapolation from our day-to-day relations with others, we might ask whether the relations between characters in a novel can be seen to capture in paradigmatic form the social structures dominant at its time. The relations between a novel's characters need not be homologous with contemporary social structures, of course, but any parallels that do exist have political importance regardless of the work's thematic focus. An inquiry of this kind could allow itself to take up those many works in James's canon with themes that seem remote from historical issues.

The Spoils of Poynton is one such work. As we shall see, though, its characters' relations with one another, themselves, and the objects in their worlds offer a paradigm of social processes that extend beyond their personal horizons. Thematically, the political relevance of the novel seems limited to the laws of inheritance in Britain that dispossess the mother in favor of the son. In the original germ as in the plot James constructed from it, these laws prompt the mother to protest against the injustice she feels done to her. But if, following Ricoeur, we see the roots of politics in questions of power, then *The Spoils of Poynton* is an immensely political novel because, like so many of James's fictions, it is a work about struggles over control and ascendancy. At the center of these battles are the spoils, and we shall ask how these objects act as mediators in Mrs. Gereth's relations with others and with herself. Like Marx in his analysis of social structures at roughly the same period, James describes a situation in which the products of human activity—the things through which we express and objectify ourselves—control us more than we control them because they mediate in the service not of community but of power.[17] Our reading of *Poynton* will conclude our study of James by revisiting the areas of experience that have concerned us thus far—consciousness, the imagination, freedom, and care—only this time in the setting of the politics of experience.

In order to avoid confusion, let me emphasize that James is not Marx. That may seem obvious, but what is surprising, I think, is the extent to which a social theorist like Marx—a thinker so alien, it would seem, to James's sensibilities and convictions—can be brought to bear sympathetically rather than antagonistically in interpreting his work. Through his artistic exploration of personal experience in the world around him, James seems in fact to have grasped intuitively a state of affairs remarkably similar to problems Marx identified theoretically. Although more concerned with James's millionaires than with his understanding of social structures, Edmund Wilson argues that "it seems . . . foolish to reproach Henry James for having neglected the industrial background. Like sex, we never get very close to it, but its effects are a part of his picture."[18] Wilson contends, though, that James restricts his art unfortunately by not pursuing social and political issues more aggressively and more openly. It is also a limit to James's phenomenological significance that he explores such matters less forcefully than he does the other aspects of experience that we have considered. James is hesitant about larger social matters in his art—but not so hesitant that a work like *The Spoils of Poynton* fails to make a significant comment on the politics of experience.

T W O

According to James, the disputed objects are "the real centre" and "the citadel of the interest" in *The Spoils of Poynton*. In his preface to the novel, James even claims to have conceived Fleda Vetch only because "the spoils of Poynton were not directly articulate" and thus, unlike his heroine, could not function as the work's central consciousness although they deserve that role.[19] Apparently following James's hint here, Stephen Spender goes so far as to argue that "it is the *things* themselves, the Spoils, which are evil, which destroy the happiness of all the people who are interested in them. . . . At the end of the story, when the house with all its treasures is seen in flames, one becomes aware of what was always wrong; it was the Spoils themselves."[20]

Spender's argument is misleading, though, because inanimate objects are incapable of "evil." They become implicated in "evil" only through their involvements in the lives of people. Spender has fallen victim to the kind of mystification that Marx describes when he explains how, in commercial and industrial societies, objects can seem to take on a life of their own independent of the human beings who are the source of their meaning and value—an independence that obscures the social processes indirectly embodied in those objects.[21] James leaves the artistic value of the spoils unspecified, so that some critics argue whether they are ugly or beautiful.[22] But by leaving these objects vague, James emphasizes that they matter less for their intrinsic value than for the way they participate in the relations that his characters have with one another and themselves. Our attention is directed toward the manner in which objects like the spoils come to embody human investments of meaning and value.

We have already seen how a cultural object like the golden bowl can act as a mediator in personal relations because it can offer to us the veiled presence of others who have dealt with it in the past. James seems to invoke this mediating role when he praises "the value derived from the social, the civilizing function" of "interesting objects."[23] But *The Spoils of Poynton* shows how objects that could open other worlds to us and that might enhance our possibilities for meaning and value can close those worlds off and even estrange us from ourselves. This occurs when, rather than furthering care and freedom, they serve conflicts over power for the sake of individual ascendancy.

Marx's analyses of private property and capitalism also describe how objects that might serve freedom and community are involved instead in conflicts over dominance and personal advantage. According to Marx, man produces himself in action and, thanks to his powers of "self-objectification," expresses himself in the products of his activity. In capitalism, however, where laborers sell their productive power to an employer, workers still objectify themselves but no longer control the results of their work, their "self-objectifications." Consequently, Marx argues, "man's own deed becomes an alien power opposed to him, which enslaves him instead of being controlled by him."[24] In this process of alienation, man's freedom and power to objectify himself are placed in bondage to another; the worker's product mystifies him because it is not an expression of his freedom but evidence of another's dominance. It mystifies the capitalist too who values a commodity mainly for its power on the marketplace.

The products of human activity seem of primary importance to both worker and employer—to the worker because they enslave him and to the employer because they provide him with profits. Accordingly, the more important process of self-objectification underlying any commodity is obscured, Marx argues, and regarded at most as secondary rather than primary.[25] When Marx claims that "only in community . . . is personal freedom possible," he means in large part that our powers of self-objectification will belong to us individually only when their products mediate positively among us as a group.[26] But products must fail in this mediating role as long as they are valued primarily as tokens that enhance individual ascendancy instead of as ways through which we express ourselves to others. Although Marx's analyses of alienation and mystification are basically economic, they are just as fundamentally political because they center on questions of power— and particularly on the struggle for control over others' capacity for self-objectification.

The Spoils of Poynton is certainly not a novel about capitalists and workers. But the problems that Marx describes are not limited to factories or the marketplace. In Marx's view, his analyses laid bare basic structures of free-market, industrial society which could be found in various forms in all aspects of social life. James's novel may help us understand how social relations far removed from the factory may still suffer from the difficulties in self-objectification and mediation that Marx found pervasive in the world of industry and commerce.

Almost all of the characters in *The Spoils of Poynton* are known through the objects that express them. Although almost completely absent from the novel, for example, Fleda's father is still suggestively present through "the objects he was fond of saying he had collected— objects, shabby and battered, of a sort that appealed little to his daughter: old brandy-flasks and match-boxes, old calendars and hand-books, intermixed with an assortment of penwipers and ash-

trays, a harvest gathered in from penny bazaars."[27] Here and elsewhere, in a manner reminiscent of Anne Thackeray Ritchie spinning
out aspects implied by the perspective she has, a character's things
can provide a clue that opens the way to his whole being. They testify
to the activity through which he has embodied in objective form his
capacities, values, and aspirations. For Fleda and Mrs. Gereth, at
least, the "horrors" at Waterbath tell us as much about the Brigstocks
as direct encounters with them do. Mrs. Gereth has a "strange, almost
maniacal disposition to thrust in everywhere the question of 'things,'
to read all behaviour in the light of some fancied relation to them"
(p. 24). Mrs. Gereth takes to an extreme, almost caricatured form our
ability to understand others through the things that represent their
being.

She does so because the process of objectifying herself through her
possessions is all-important to her own sense of who she is. "Poynton
was the record of a life" (p. 22), a place "charged with memories"
where "everything was in the air—each history of each find, each cir-
cumstance of each capture"—all combining to throw "out a radiance
in which the poor woman saw in solution all her old loves and pa-
tiences, all her old tricks and triumphs" (p. 58). The intrinsic value
of the things, whether beautiful or ugly, matters less than the way they
embody Mrs. Gereth's very self as products of activity in the past that
express and preserve that activity for the present and the future.
"They're living things to me," Mrs. Gereth claims; "they know me,
they return the touch of my hand" (p. 31). Although inanimate, the
things "live" because they carry traces of her life. It is herself she
touches in touching them and herself who returns her touch. She re-
vives her past self with the touch of her present being, and her past
self responds by confirming and sustaining her sense of identity.
Fleda finds Mrs. Gereth's "passion" for the things at Poynton "absolutely unselfish—she cared nothing for mere possession" (p. 214).
"Mere possession" may not be at stake in the dispute over the spoils,
but Mrs. Gereth's self is because they are embodiments and expressions of her existence.

Mrs. Gereth takes her self-objectifications so seriously, however,
that they actually alienate her from herself. Although not always a reliable observer, Fleda senses correctly that "the piety most real to
[Mrs. Gereth] was to be on one's knees before one's high standard"
(p. 30)—in the older woman's case to worship at the altar of the de-

ified things. Mrs. Gereth's "high standard" is her own creation, though, just as her things are manifestations of her life. In her "piety," then, she worships herself. Mrs. Gereth makes a fetish of the things in much the same way that, according to Marx, workers and employers make a fetish out of commodities by regarding "the products of men's hands" as "independent beings endowed with life" and with meaning and value independent of man."[28] As a result, she is confused about and even enslaved by the spoils in a way that Marx's theories of mystification and alienation can help to explain. She is mystified by the spoils because, by deifying the products of her life's work, she undervalues the more decisive process of self-objectification to which they owe their meaning and value. When she fights to keep control over the things, she fears that she will be deprived not only of precious expressions of her being but, even more, of her powers of self-creation because the products of her work have taken alienating precedence in her mind over the process of making and manifesting her identity.

Fleda thinks that "in the event of a surrender the poor woman would never again be able to begin to collect: she was now too old and too moneyless, and times were altered and good things impossibly dear" (p. 147). Age and lack of means might prevent Mrs. Gereth from duplicating Poynton, and she does deserve sympathy for having her life's work taken away from her without adequate recompense. But Fleda's observation here makes the mistake of emphasizing the results of Mrs. Gereth's labor more than the processes of self-creation and self-expression that are embodied in the things. For example, Mrs. Gereth inadvertently shows that those powers still belong to her—and that age and lack of means matter less than she and Fleda think— when she unwittingly works wonders with "the wretched things" (p. 248) that the maiden aunt left at Ricks. Mrs. Gereth need not lose her freedom and power for the future, then, when she loses the objects that manifested them in the past. In moving the things to and from Ricks, in setting up house there, and in mapping her devious strategies, Mrs. Gereth puts on an impressive, even intimidating, display of her powers of self-objectification; with "a sort of arrogance of energy," she shows that "what she undertook was always somehow achieved" (p. 231). The threat to the spoils prompts a forceful response from Mrs. Gereth that indicates, perhaps ironically, how much they owe to her ability and strength of will even though she feels that she would be nothing without them. But since she has invested exclusive meaning and value in the products of her labor, it is not surprising that she feels totally deprived of possibilities for action and expression at the end when she is finally deprived of her things. Her worship of the spoils is a vain act of self-glorification. But it is also an alienating sacrifice of herself to their control. She feels all her freedom and power taken away from her at the end only because she vainly identified her very being with the things in a mystifying manner.

The dispute over the spoils is not the first time that they have acted as symbols of power. In fact, the dispute only brings into the open the disguised value of the things as tokens of individual ascendancy that they seem to have had for Mrs. Gereth all along despite her claim of caring selflessly for them with a noble devotion to the ideal they represent. For example, Mrs. Gereth complains that few others understand her devotion or share her deep appreciation of the things. But her superiority of knowledge, sensibility, and commitment represents power here because it gives proof of her special ascendancy over others. This may be one reason why such a cultivated mother has such an uncultivated son. In his obtuseness, Owen offers Mrs. Gereth more evidence of her privileged uniqueness than he might as a rival in appreciation.

Furthermore, Mrs. Gereth's collection at Poynton is itself an act of power over others' powers of self-objectification. Mrs. Gereth does not make the things herself but collects them, which is to control the self-expressions of others and to put them to the service of her own project of creating an identity. Collecting might not constitute an assertion of power if the collector sought to devote himself to bringing out the presence of others that lies dormant in his pieces as the source of their meaning and value. But Fleda complains that "somehow there were no ghosts at Poynton" (p. 250), by which she means that the things fail to resonate with the voices of others who had cared for them before Mrs. Gereth. The presence of others in the things has apparently been stifled by Mrs. Gereth's domineering will that allows only her being to emanate from them. "Poynton, moreover, had been an impossible place for producing," Fleda feels; "no art more active than a Buddhistic contemplation could lift its head there" (p. 148). As testimony to the exclusive powers of Mrs. Gereth, the things do not call forth the expressive capacities of others in response to them any more than they enable the voices of those behind them to speak.

Fleda wonders why Mrs. Gereth, with her noble aesthetic ideals, should welcome an open battle, complete with "the constables and the dragging," in order "to make Owen and Mona do everything that will be most publicly odious" (p. 48). But there is no essential contradiction between Mrs. Gereth's commitment to the things and her eagerness for the police because both signify a contest for power. Mrs. Gereth may be ready to understand the threat to the things as a threat to her freedom and agency because, even before open warfare over them begins, the spoils have been a means for appropriating and dominating others' powers of self-objectification.

All of this helps to explain why the things fail to mediate positively between people. If Poynton lacks "ghosts" and Fleda feels her creativity stifled there, then the things, in Mrs. Gereth's hands at least, do not open the worlds of different subjects to one another but leave them inaccessible and opaque. Another reason for Owen's blindness to cultural value may be that the value-generating acts embodied in his mother's things are not allowed to speak to other subjectivities because her will to power does not let her possessions function as intersubjective mediators. The things speak to Fleda, of course, but with a voice that testifies almost exclusively to Mrs. Gereth's powers of self-objectification. Mrs. Gereth collected the things with her husband, but even his presence seems oddly absent from them. They are not depicted in any important sense as a sentimental link between the departed husband and his survivors.

Mrs. Gereth and her son Owen do not have much in common, but they do share a lack of imagination about the worlds of other selves. "Poor Owen went through life with a frank dread of people's minds" (p. 42) because of the fearful complications with which they threaten to surprise him. Mrs. Gereth "had no imagination about anybody's life save on the side she bumped against" (p. 138). But her blindness to the hidden sides of others, to the unfathomable depths beyond their surfaces, goes hand in hand with the solipsistic vanity of her concern over her powers of self-creation. Unlike the more imaginative Fleda (perhaps extravagantly imaginative, in fact), Mrs. Gereth does not feel the "dim presence" of "the character of the maiden-aunt" during their first trip to Ricks (p. 54). And it seems that only a lapse of will on Mrs. Gereth's part after the defeat of her strategies allows the presence of the aunt to emerge in her arrangement there at the end. "We're in fact just three" (p. 249), Fleda exclaims because, for the first time,

Mrs. Gereth had allowed the "ghost" of another to make itself felt through her hands.

We saw with Maggie Verver how, by giving us mediated access to the worlds of others, an object like the golden bowl can help to overcome the opacity that hampers personal relations. But Mrs. Gereth's objects disguise rather than reveal the presence of others because, like Marx's similarly mystifying commodities, they act as mediators in conflicts over power. Such battles thrive on opacity, but care demands that we work toward transparency. The spoils bring the characters in James's novel into relation with one another—but as negative mediators that serve opacity rather than transparency, conflict rather than care.

The things mediate between Mrs. Gereth and Mona Brigstock, of course, in just such a negative manner. In the atmosphere of obscurity that surrounds their struggle, we (along with Mrs. Gereth and Fleda) are kept largely in the dark about what Mona really thinks about the spoils. Mona rarely appears in person and never speaks her mind, but Owen reports that "she thinks they're all right" (p. 29) and even that "she was awfully sweet on them" (p. 91). The intrinsic value of Mrs. Gereth's objects seems to matter little to Mona. Once again, though, what does count is that to possess them means to have power. "She never wanted them particularly till they seemed to be in danger," Owen explains; "now she has an idea about them, and when she gets hold of an idea—oh dear me!" (p. 161). Mona's "idea" seems to be like Mrs. Gereth's—that ownership of the things is crucial for her individual ascendancy. Mona does not seem to desire the spoils with any fervor until she learns that they are the object of another's fervent desire. The things seem to take on meaning and value for her because Mrs. Gereth identifies her own power with them so closely and, by refusing to give them up, challenges Mona's dominion. (Mona responds similarly later to Fleda's apparent challenge as a rival for possession of Owen. Mona seems willing to let him go until Fleda's threat to take him away makes Owen the stake in a battle to prove personal ascendancy.)

Now according to Marx, the intrinsic worth (or "use-value") of commodities matters less in free-market societies than their capacity to purchase other commodities (their "exchange-value"); considerations of inherent utility are driven out by considerations of power.[29] Mona shows that she is more concerned with the "exchange-value" than the "use-value" of the spoils when she travels with Owen after their marriage: "It was a piece of calculated insolence," in Mrs. Gereth's view, "a stroke odiously directed at showing whom it might concern that now she had Poynton fast she was perfectly indifferent to living there" (p. 258). By refusing to use Poynton, Mona displays her ascendancy over Mrs. Gereth more forcefully than she would if she seemed to show she cared for the things themselves. She also announces clearly that personal hegemony was her goal all along.

Both Mona and Mrs. Gereth are mystified by the spoils, though, because having them does not enhance Mona's powers of objectifying herself in future action any more than not having them should prevent Mrs. Gereth from creating and expressing herself after her defeat. Mona has only the objects that embody Mrs. Gereth's past activities but does not have control over her rival's capacity to objectify herself in the future. Mona's indifference to Poynton shows that her victory is a dead-end that does not point to productive possibilities beyond itself. In Marx's view, the employer's power over his workers is defined less by his ownership of their products than by his control of their power to produce. Mona has power over Mrs. Gereth's products, but not over her productivity. Their relation shows the futility of mystifying power by making it an end in itself.

Power is also at the heart of Fleda's and Mrs. Gereth's relationship. Apparently brought together by their appreciation of the beautiful and disgust at the tasteless, these two women might seem positively mediated by their mutual care for the things at Poynton. Fleda understands that Mrs. Gereth "had taken a tremendous fancy to her, but that was on account of the fancy—to Poynton of course—taken by Fleda herself" (p. 37). Mrs. Gereth "fancies" Fleda in large part out of vanity, inasmuch as her young friend glorifies her when she celebrates the things in which the older woman has manifested her being. Mrs. Gereth claims unselfishly to prefer Fleda over Mona as the future custodian of the spoils because "there's a care they want, there's a sympathy that draws out their beauty" that "a woman ignorant and vulgar" could not give (p. 31). But if Mrs. Gereth finds Mona objectionable as much for the strength of her will as for the vulgarity of her tastes, then Fleda is acceptable to her as much for her seeming weakness as for all her apparent refinement. Fleda obligingly imagines that "if *she* were mistress of Poynton, a whole province, as an abode, should be assigned there to the great queen-mother. She would have returned from her campaign with her baggage-train and her loot, and the palace would unbar its shutters and the morning flash back from its halls" (pp. 146–47). Fleda envisions not how she will care for the things with an appropriate sympathy but rather how she will take care not to usurp Mrs. Gereth's ascendancy at Poynton as Mona would. Unlike Owen's fiancée, Fleda does not threaten to take from Mrs. Gereth's control the things that are her self-objectifications and that represent to her her power to continue exercising her will.

In the meantime, Mrs. Gereth expects Fleda to submit quietly to schemes aimed at defeating Mona—and to submit with the same unquestioning acceptance that the young woman imagines giving to her friend's dominance at Poynton afterwards. Fleda soon realizes with dismay "that her own value in the house was the mere value, as one might say, of a good agent" (p. 36) who is expected to sacrifice her freedom to the bondage of her friend's power. Again and again Mrs. Gereth makes demonstrations of care to Fleda that betray a quality of aggression that shows the two friends to be in conflict—"suddenly inflicting on Fleda a kiss" at one point, for example, "intended by every sign to knock her into position" (p. 31) to take Owen away from Mona. Again and again Fleda has "the sense of being buried alive, smothered in the mere expansion of another will" (p. 209) because, in a Sartrean manner familiar to us from the last chapter, her subjectivity has been made the object of another's ambitions in a way that makes the young woman feel deprived of her freedom. Fleda has become subservient to Mrs. Gereth, of course, because the poor young woman prefers the role of companion to the other prospects open to someone in her penniless state. Without capital of her own, to paraphrase Marx, she has nothing to sell but her labor-power—her powers of appreciation, for example, and her capacity to act as Mrs. Gereth's accomplice. By taking Fleda under her wing, Mrs. Gereth assumes that she has purchased control of those powers. And in her alienated state, with her capacities made over to the power of another, Fleda would seem unable to protest.

Fleda does protest, however. She resists the dominance of her benefactress and insists on her freedom to create herself for herself by keeping secrets, telling lies, and mapping strategies toward Owen, Mona, and Mrs. Gereth that defy Mrs. Gereth's plans for her. Many factors are at work here, including Fleda's delicate moral scruples, her love for Owen, her highly ambivalent and thickly disguised sexual feelings, and her wonderful yet dangerous imagination. But one major factor in Fleda's duplicitous diplomacy between Owen and his mother is simply self-defense; if her benefactress claims control over Fleda's powers, then this young woman's schemes and secrets represent an attempt to create her own objectifications (the achievements of her diplomacy) safe behind a cloak of opacity from Mrs. Gereth's usurpation. Some of the most dramatic scenes in the novel involve Fleda desperately trying to protect her secrets from Mrs. Gereth's penetrating gaze—the secret of her love for Owen, for example, then of his love for her and of the likelihood that Mona will drop Owen if his mother holds out long enough. Fleda resents "the chill of her exposed and investigated state" and takes offense at the way "Mrs. Gereth popped in and out of the chamber of her soul" (p. 132). Attempting to close the door to that chamber by lying and putting on an act, Fleda tries to make herself more knowing than known and thus struggles against Mrs. Gereth's presumption of hegemony.

Fleda finds "a high brutality" in Mrs. Gereth's "good intentions" (p. 131) because they inform a stifling rather than liberating solicitude. The older woman's presumably helpful acts repeatedly defy her young friend's wishes and plans—as when, for example, in "an indirect betrayal" of "the spirit of their agreement" (pp. 153–54), Mrs. Gereth tells Owen Fleda's address in London, or when, with "a calculated, . . . a crushing bribe" designed "to make sure of her" (p. 212), the older woman returns the spoils to Poynton in anticipation of Owen's and Fleda's marriage. Mrs. Gereth may seem justified in her impatience at the extraordinarily delicate, sexually ambivalent Fleda's indecisiveness toward Owen. But Fleda seems justified too in resenting and resisting the power Mrs. Gereth assumes she has the right to exercise over her son and her agent.

Fleda's schemes and secrets transcend Mrs. Gereth's transcendence by foiling her plans more completely than the young woman herself had foreseen. Fleda sheds her protective cloak of opacity and confesses her secrets only when all has gone too far and Mrs. Gereth, without her things and with Owen and Mona probably married, seems powerless. After her confession, Fleda prepares "for penal submission—for a surrender that, in its complete humility, would be a long expiation" (p. 233). This final "surrender" confirms that Fleda had been resisting "submission" all along. Fleda practices her secretive, duplicitous diplomacy in the role of mediator between the parties in conflict over the spoils. It is a strange mediator who increases the atmosphere of obscurity that surrounds mutual misunderstanding and who adds to the conflicts that embroil the opposing sides. But if the spoils mediate negatively between those they bring together, Fleda could hardly be expected to reverse their effect all by herself.

The Spoils of Poynton ends with less hope than *The Golden Bowl* that positive acts of mediation in the future might replace conflict with care—or, to recall James's words, might lead to "fusion" and "abridge old rigours of separation." The fire that consumes the spoils does not purge the novel's world. Rather, it reflects the incendiary value that the spoils have taken on as embodiments of the violent battles for power that have revolved around them. After these objects are gone, though, the dilemmas of power, freedom, and community that they objectified still remain. When Fleda says at the end, "I'll go back" (p. 266), she does not specify what she will return to. But her most obvious alternatives do not seem particularly promising—back to Mrs. Gereth at Ricks in an estranged relation based "almost wholly on breaches and omissions" (p. 253), or back to a penniless, dependent existence with her father or her sister and with as little freedom and power as ever to attain the possibilities her imagination so richly projects. Maggie's and Amerigo's final embrace is ambiguous, as we saw, because it contains elements of both conflict and care. But it at least offers the possibility that they might work toward a mutually liberating union.

For Marx, individuals can enjoy personal freedom and caring rather than exploitive relations with others only after fundamental social and economic changes have cleared the way. When Sartre describes how the Self and the Other might reconcile their differences, he argues that transparency cannot triumph over opacity until "there has been a change in the economic, cultural, and affective relations among men, beginning with the eradication of material scarcity." With Marx, he regards economic inequities as "the root of the antagonisms among men, past and present."[30] James understands how "material scarcity" and economic inequities contribute to conflict and interfere with care in personal relations. Let us remember, for example, how the inequality of Maggie's and the Prince's financial positions interferes with reciprocity and thus with intimacy in their relationship's early stages. Or recall how Fleda's poverty allows Mrs. Gereth to feel entitled to manipulate her young friend with impunity. Still, James would probably agree with Ricoeur and Sartre that problems of power and conflict will continue to threaten the ideal of harmonious personal relations even if material inequities are ever overcome.[31] If antagonism isolates Fleda and Mrs. Gereth from each other at the end, or if conflict still threatens Amerigo's and Maggie's union as they embrace, perfect harmony fails these characters less because of the divisive impact of economic inequity than because of the disruptive role battles for power can always play in relations between ourselves and others. James shares the ideals of freedom and community, but both *The Spoils of Poynton* and *The Golden Bowl* demonstrate the distance that in his view exists between these ideals and their possibility of attainment.

T H R E E

Our analysis of the politics of *The Spoils of Poynton* has led us to reconsider aspects of experience familiar to us from earlier chapters. The failure or success of mediation, for example, helps to decide whether conflict or care, opacity or transparency, will prevail in personal relations. The process of self-objectification implicates both freedom and perception—the possibility of producing ourselves in action and the ability to recognize ourselves and others through the products of our activity. Mystification is an epistemological dilemma— a failure to know ourselves, others, and our objects for what they are— which also hampers freedom and care by thwarting self-expression and community. The ability to create and recognize ourselves in the objects we make also requires the use of the imagination, as both Fleda and Mrs. Gereth amply show in their successes and failures in exercising this faculty. Once again we have seen, then, that there is a unity of knowing and doing in James that extends from his notion of the "impression" to his "moral vision," including his portrayal of the politics of experience.

Although *The Spoils of Poynton* does not address overtly political themes, it proved particularly felicitous for an analysis guided by Marxian concepts because of the role objects play in its characters' relations with themselves and others. This novel offers no more, though, than an extreme case of an abiding interest throughout James's canon with cultural objects like the spoils. Readers acknowledge this interest, for example, when they note the recurrence of collectors like Mrs. Gereth and Fleda's father in James's works—collectors like the Ververs in *The Golden Bowl*, Gilbert Osmond and Ned Rosier in *The Portrait of a Lady*, or even Rowland Mallet in *Roderick Hudson*.[32] In fact, even beyond the collection of collectors in these works, the notions of objectification, mediation, and mystification could be employed to interpret all of the novels we have considered. Roderick Hudson objectifies himself in his sculpture, but his works fail to mediate between himself and others so that he becomes increasingly, tragically isolated in his own world, immune to help from his friends and relatives. When Gilbert Osmond insists that Isabel Archer sacrifice herself completely to his will, he demands that she cede to him all control over her power to create and express herself. Without any independent ability to objectify herself, she will become object-like—"her intelligence" like "a silver plate," to recall a description quoted earlier, and her entire self "as smooth to his general need of her as handled ivory to the palm." When the Ververs appropriate the Prince as "a *morceau de musée*," they mystify themselves about him and lead him to protest in his adultery with Charlotte because they deny his power to express himself—to reciprocate their benevolence, for example, or to act the "galantuomo." No more than *The Spoils of Poynton* do these novels precisely reproduce Marx's analysis of "commodity fetishism." But all of these works, each in a different way, show a profound awareness of the processes responsible for the alienation and mystification that Marx's analysis uncovers: a confusion about the relation between the human world and the world of objects, the contest for control of others' powers of self-objectification, and the failure of mediation to which this confusion and this contest can contribute.

Maxwell Geismar sees no political or social significance in James's writings but argues instead that this novelist received the acclaim of the New Critics because both he and they isolated art from experience and history. "Henry James was, above all, the pure artist," Geismar claims. "Just the thing for the new criticism with its own stress on method which also negated, or obliterated, the historical and the human elements alike in the 'pure' work of art." Geismar calls "the cult of James" in the 1950s "a revealing symbol and symptom of an age and a society which wanted to dwell like him in some imaginary world of false art and false culture" far removed from "the realities of world history which a large sector of the American intellectuals no longer wished to understand and deal with." [33] There may be a grain or two of truth in Geismar's angry, overly general sociology. He is right, for example, about the ahistorical bias inherent in the New Critics' method of viewing the literary work "*sub specie aeternitatis*," as a self-contained and self-sufficient "verbal icon," with no need to refer for its meaning and significance to its author (the "intentional fallacy") or its readers (the "affective fallacy"). [34] Geismar is unfair, of course, in downplaying the interpretive rigor and depth that the New Critics gained by virtue of the very restrictions they placed on their definition of the work. Even more, though, he is unfair to Henry James.

We have seen in this chapter that James's work can be read for its social and political significance with a method derived from Marx's concern with "the realities of world history." And we have seen in this study as a whole that James's art need not be isolated from experience. Our survey of the intentional foundations that support the world of James's art has taken us through a full range of the aspects of experience—from his concern with consciousness to his "moral vision," from matters of knowing to matters of doing, from his fascination with the "impression" to his understanding of the imagination, freedom, personal relations, and the politics of social reality. A phenomenological reading of Henry James emphasizes rather than "obliterates" the "human elements" in his work. If James's art had little or nothing to do with experience, then the unity of knowing and doing that we have explicated in his work would not share so much with phenomenology's understanding of the epistemological and existential dimensions of our worlds. To understand James as a phenomenological novelist, however, means to understand him as a novelist of experience.

EPILOGUE

THE MODERNITY OF

HENRY JAMES

The phenomenological significance of James's achievement is an index of his modernity. In both his epistemology and his ethics, James heralds some of the major concerns of twentieth-century literature and thought. His treatment of consciousness has long been regarded as a turning point in the history of the novel. It leads away from the conventions of realism toward the preoccupation with the processes of creating and construing meaning that is one hallmark of modern fiction from Joyce through Woolf and Beckett and beyond. The art of the novel, according to Henry James, is "the art of representation."[1] But his most innovative fictions pursue representation in a way that challenges and ultimately changes it by exposing its epistemological foundations. His experiments with point of view—thematizing the aspects that display his fictional worlds—examine self-consciously the processes of meaning-creation and interpretation that most traditional fiction quietly exploits to achieve a sense of reality. In their self-consciousness about representation, James's novels explore how we make reality by interpreting it. They thereby lead the reader on a journey of discovery into the mysteries of how we endow the world with meaning and interpret the signs through which it offers itself. James's moral vision announces and seeks to resolve one of the more important consequences of the modern period's epistemological crisis: How should we respond to the discovery that what we know—our meanings, purposes, and values—cannot claim the immediate guarantee of any transcendental justification? His explorations of the drama of experience are a prolonged inquiry into the status of ethics in a world where norms have no foundation deeper than existence itself and where judgment is simply one of the many vicissitudes of consciousness.

James's position as a pivotal figure in the history of representation can be seen in his contradictory attitude toward the status of reality. He shares the enabling assumption of mimesis that reality is determinate and independent—a prior given that is "there" to be uncovered and rendered. But he also believes—and with growing conviction over the course of his career—that the world is plural, dependent for its shape on the creation and construal of meaning, and hence a field of differing interpretations that may or may not overlap.

According to James, "The real represents to my perception the things we cannot possibly *not* know, sooner or later, in one way or another; it being but one of the accidents of our hampered state, and one of the incidents of their quantity and number, that particular instances have not yet come our way."[2] This is a declaration of faith in a reality independent of what anyone thinks it to be; there may be many observers at the various windows of the house of fiction, but at least part of the show they all see differently is ultimately the same if there are "things we cannot possibly *not* know." Still, James's use of a double negative suggests the absence of the real and not its indubitable presence. Negativity and absence are characteristics of a world of signs. James suggests that the "real" is not a given but a goal that signs point toward with a kind of inevitability. But when his characters discover the truth of their situations, it is often by the merest chance—as when Isabel happens upon Osmond sitting while Madame Merle stands, or when Maggie purchases the golden bowl ("the coincidence is extraordinary," the Prince says),[3] or when Strether encounters Chad and Madame de Vionnet in the French countryside. The chance-quality of these revelations suggests the weakness of the double negative that guarantees for James that reality is a discoverable given. Even more, the intractable ambiguity of works like *The Sacred Fount* or *The Turn of the Screw* suggests that the force of reality may not be strong enough to lead interpretation to a definitive, indubitable result.

And so, perhaps paradoxically, James abandons monism and embraces pluralism in lines I quoted earlier from "The Art of Fiction": "[T]he measure of reality is very difficult to fix. . . . Humanity is immense, and reality has a myriad forms."[4] This is also Maggie Verver's

discovery when she learns after her awakening that any state of affairs
is "subject to varieties of interpretation"—that "the full significance"
of any episode in the foursome's history "could be no more after all
than a matter of interpretation, differing always for a different interpreter."[5] Maggie's hermeneutic education reveals to her that she inhabits a world of signs that can vary widely in meaning according to
the consciousness that construes them.

The paradox of James's contradictory attitudes toward reality and
interpretation provides the tension that animates Strether's quest for
knowledge in *The Ambassadors*. In an amusing but immensely serious
exchange with Madame de Vionnet, Strether asks what he should report to Mrs. Newsome:

> "Simply tell her the truth."
> "And what do you call the truth?"
> "Well, *any* truth—about us all—that you see yourself. I
> leave it to you."
> "Thank you very much. I like," Strether laughed with a
> slight harshness, "the way you leave things!"
> But she insisted kindly, gently, as if it was n't so bad. "Be
> perfectly honest. Tell her all."
> "All?" he oddly echoed.
> "Tell her the simple truth," Madame de Vionnet again
> pleaded.
> "But what *is* the simple truth? The simple truth is exactly
> what I'm trying to discover."[6]

Strether eventually discovers "the simple truth" about Madame de Vionnet's liaison with Chad. Although quite by accident, evidence finally comes his way so that he "cannot possibly not know" that their
relation is carnal and passionate, not innocent and platonic. Strether's
revelation makes their love affair seem like a fact, a reality, that simply awaited his belated discovery. But after his awakening Strether
still disagrees with Woollett's interpretation of Chad's entanglement
and Madame de Vionnet's character. The justice of his opposing view,
even after Woollett's assumption of carnality has been vindicated,
suggests that "truth" is not simple and single but various and multiple, a matter of interpretation.

The paradox here—that reality is both independent of and dependent on interpretation—suggests how James stands with one foot in

the nineteenth century and one foot in the twentieth. The extent to which James maintains faith in the real is a measure of his allegiance to the great tradition of verisimilitude in the novel. But the extent to which he challenges the epistemological assumptions of mimesis by questioning the determinacy and independence of reality suggests the degree to which he announces the modern preoccupation with meaning and interpretation.

James's concern with epistemology and hermeneutics is shared, although in different ways, by Ford Madox Ford and Joseph Conrad, two distinctly modern novelists with whom he is frequently compared and who both acknowledged their debt to his achievement. James, Ford, and Conrad all assign the greatest thematic and aesthetic importance to the experience of bewilderment. For them, bewilderment throws into question the interpretive constructs that we ordinarily take for granted as our ways of knowing the world. Aesthetically, bewilderment calls for representational strategies that make strange our sense of reality by showing that it has no more certainty or stability than an interpretive scheme. From Maisie's "career of unsuccessful experiments" with knowing to Maggie Verver's awakening to the trials of understanding other minds, James's portraits of bewilderment show his fascination with the composing powers of consciousness. Hence his practice of telling his stories through "registers" and "reflectors" who change and develop their points of view as they struggle with dilemmas that threaten to defeat their capacity to fit elements together in a consistent whole.

Fordian bewilderment emphasizes that experience is inherently uncomposed. According to Ford, he and Conrad "saw that Life did not narrate but made impressions on our brains. We in turn, if we wished to produce on you an effect of life, must not narrate but render impressions."[7] Ford's most successful novels dramatize the gap between the ambiguity of unreflective understanding and the attempt of reflective interpretation to compose impressions into a clear, coherent narrative pattern. Maisie struggles to narrow the Fordian gap between what she sees and what she understands; but by concentrating on her resourceful imagination in generating epistemological hypotheses, James shows his interest in how consciousness constantly and relentlessly composes despite the forces that seek to disrupt it. In the fragmented, rambling narration of *The Good Soldier*, Ford stresses the stubborn opacity of unreflective experience—an opacity that resists the often confused efforts of the narrator to develop a coherent point of view on events that have outstripped his understanding.

In their bewilderment, Ford's and James's characters frequently question the meaning of existence; but Conrad's Marlow is the great metaphysical questioner. Bewilderment in Conrad has the power to awaken us out of "our agreeable somnolence," the "dullness that makes life to the incalculable majority so supportable and so welcome." This experience of disorientation—the disequilibrium Marlow suffers from his encounters with Jim and Kurtz—then announces a metaphysical hermeneutics of suspicion and faith. Conrad's works wonder whether "belief in a few simple notions" like duty and fidelity can withstand the challenge of skepticism and hold back the darkness of nihilism.[8] In their fascination with bewilderment, these three novelists herald the growing awareness in modern thought and literature that the limits on how we know throw into question the status of what we know.

The modern epistemological crisis is also a moral crisis. The moral question that many twentieth-century thinkers and writers face is how to justify our purposes and values in a world of signs that, when interpreted, seem to lead only to other signs and not to any ultimate truth. Can a foundation be discovered on which to base our meanings and standards, or are they radically contingent because they are nothing more than products of consciousness? Some respond to this crisis with the excessive faith of idealism, while others embrace the extreme suspicion of nihilism. In literature, we can take T. S. Eliot as the figure of modern idealism that laments the fragmentation caused by the lapse of universals and seeks unity through faith in a new transcendental (whether this be a revitalized Christianity, a cyclical view of history, or a rediscovered, recreated mythology). Kafka is the figure of nihilism with his skeptical despair at the prospects of ever finding a frame of reference to guide us. In modern thought, idealism shows itself in theories as diverse as, on the one hand, Jung's belief in an eternal, collectively unconscious world of universal archetypes or, on the other, Lévi-Strauss's supposition of a fundamental unity between the savage and modern minds based on the transcendental logic of binarism. But the modern period is also the age of suspicion, led by the great unmaskers Freud, Marx, and Nietzsche who, although not nihilistic, challenge the foundations of all convictions. Their tradition of unmasking finds extreme expression in Derrida's opposition to all

metaphysical schemes that posit a stable center in order to deny the
unsettling, unlimited absence that permeates our worlds.

Henry James and phenomenology respond to the modern moral crisis by turning to the structure of experience. For them, experience
itself provides a foundation that, without idealistic transcendentals,
rests on nothing but itself and that, unlike nihilism, allows us to discover and justify purposes and values to guide our lives. In the words
of William James: "All 'homes' are in finite experience; finite experience as such is homeless. Nothing outside of the flux secures the issue
of it. It can hope salvation only from its own intrinsic promises and
potencies."[9] Experience is a foundation that does not give us the stable security Derrida attributes to all ways of positing a ground. As
Henry James's works show, nothing guarantees that we can know with
certainty or imagine wondrously and without risk. There is no assurance that we can discover invigorating possibilities within the limits that bind us, or establish care over conflict by making ourselves
mutually transparent. Nor can we foresee an end to the battles for
power that disrupt social harmony. These are justifiable goals, however, that can claim as their basis the structure of experience itself.

These goals are immanent to the world of signs and interpretation
because they reflect the inherent conditions of being-in-the-world in
which the creation and construal of meaning take place. By granting
primacy to experience as a home of moral values, Henry James and
phenomenology suggest that we can avoid the despair of nihilism and
the false comfort of idealism by taking as our guide the "intrinsic
promises and potencies" of being-in-the-world. The potential values
of existence—adequate knowing, *unverstiegen* imagining, responsible freedom, genuine care, social community—will remain empty
categories unless we put them into practice as principles animating
our conduct. Furthermore, their meaning as moral goals is variable
and depends on how we activate them. But their validity is guaranteed
by the very conditions of existence into which we find ourselves
thrown as knowing and doing beings. Although nothing *beyond* experience guarantees our meanings and values, James and phenomenology discover *within* experience the basis for a purposeful existence.

Neither nihilistic nor idealistic, James interprets experience with a
combination of suspicion and faith. His works suggest that a dialectic
of belief and doubt is necessary to realize the potential values intrinsic to existence. As Anne Thackeray Ritchie's example indicated, the

strengths and weaknesses of the "impression" as a way of knowing require faith in the possibilities of consciousness joined with suspicion to avoid overstepping the bounds set by the many limits to perception. Roderick Hudson's lively imagination carries him too far ahead of and beyond himself because he trusts his marvelous ethereal world too much and suspects too little the dangers of the tomb. Rowland Mallet's moralistic attitude suffers the reverse failing of excessive criticism and inadequate faith. In her once-born, healthy-minded assertion of independence, Isabel Archer exults in her belief in possibilities without suspecting the necessity of limitation. She understands the paradox of the servile will when she doubts the possibility of unlimited independence but still believes in a future of freedom grounded in a consent to the necessity established by her past commitments. In her innocence about the problem of other minds, Maggie Verver does not suspect the dangers that the opacity of the Other poses to her belief in an unproblematic, all-encompassing care. Her awakening initiates her contradictory strategy of pursuing care through conflict—a strategy that, at the end of the novel, leaves open the possibility of belief in intersubjectivity and care but also raises doubts that solipsism and conflict can be completely overcome. Thanks to the process of self-objectification, cultural objects like the spoils can mediate between members of a community; but they can also inspire battles for power if, like Mrs. Gereth, we believe in them so much that we do not suspect the mystification and alienation of "commodity fetishism." Where some thinkers and writers respond to the modern lapse of transcendentals by stressing either suspicion or faith, James suggests that a universe founded on nothing more or less than experience requires the constant exercise of both.

This inquiry into James's modernity shows again the unity of James the epistemological novelist and James the moral dramatist. Let us reconsider the example given in Chapter 1 of how Mrs. Wix condemns Maisie for lacking "a moral sense." As I argued there, a moral vision deeper and broader than Mrs. Wix's ethics emerges from Maisie's trials. Mrs. Wix invokes an extrinsic set of standards established by social conventions that fix the boundaries between moral and immoral conduct. But she does not realize that a society's moral conventions are radically contingent, not founded on anything deeper than experience itself. A society may agree to condemn adultery, for example. But as Maisie's parents and stepparents demonstrate, this convention is no stronger than the agreement of the society's members to put it into practice. Furthermore, the rule against adultery embodies in a particular way the conditions inherent in the structure of experience because it makes a stipulation about the relation between the Self and the Other. To condemn adultery means, at the most fundamental epistemological and existential level, to combat rather than encourage the opacity that divides the Self from others—to condemn the lies and intrigues that, as Maisie's story shows, take advantage of the opacity of the Other for the purposes of conflict instead of care.

In a world like Maisie's, where conventions governing conduct have lost their force, James suggests that one can still lead a moral life not by becoming dogmatic like Mrs. Wix but, like her ward, by taking seriously the work of expanding what we know, enhancing our sphere of possibilities, and narrowing the gap between the Self and others. On these terms, morality for James is never finally achieved but is always still to be won, just as Maisie's story ends *en l'air*, with one chapter of her history concluded only to face her with further dilemmas for the future. For James, the pursuit of the moral life is an often ambiguous, always perilous, never ultimately completed activity because it is a constant epistemological and existential challenge.

NOTES

PREFACE

1. The following introductions to phenomenology are also recommended: Pierre Thévenaz, *What Is Phenomenology?*, trans. James M. Edie et al. (1952; reprint, Chicago: Quadrangle, 1962); Herbert Spiegelberg, *The Phenomenological Movement*, rev. ed., 2 vols. (The Hague: Martinus Nijhoff, 1968); Maurice Natanson, *Edmund Husserl: Philosopher of Infinite Tasks* (Evanston, Ill.: Northwestern University Press, 1973). Also see Joseph J. Kockelmans, ed., *Phenomenology: The Philosophy of Edmund Husserl and Its Interpretation* (Garden City, N.Y.: Anchor Books, 1967). Of the many introductory works in print, one of the few addressed to a literary audience is Robert R. Magliola's *Phenomenology and Literature: An Introduction* (West Lafayette, Ind.: Purdue University Press, 1977). Magliola claims that he writes for a general literary readership, but the style and substance of his book presume a familiarity with philosophical issues and critical theory. Some important materials on phenomenology and literature are collected in Vernon W. Gras, ed., *European Literary Theory and Practice* (New York: Dell Publishing Co., 1973). But a fully rounded picture of phenomenology does not emerge because half of the anthology is devoted to structuralism.

2. Literary interest in phenomenology has increased over the last several years. For example, see James E. Swearingen, *Reflexivity in "Tristram Shandy": An Essay in Phenomenological Criticism* (New Haven: Yale University Press, 1977); Edgar A. Dryden, *Nathaniel Hawthorne: The Poetics of Enchantment* (Ithaca, N.Y.: Cornell University Press, 1977); David Halliburton, *Edgar Allan Poe: A Phenomenological View* (Princeton: Princeton University Press, 1973); Lucio P. Ruotolo, *Six Existential Heroes: The Politics of Faith* (Cambridge: Harvard University Press, 1973); Sarah N. Lawall, *Critics of Consciousness: The Existential Structures of Literature* (Cambridge: Harvard University Press, 1968); E. D. Hirsch, Jr., *Validity in Interpretation* (New Haven: Yale University Press, 1967); Paul Brodtkorb, Jr., *Ishmael's White World: A Phenomenological Reading of "Moby Dick"* (New Haven: Yale University Press, 1965); J. Hillis Miller, *Poets of Reality* (Cambridge: Harvard University Press, 1965), and *The Disappearance of God* (Cambridge: Harvard University Press, 1963).

3. Georges Poulet, "Phenomenology of Reading," in *Critical Theory since Plato*, ed. Hazard Adams (New York: Harcourt Brace Jovanovich, 1971), p. 1221. See as well Poulet's studies of space and time in James in *The Metamorphoses of the Circle*, trans. Carley Dawson and Elliott Coleman (1961; reprint, Baltimore: Johns Hopkins University Press, 1966), pp. 307–20, and *Studies in Human Time*, trans. Elliott Coleman (1949; reprint, Baltimore: Johns Hopkins University Press, 1956), pp. 350–54.

4. For a theoretical explanation of "existential psychoanalysis," see Jean-Paul Sartre, *Being and Nothingness*, trans. Hazel E. Barnes (1943; reprint, New York: Washington Square Press, 1966), pp. 712–34. For practical examples of Sartre's method, see *Saint Genet: Actor and Martyr*, trans. anon. (1952; reprint, New York: New American Library, 1971), and the discussion of Flaubert in *Search for a Method*, trans. Hazel E. Barnes (1960; reprint, New York: Vintage Books, 1968), pp. 57–65. Also see Sartre, *Baudelaire*, trans. Martin Turnell (1947; reprint, Norfolk, Conn.: New Directions, 1950).

5. See Wolfgang Iser, *The Implied Reader* (Baltimore: Johns Hopkins University Press, 1974), and *The Act of Reading: A Theory of Aesthetic Response* (Baltimore: Johns Hopkins University Press, 1978). Iser's theory is heavily indebted to Roman Ingarden, whose aesthetics I discuss at length in Chapter 2.

6. See Martin Heidegger, "Hölderlin and the Essence of Poetry," in *European Literary Theory and Practice*, ed. Gras, pp. 27–41. Also see Heidegger, *On the Way to Language*, trans. Peter D. Hertz and Joan Stambaugh (1959; reprint, New York: Harper and Row, 1971), and *Poetry, Language, Thought*, ed. and trans. Albert Hofstadter (New York: Harper and Row, 1971).

7. See particularly Gaston Bachelard, *The Poetics of Space*, trans. Maria Jolas (1958; reprint, Boston: Beacon Press, 1969).

8. Paul Ricoeur, "Metaphor and the Main Problem of Hermeneutics," in *The Philosophy of Paul Ricoeur*, ed. Charles E. Reagan and David Stewart (Boston: Beacon Press, 1978), p. 144.

9. William Troy, "The New Generation," in *Henry James: A Collection of Critical Essays*, ed. Leon Edel (Englewood Cliffs, N.J.: Prentice-Hall, 1963), p. 79.

CHAPTER 1

1. Joseph Conrad, "Henry James: An Appreciation" (1905), in *Henry James*, ed. Edel, p. 15.

2. Henry James, *The Letters of Henry James*, ed. Percy Lubbock, 2 vols. (New York: Charles Scribner's Sons, 1920), 2:83, 44. See F. O. Matthiessen, *The James Family* (New York: Alfred A. Knopf, 1947); H. B. Parkes, "The James Brothers," *Sewanee Review* 56 (1948): 323–28; Joseph J. Firebaugh, "The Pragmatism of Henry James," *Virginia Quarterly Review* 27 (1951): 419–35, and "The Ververs," *Essays in Criticism* 4 (1954): 400–410; William McMurray, "Pragmatic Realism in *The Bostonians*," in *Henry James: Modern Judgements*, ed. Tony Tanner (Nashville, Tenn.: Aurora, 1970), pp. 160–65; Richard A. Hocks, *Henry James and Pragmatistic Thought: A Study in the Relationship between the Philosophy of William James and the Literary Art of Henry James* (Chapel Hill: University of North Carolina Press, 1974).

3. See Spiegelberg, *The Phenomenological Movement*, 1:111–17. For in-

terpretations of William James's phenomenological significance, see John Wild, *The Radical Empiricism of William James* (Garden City, N.Y.: Doubleday and Co., 1969), and Bruce Wilshire, *William James and Phenomenology* (Bloomington: Indiana University Press, 1968). In the context of a different argument, John Carlos Rowe makes a similar suggestion about the relation of the James brothers to the phenomenological tradition. See *Henry Adams and Henry James: The Emergence of a Modern Consciousness* (Ithaca, N.Y.: Cornell University Press, 1976), pp. 37–38.

4. Henry James, *The Art of the Novel* (1907–9), ed. R. P. Blackmur (1934; reprint, New York: Charles Scribner's Sons, 1962), pp. 45–46.

5. Quoted in Thévenaz, *What Is Phenomenology?*, p. 45.

6. Maurice Merleau-Ponty, *The Primacy of Perception*, ed. James M. Edie (Evanston, Ill.: Northwestern University Press, 1964), pp. 30–31, 25–26.

7. See William James, "Does 'Consciousness' Exist?," in *Essays in Radical Empiricism*, ed. Ralph Barton Perry (1912; reprint, New York: E. P. Dutton and Co., 1971), pp. 3–22.

8. Edmund Husserl, *Cartesian Meditations*, trans. Dorion Cairns (1929; reprint, The Hague: Martinus Nijhoff, 1970), p. 65, and *Ideas*, trans. W. R. Boyce Gibson (1913; reprint, New York: Collier, 1972), p. 223.

9. For further explanations of intentionality, see Husserl, *Ideas*, pp. 222–24, and *Cartesian Meditations*, pp. 44–46.

10. James M. Edie, "Introduction" to Thévenaz, *What Is Phenomenology?*, pp. 26–27. Some conservative phenomenologists regard existential theory not as an enrichment and logical outgrowth of Husserl's work but as an unfortunate turning away from the pure epistemological and methodological ambitions of his attempt to provide indubitable foundations for philosophy. For a critique of their arguments and a further explanation of the essential continuity between phenomenology and existentialism, see Paul Ricoeur's essay, "Existential Phenomenology" (1957), in his *Husserl: An Analysis of His Phenomenology*, ed. and trans. Edward G. Ballard and Lester E. Embree (Evanston, Ill.: Northwestern University Press, 1967), pp. 202–12; Natanson's chapter on "Phenomenology and Existence," in *Husserl: Philosopher of Infinite Tasks*, ed. Natanson, pp. 147–67; and Richard M. Zaner and Don Ihde, eds., "Introduction" to their anthology, *Phenomenology and Existentialism* (New York: G. P. Putnam's Sons, 1973), pp. 9–26. My own study of the unity of knowing and doing in James will also show in detail how phenomenology and existentialism are systematically related to each other.

11. Jean-Paul Sartre, *Being and Nothingness*, p. 407.

12. Pelham Edgar, *Henry James: Man and Author* (Boston and New York: Grant Richards, 1927), p. 123. Also see F. W. Dupee, *Henry James* (1951; reprint, New York: William Morrow, 1974), p. 167; James W. Gargano, "*What Maisie Knew*: The Evolution of a 'Moral Sense,'" *Nineteenth-Century Fiction* 16 (1961): 33–46; Walter Isle, *Experiments in Form: Henry James's Novels, 1896–1901* (Cambridge: Harvard University Press, 1968), p. 145.

13. Oscar Cargill, *The Novels of Henry James* (New York: Macmillan Co., 1961), p. 258. Also see J. W. Beach, *The Method of Henry James* (New

218 Notes to Pages 9–19

Haven: Yale University Press, 1918), p. 239, and Harris W. Wilson, "What *Did* Maisie Know?," *College English* 17 (February 1956): 279–82.

14. Henry James, *The Art of the Novel*, p. 145.

15. Henry James, *What Maisie Knew*, in *The Novels and Tales of Henry James*, 26 vols. (New York: Charles Scribner's Sons, 1907–17), 11:9. All references in the text are to this edition.

16. See Maurice Merleau-Ponty, *Phenomenology of Perception*, trans. Colin Smith (1945; reprint, London: Routledge and Kegan Paul, 1962), pp. xvii–xxi, 23, 30, 250, 361, 364, 369–409. Also see Merleau-Ponty, *The Primacy of Perception*, pp. 12–27.

17. For more on acquired habitualities and the historical genesis of meaning, see Husserl, *Cartesian Meditations*, pp. 75–80.

18. For an analysis of the relation between meaning and play, see Paul Ricoeur, *Freud and Philosophy*, trans. Denis Savage (1965; reprint, New Haven: Yale University Press, 1970), pp. 284–86, 314–16. Ricoeur draws on Freud's explanation of the *"fort-da"* game in *Beyond the Pleasure Principle* (1920).

19. Henry James, *The Art of the Novel*, p. 147.

20. See Charles Sanders Peirce, "The Fixation of Belief" and "How to Make Our Ideas Clear," in *Philosophical Writings of Peirce*, ed. Justus Buchler (New York: Dover Publications, 1955), pp. 21–39.

21. William James, *Pragmatism* (1907; reprint, New York: New American Library, 1955), p. 145.

22. Ibid., p. 136.

23. Henry James, *The Art of the Novel*, p. 147.

24. Ibid., p. 146. See Isle, *Experiments in Form*, pp. 136ff., for an illuminating study of the technical devices James employs to tell more than Maisie knows.

25. See Iser, *The Act of Reading*, pp. 125–34, and *The Implied Reader*, pp. 285–90. Here and elsewhere, when I refer to "the reader" or "us" in my Iserian analyses of James, I mean the roles, tasks, and opportunities that the text holds in readiness for its audience. Actual readers can and do respond differently to the possibilities of concretization that a text makes available— so much so that disputes about its meaning may arise. I have these actual readers in mind when I refer to "James's readers" in the sense of the various critics and students who have analyzed and reported about his works.

26. See Iser, *The Implied Reader*, pp. 275–82.

27. Ibid., p. xiv.

28. Merleau-Ponty, *Phenomenology of Perception*, p. 364.

29. Husserl, *Cartesian Meditations*, p. 117.

30. Dupee, *Henry James*, p. 166.

31. Søren Kierkegaard, *The Concept of Dread*, trans. Walter Lowrie (1844; reprint, Princeton: Princeton University Press, 1973), p. 38.

32. See Martin Heidegger, *Being and Time*, trans. John Macquarrie and Edward Robinson (1927; reprint, New York: Harper and Row, 1962), pp. 344–46.

33. Ibid., pp. 235–41.

34. Henry James, *Letters*, 1:297.

35. Among the many Marxist critics who make a similar argument, see particularly Lucien Goldmann, *Towards a Sociology of the Novel*, trans. Alan Sheridan (1964; reprint, London: Tavistock, 1975), p. 159.

36. Henry James, *The Art of the Novel*, p. 140.

37. For an illuminating parallel to Maisie's dilemma here, see Ludwig Binswanger, "The Case of Ilse," in *Existence*, ed. Rollo May et al. (New York: Simon and Schuster, 1958), pp. 214–36.

38. For more on wishing and freedom, see Heidegger, *Being and Time*, pp. 239–40.

39. See Binswanger, "Extravagance (*Verstiegenheit*)," in *Being-in-the-World*, ed. Jacob Needleman (New York: Harper and Row, 1968), pp. 342–49.

40. For an explanation of the relation between solicitude and potentiality-for-Being, see Heidegger, *Being and Time*, pp. 158–59.

41. Ibid., pp. 319–25; Kierkegaard, *Concept of Dread*, pp. 37–41, and Sartre, *Being and Nothingness*, pp. 64–85.

42. Sartre, *Being and Nothingness*, p. 65.

43. See Heidegger, *Being and Time*, pp. 188–95, 235–41, 377.

44. See Sartre, *Being and Nothingness*, pp. 3–56, and *What Is Literature?*, trans. Bernard Frechtman (1947; reprint, New York: Harper and Row, 1965), pp. 1–60.

45. Merleau-Ponty, *Phenomenology of Perception*, p. 136.

46. Despite the important role of time in the creation of meaning, my reading of James is more synchronic than diachronic. In order to make clear the underlying structure of his artistic world, it was necessary to map his intentional foundations in an almost spatial manner, as if they were laid out all at once before us, instead of following the temporal path of their development over his career. Clarity required this strategy, but I have tried to compensate for its potential disadvantages by including texts from every stage of James's mature artistic life. There is continuity in the development of James's opus, as we shall see, since such an early work as *Roderick Hudson* and such a late one as *The Golden Bowl* share many of the same concerns. James's fundamental themes and values established themselves early and then were deepened more than they transformed. His concerns do change as they deepen, though, by taking on greater complexity and by betraying a growing sense of the ambiguity and contingency of experience.

47. Beach, *The Method of Henry James*, pp. 130–44; Percy Lubbock, *The Craft of Fiction* (New York: Viking Press, 1921), pp. 161–71; F. O. Matthiessen, *Henry James: The Major Phase* (1944; reprint, New York: Oxford University Press, 1963), pp. 1–17, 131–51; Leon Edel, *The Psychological Novel, 1900–1950* (New York and Philadelphia: J. P. Lippincott Co., 1955), pp. 53–75.

48. Dupee, *Henry James*, and Dorothea Krook, *The Ordeal of Conscious-*

ness in Henry James (1962; reprint, Cambridge: Cambridge University Press, 1967).

49. J. H. Raleigh, "Henry James: The Poetics of Empiricism," in *Henry James*, ed. Tanner, p. 53.

50. Quentin Anderson, *The American Henry James* (New Brunswick, N.J.: Rutgers University Press, 1957), pp. xi-xiii.

51. An interesting recent book with a similar ambition but a different perspective is Stephen Donadio's *Nietzsche, Henry James, and the Artistic Will* (New York: Oxford University Press, 1978). Nietzsche's relations to the phenomenological tradition are important and complex. With Kierkegaard, Nietzsche has been called one of the nineteenth-century fathers of phenomenology. The reasons for this include Nietzsche's understanding of the provisional, perspectival nature of "truth," his concern with the status of the Self, his practice of discarding the blinders of everyday, unquestioned assumptions when describing phenomena like "morality," and the priority he gives to concrete, historical human experience over abstract philosophical systems. For two particularly noteworthy statements about Nietzsche by leading existential phenomenologists, see Karl Jaspers, *Nietzsche: An Introduction to the Understanding of His Philosophical Activity*, trans. Charles F. Wallraff and Frederick J. Schmitz (1936; reprint, South Bend, Ind.: Regnery/Gateway, 1979); and Martin Heidegger, *Nietzsche*, 2 vols. (Pfullingen: Neske, 1961).

52. Henry James, *Notes of a Son and Brother* (1914), in Henry James, *Henry James: Autobiography*, ed. F. W. Dupee (London: W. H. Allen, 1956), p. 350.

53. Krook, *The Ordeal of Consciousness*, pp. 410–11.

54. Henry James, *Partial Portraits* (1888), reprint ed. Leon Edel (Ann Arbor: University of Michigan Press, 1970), p. 238; "Ivan Turgenev" (1874), excerpted in James E. Miller, Jr., ed., *Theory of Fiction: Henry James* (Lincoln: University of Nebraska Press, 1972), p. 297.

CHAPTER 2

1. Henry James, *Partial Portraits*, p. 384 (hereafter cited as *PP*).

2. Henry James, *Letters*, 1:323.

3. Adams, ed., *Critical Theory since Plato*, p. 660. On the other hand, of course, many critics have found considerable "theoretical value" in James's aesthetic writings. See particularly Miller, *Theory of Fiction*, and René Wellek, "Henry James's Literary Theory and Criticism," *American Literature* 30, no. 3 (November 1958): 293–321. Also see Elsa Nettels, *James and Conrad* (Athens: University of Georgia Press, 1977), pp. 25–43.

4. Leon Edel identifies Ritchie and her novel in his notes to this edition of *Partial Portraits*, p. 411.

5. See Heidegger, *Being and Time*, pp. 188–95.

6. Peirce, *Philosophical Writings*, p. xiv.

7. William James, *A Pluralistic Universe* (1909; reprint, New York: E. P. Dutton Co., 1971), p. 170.

8. William James, *The Will to Believe* (1897; reprint, New York: Dover Publications, 1956), pp. 29, xi; *Essays in Radical Empiricism*, p. 20.

9. Merleau-Ponty, *Phenomenology of Perception*, p. 233.

10. Joseph J. Kockelmans, "Intentional and Constitutive Analyses," in *Phenomenology*, ed. Kockelmans, pp. 139–40. Also see Aron Gurwitsch, "On the Intentionality of Consciousness," in his *Studies in Phenomenology and Psychology* (Evanston, Ill.: Northwestern University Press, 1966), pp. 124–40.

11. Henry James, *The Lesson of Balzac* (Boston: Houghton Mifflin Co., 1905), p. 110.

12. Henry James, *The Art of the Novel*, p. 327 (hereafter cited as *AN*).

13. Husserl, *Cartesian Meditations*, pp. 44–45.

14. Kockelmans, "Intentional and Constitutive Analyses," pp. 140–42.

15. Joseph J. Kockelmans, "What Is Phenomenology?," in *Phenomenology*, ed. Kockelmans, pp. 30–31. See Emmanuel Levinas, "Intuition of Essences," in *Phenomenology*, ed. Kockelmans, pp. 83–105, and the entire volume from which this excerpt is taken, *Théorie de l'intuition dans la phenomenologie de Husserl* (Paris: J. Vrain, 1963); Suzanne Bachelard, *A Study of Husserl's Formal and Transcendental Logic*, trans. Lester E. Embree (1957; reprint, Evanston, Ill.: Northwestern University Press, 1968), pp. 171–97. Also see Husserl, *Ideas*, pp. 155–67, 176–85, 191–93, and *Cartesian Meditations*, pp. 69–72.

16. Few topics in phenomenology have been so heatedly and widely debated as the question of Husserl's idealism. In works cited in the previous note, for example, Suzanne Bachelard willingly accepts the idealist implications of the "eidetic reduction," while Levinas attempts to save Husserl's notion of "essence" from the charge of Platonism. Also see Jean Hering, "Bemerkungen über das Wesen, die Wesenheit, und die Idee," *Jahrbuch für Philosophie und phänomenologische Forschung* 4 (1921): 495–543. Some of the more important and interesting arguments against idealism include Roman Ingarden, "Bemerkungen zum Problem Idealismus-Realismus," *Jahrbuch für Philosophie und phänomenologische Forschung* (Supplement, 1929), pp. 159–90; Jean-Paul Sartre, *The Transcendence of the Ego*, trans. Forrest Williams and Robert Kirkpatrick (1936–37; reprint, New York: Farrar, Straus and Giroux, 1957); and Theodore W. Adorno, "Husserl and the Problem of Idealism," *Journal of Philosophy* 37 (1940): 5–18.

17. William James, *The Will to Believe*, pp. 14–15.

18. William James, *Essays in Radical Empiricism*, p. 11, and *Pragmatism*, p. 167.

19. Georges Poulet, *The Metamorphoses of the Circle*, p. 310.

20. Mark Spilka, "Henry James and Walter Besant: 'The Art of Fiction' Controversy," *Novel* 6, no. 2 (Winter 1973): 112.

21. Merleau-Ponty, *Phenomenology of Perception*, p. 304.

22. Ibid.

23. William James, *Talks to Teachers* (1899; reprint, New York: W. W. Norton and Co., 1958), p. 169.

24. William James, *Pragmatism*, pp. 17–19.

25. Henry James, *The Lesson of Balzac*, pp. 80–82. See Heidegger, *Being and Time*, pp. 172–79.

26. William James, *The Principles of Psychology*, 2 vols. (1890; reprint, New York: Dover Publications, 1950), 1:289.

27. Henry James, *The Notebooks of Henry James*, ed. F. O. Matthiessen and Kenneth B. Murdock (New York: Oxford University Press, 1947), p. 18.

28. Henry James, *A Small Boy and Others* (1913), in *Henry James: Autobiography*, ed. Dupee, p. 137.

29. For other interpretations of how Henry James's notion of the impression unites the subjective and the objective, see John Paterson, "Henry James: The Romance of the Real," in *The Novel as Faith* (Boston: Gambit, 1973), pp. 30–34, and James E. Miller, Jr., "Henry James in Reality," *Critical Inquiry* 2, no. 3 (Spring 1976): 585–604.

30. William James, *Principles of Psychology*, 1:237.

31. I do not mean to imply, of course, that James first decided on the problems of perception he wanted to address and then created a suitable plot to express philosophical insights in a sort of allegory. He no doubt followed a reverse course, developing fictions for the sake of their inherent interest to him but exploring issues in them that we can identify after the fact as phenomenological in significance. My wish is simply to emphasize the importance of the impression as an intentional foundation that helps explain how James's achievement organizes itself.

32. Henry James, "Taine's English Literature" (1872), excerpted in *Theory of Fiction*, ed. Miller, p. 326.

33. Henry James, "Nana" (1880), excerpted in *Theory of Fiction*, ed. Miller, p. 135.

34. Henry James, *The Lesson of Balzac*, pp. 97–98.

35. See Iser, *The Implied Reader*, pp. 291–94, for an explanation of intersubjectivity in reading. According to Iser, "in reading we must think the thoughts of someone else." Two levels of consciousness consequently play off each other—"the alien 'me'" I have become by adopting the text's subjectivity and "the real, virtual 'me'" that I remain even as I enter another world. This duplication of consciousness opens us up to new modes of experience at the same time that it allows us to formulate more explicitly who we are by confronting us with otherness at the heart of our being.

36. See Peirce, "The Fixation of Belief," in *Philosophical Writings*, pp. 5–22.

37. Henry James, "The Lesson of the Master," in *The Novels and Tales of Henry James*, 15:22.

38. Robert Louis Stevenson, "A Humble Remonstrance" (1884), in *Henry James and Robert Louis Stevenson: A Record of Friendship and Criticism*, ed. Janet Adam Smith (London: Rupert Hart-Davis, 1948), pp. 89–92, 100.

39. Roman Ingarden, *The Literary Work of Art*, trans. George G. Gra-

bowicz (1931; reprint, Evanston, Ill.: Northwestern University Press, 1973), p. 180. For a chapter-by-chapter survey of Ingarden's seminal book, see Magliola, *Phenomenology and Literature*, pp. 107–41. René Wellek and Austin Warren rely more heavily on Ingarden than their brief mention of him would suggest in *Theory of Literature*, 3d ed. (New York: Harcourt, Brace and World, 1962), pp. 151–52, 156. And Ingarden rightly protests that their description of his theory is incorrect (see *The Literary Work of Art*, pp. lxxviii–lxxxiii).

40. Quoted by Matthiessen in *The James Family*, p. 324; William James, *The Principles of Psychology*, 1:285–87.

41. Ingarden, *The Literary Work of Art*, p. 159. This work is the source for my remarks that follow on Ingarden's theory of representation. See pp. 246–54 for his discussion of "spots of indeterminacy" and pp. 255–87 for his explanation of how aspects make representation possible. For an interesting critique of Ingarden's notion of indeterminacy, see Iser, *The Act of Reading*, pp. 170–79.

42. Iser, *The Implied Reader*, p. 283.

43. See Ian Watt, *The Rise of the Novel* (Berkeley: University of California Press, 1957), p. 32; Erich Auerbach, *Mimesis*, trans. Willard R. Trask (Princeton: Princeton University Press, 1953).

44. Henry James, *The Lesson of Balzac*, pp. 78–79.

45. See Ingarden, *The Literary Work of Art*, pp. 336–43. Ingarden examines the aesthetic experience and the phenomenon of reading at greater length in *The Cognition of the Literary Work of Art*, trans. Ruth Ann Crowley and Kenneth R. Olson (1937; reprint, Evanston, Ill.: Northwestern University Press, 1973).

46. Henry James, "The Novels of George Eliot" (1866), excerpted in *Theory of Fiction*, ed. Miller, p. 321.

47. Henry James, "Alexandre Dumas" (1866), excerpted in Miller, ed., *Theory of Fiction*, p. 294.

48. Stevenson, "A Humble Remonstrance," p. 93.

49. See Ingarden, *The Cognition of the Literary Work*, pp. 168–331.

50. Henry James, "The Figure in the Carpet," in *The Novels and Tales of Henry James*, 15:236.

51. Henry James, "The New Novel," in *Notes on Novelists* (New York: Charles Scribner's Sons, 1914), p. 344.

52. Iser, *The Act of Reading*, p. 181.

53. See Ingarden, *The Literary Work of Art*, pp. lxxxii, 30–31, and *The Cognition of the Literary Work*, entire, for Ingarden's theory of value. Also see Ingarden, *Erlebnis, Kunstwerk, und Wert* (Tübingen: Max Niemeyer, 1969).

54. See Ingarden, *The Literary Work of Art*, pp. 160–73, for Ingarden's explanation of quasi-judgments. Käte Hamburger attacks Ingarden's notion of quasi-judgments, although for different reasons than I will give, in *Die Logik der Dichtung* (Stuttgart: Klett, 1957), pp. 14–17. For Ingarden's reply, see *The Literary Work of Art*, pp. 173–81.

55. Wellek, "James's Literary Theory," p. 299.

56. Henry James, "Ivan Turgenev" (1874), excerpted in *Theory of Fiction*, ed. Miller, p. 296.

57. See Heidegger, *Being and Time*, pp. 95–102, 135–44, 225–73.

58. Henry James, "Charles Baudelaire" (1876), excerpted in *Theory of Fiction*, ed. Miller, p. 307.

59. Henry James, "Charles de Bernard and Gustave Flaubert" (1876), excerpted in *Theory of Fiction*, ed. Miller, p. 304.

60. Ricoeur, *Freud and Philosophy*, p. 12.

61. Paul Ricoeur, *The Symbolism of Evil*, trans. Emerson Buchanan (1960; reprint, Boston: Beacon Press, 1969), pp. 152, 13.

62. Ricoeur, *Freud and Philosophy*, p. 46.

63. Ricoeur, "Metaphor and the Main Problem of Hermeneutics," pp. 143–44. Also see Ricoeur, *The Rule of Metaphor*, trans. Robert Czerny (1975; reprint, Toronto: University of Toronto Press, 1977), particularly pp. 216–56.

64. Henry James, "The Question of Our Speech," published with *The Lesson of Balzac*, p. 10.

65. Henry James, "The New Novel," p. 315.

66. Henry James, "The Future of the Novel" (1899), in *Theory of Fiction*, ed. Miller, p. 343.

CHAPTER 3

1. Henry James, *Notes of a Son and Brother* in *Henry James: Autobiography*, ed. Dupee, pp. 454–55.

2. Jean-Paul Sartre, *The Psychology of Imagination*, trans. anon. (1940; reprint, Secaucus, N.J.: Citadel Press, 1972), p. 171.

3. See Heidegger, *Being and Time*, pp. 319–35. Also see Stanley Rosen, "Thinking about Nothing," in *Heidegger and Modern Philosophy*, ed. Michael Murray (New Haven: Yale University Press, 1978), pp. 116–37; William J. Richardson, *Heidegger: Through Phenomenology to Thought* (The Hague: Martinus Nijhoff, 1963), pp. 8–9, 38–39, 72–73.

4. See Sartre, *Being and Nothingness*, pp. 33–85.

5. Sartre, *Psychology of Imagination*, pp. 18, 261, 263, 270. Also see Edward S. Casey, *Imagining: A Phenomenological Study* (Bloomington: Indiana University Press, 1976). Casey offers an interesting criticism of Sartre's theory of imagination. But Casey also reaches the Sartrean conclusion that imagination and freedom are intimately related: "Mind is free—is indeed most free—in imagining" (p. 201). Casey's two chapters on the continuities and discontinuities between imagination and perception are particularly illuminating (pp. 127–73).

6. Quoted by Janet Adam Smith in *Henry James and Robert Louis Stevenson*, p. 35.

7. See Oscar Cargill, *The Novels of Henry James*, pp. 19–21.

8. Nathaniel Hawthorne, *The Marble Faun* (1860; reprint, New York: Signet, 1961), p. 122.

9. Leon Edel, "Introduction" to *Roderick Hudson* (New York: Harper and Brothers, 1960), p. xvii; Dupee, *Henry James*, p. 74.

10. Leon Edel, *Henry James: The Conquest of London, 1870–1881* (Philadelphia: J. B. Lippincott Co., 1962), p. 177; Cargill, *The Novels of Henry James*, p. 29; Dupee, *Henry James*, p. 75.

11. Henry James, *Roderick Hudson* (1875–78; reprint, Harmondsworth, England: Penguin, 1969), pp. 85, 198, 35. All references in the text are to this edition. This paperback edition is, unfortunately, the only reasonably accessible version of the novel in an early, little revised form. I depart here from the standard practice of citing works as they appear in the New York Edition because it seems to me that the relative naiveté of James's earlier prose better suits the subject of imaginative extravagance—a subject that this work and others in his canon portray as the particular province of youthful innocence.

12. See Binswanger, "The Case of Ellen West," in *Existence*, ed. May, pp. 237–364; Binswanger, "Extravagance (*Verstiegenheit*)," in *Being-in-the-World*, ed. Needleman, pp. 342–49; and Binswanger, *Henrik Ibsen und das Problem der Selbstrealisation in der Kunst* (Heidelberg: Lambert Schneider, 1949), entire. Gras has translated an excerpt from the last work as "Ibsen's *The Masterbuilder*" for his *European Literary Theory and Practice*, pp. 185–216. One of the few Anglo-American critics to recognize the importance of this too little-known Swiss psychiatrist, Paul de Man devotes a chapter to Binswanger in *Blindness and Insight* (New York: Oxford University Press, 1971), pp. 36–50. Also see William A. Sadler, Jr., *Existence and Love* (New York: Charles Scribner's Sons, 1969), pp. 115–42.

13. Binswanger, "The Case of Ellen West," pp. 280, 277, 275, 303, and "Extravagance (*Verstiegenheit*)," p. 346.

14. See Sartre, *Psychology of Imagination*, p. 271.

15. Binswanger, "The Case of Ellen West," p. 304.

16. See Gaston Bachelard, *The Poetics of Reverie*, trans. Daniel Russell (1960; reprint, Boston: Beacon Press, 1969), and *The Poetics of Space*. For discussions of Bachelard's aesthetics, see particularly Georges Poulet, "Bachelard et la conscience de soi," *Revue de Metaphysique et la morale* 70 (January–March 1965): 1–26; Eva M. Kushner, "The Critical Method of Gaston Bachelard," in *Myth and Symbol*, ed. Bernice Slote (Lincoln: University of Nebraska Press, 1963), pp. 39–50.

17. Bachelard, *Poetics of Space*, p. xxxi; Binswanger, "The Case of Ellen West," p. 303. Nietzsche explains his distinction between the Apollonian and the Dionysian in *The Birth of Tragedy* (1872).

18. See Binswanger, "The Case of Ellen West," p. 275.

19. Gaston Bachelard, *The Psychoanalysis of Fire*, trans. Alan C. M. Ross (1938; reprint, Boston: Beacon Press, 1964), p. 100.

20. Binswanger, "Ibsen's *The Masterbuilder*," p. 200, and "The Case of Ellen West," p. 278.

21. Binswanger, "Extravagance (*Verstiegenheit*)," pp. 342–43.

22. See Binswanger, "Ibsen's *The Masterbuilder*," as well as his complete monograph on Ibsen. Also see Binswanger, "Extravagance (*Verstiegenheit*)," pp. 342–49, and "The Case of Ellen West," p. 277.

23. Binswanger, "The Case of Ellen West," p. 312.

24. Leon Edel, *Henry James: The Conquest of London*, p. 175.

25. René Girard, *Deceit, Desire, and the Novel*, trans. Yvonne Freccero (1961; reprint, Baltimore: Johns Hopkins University Press, 1965), pp. 63, 65, 53ff., 17.

26. Binswanger, "Extravagance (*Verstiegenheit*)," p. 347.

27. Binswanger, "The Case of Ellen West," pp. 305, 307.

28. Binswanger, "The Existential Analysis School of Thought," in *Existence*, ed. May, p. 194, and "The Case of Ellen West," p. 306.

29. Binswanger, "Ibsen's *The Masterbuilder*," p. 190.

30. Henry James, *The Art of the Novel*, pp. 12–13.

31. See Binswanger, "The Existential Analysis School of Thought," pp. 197–98, "The Case of Ilse," p. 225, and "The Case of Ellen West," p. 354.

32. See Binswanger, "The Case of Ellen West," pp. 312–14, and Heidegger, *Being and Time*, pp. 319–35, 341–48.

33. See Heidegger, *Being and Time*, pp. 216–17.

34. Binswanger, "Extravagance (*Verstiegenheit*)," pp. 347–48, and *Henrik Ibsen*, p. 31 (translation mine).

35. Cargill, *The Novels of Henry James*, p. 23.

36. This is one of the consequences of what Heidegger has observed in explaining that existence "is in each case mine (*je meines*)." See *Being and Time*, pp. 67–71. It is also the issue at the heart of what Dupee calls the "adoption" theme in James—referring to the act of "adopting" another to live through him or her—and of "the question of one's right to devise the destiny of another" that Cargill identifies as "the central theme" of *Roderick Hudson* (see Dupee, *Henry James*, p. 75, and Cargill, *The Novels of Henry James*, p. 31). Also see Chapter 5 below.

37. Richard Poirier, *The Comic Sense of Henry James* (New York: Oxford University Press, 1967), p. 27; Edel, *Henry James: The Conquest of London*, pp. 176–77; Ora Segal, *The Lucid Reflector: The Observer in Henry James's Fiction* (New Haven: Yale University Press, 1969), p. 111.

38. See Søren Kierkegaard, *Either/Or*, vol. 1, trans. David F. and Lillian Marvin Swenson, and vol. 2, trans. Walter Lowrie (1843; reprint, Princeton: Princeton University Press, 1944).

39. Ricoeur, *Freud and Philosophy*, p. 36.

40. Iser, *The Implied Reader*, pp. 112–13. Also see *The Act of Reading*, pp. 180–231.

41. See Poirier, *The Comic Sense of Henry James*, pp. 11–12.

CHAPTER 4

1. Henry James, *Notebooks*, p. 67.

2. Henry James, *Partial Portraits*, p. 89; from a speech in *"Daniel Deronda*: A Conversation" made by Constantius, the writer who represents James's position in the argument.

3. Henry James, *The Ambassadors*, in *The Novels and Tales of Henry James*, 21:217; "Madame de Mauves," in *The Novels and Tales of Henry James*, 13:318–19.

4. Merleau-Ponty, *Phenomenology of Perception*, p. 455. Of the many studies of freedom and necessity in existential phenomenology, see particularly Calvin O. Schrag, *Existence and Freedom: Towards an Ontology of Human Finitude* (Evanston, Ill.: Northwestern University Press, 1961).

5. See Heidegger, *Being and Time*, pp. 172–79, 293–99. For a discussion of some further implications of what "thrownness" means for Heidegger, see Otto Pöggeler, "Being as Appropriation," in *Heidegger and Modern Philosophy*, ed. Murray, pp. 84–115. Also see Richardson, *Heidegger*, pp. 37–38, 64, 74, 181.

6. Merleau-Ponty, *Phenomenology of Perception*, p. 438.

7. See Don Ihde, *Hermeneutic Phenomenology: The Philosophy of Paul Ricoeur* (Evanston, Ill.: Northwestern University Press, 1971), pp. 56–58.

8. See Ricoeur, *The Symbolism of Evil*, pp. 151–57.

9. Henry James, *The Art of the Novel*, p. 48.

10. Dorothy Van Ghent, *The English Novel: Form and Function* (New York: Rinehart and Co., 1953), p. 212; Cargill, *The Novels of Henry James*, pp. 88, 97–98; Poirier, *The Comic Sense of Henry James*, p. 246; Morton D. Zabel, "Introduction" to Henry James, *In the Cage and Other Tales*, ed. Morton D. Zabel (New York: W. W. Norton and Co., 1969), p. 13. For similar readings, also see Arnold Kettle, *An Introduction to the English Novel*, 2 vols. (London: Hutchinson, 1953), 2:19; Tony Tanner, "The Fearful Self: Henry James's *The Portrait of a Lady*," in *Henry James*, ed. Tanner, pp. 143–59; Dupee, *Henry James*, pp. 111–12; Philip Rahv, *Image and Idea* (1949; reprint, Norfolk, Conn.: New Directions, 1957), pp. 51–57.

11. Quoted by Ralph Barton Perry in *The Thought and Character of William James: Briefer Version* (1935, 1948; reprint, New York: Harper and Row, 1964), p. 121.

12. William James, *The Varieties of Religious Experience* (1902; reprint, New York: Collier, 1961), pp. 140–41, 120, 150. See Ricoeur, *The Symbolism of Evil*, p. 350; *Freud and Philosophy*, pp. 524–31; *The Conflict of Interpretations*, ed. Don Ihde (Evanston, Ill.: Northwestern University Press, 1974), pp. xx, 402–24, 440–67.

13. Henry James, *The Portrait of a Lady*, in *The Novels and Tales of Henry James*, 3:68. All references in the text are from this edition and will cite the work's two volumes as "1" and "2."

14. Kierkegaard, *Concept of Dread*, p. 110.

15. William James, *Essays in Radical Empiricism*, p. 88, and *Principles of Psychology*, 2:534–49. Sartre adopts Bachelard's notion of the "coefficient of adversity" in *Being and Nothingness*, p. 428.

16. Dupee, *Henry James*, p. 105.

17. For similar interpretations of Isabel's imagination, see Richard Chase, *The American Novel and Its Tradition* (Garden City, N.Y.: Doubleday and Co., 1957), p. 129, and Poirier, *The Comic Sense of Henry James*, p. 213.

18. William James, *The Will to Believe*, p. 131.

19. For example, see Krook, *The Ordeal of Consciousness*, pp. 28–37.

20. See Erik H. Erikson, *Identity: Youth and Crisis* (New York: W. W. Norton and Co., 1968), pp. 135–38. Here and elsewhere, I regard Erikson as an existential psychologist even though he does not understand himself as such. His effort to transcend Freudian determinism and to orient psychoanalysis toward the entire life cycle often seems to lead him, I think, toward the positions of Heidegger, Binswanger, and Ricoeur. For a similar interpretation of Erikson, see Sadler, *Existence and Love*, pp. 155–60.

21. See Heidegger, *Being and Time*, pp. 182–88, 239–40, 305–11.

22. See Ricoeur, "Structure, Word, Event," in *The Conflict of Interpretations*, ed. Ihde, pp. 79–96. Two useful accounts of the complicated, controversial relations between phenomenology and structuralism are Magliola, "Phenomenology Confronts Parisian Structuralism," in his *Phenomenology and Literature*, pp. 81–93, and Robert Detweiler, "Phenomenological and Structuralist Literary Criticism," in *Story, Sign, and Self* (Philadelphia: Fortress, 1978), pp. 165–218.

23. See Roland Barthes, *Elements of Semiology*, trans. Annette Lavers and Colin Smith (1964; reprint, Boston: Beacon Press, 1970), and *Mythologies*, trans. Annette Lavers (1957; reprint, New York: Hill and Wang, 1972). Also see Umberto Eco, *A Theory of Semiotics* (Bloomington: Indiana University Press, 1976).

24. Poirier, *The Comic Sense*, p. 206.

25. Heidegger, *Being and Time*, p. 346.

26. See Kierkegaard, *Concept of Dread*, pp. 37–41, 139–45.

27. Ricoeur, *The Symbolism of Evil*, p. 312.

28. See Sartre, *Being and Nothingness*, pp. 86–116.

29. Poirier, *The Comic Sense*, p. 219.

30. Henry James, *Notebooks*, p. 15.

31. See Iser, *The Implied Reader*, pp. 277–82, and *The Act of Reading*, pp. 108–18.

32. Ricoeur, *Freud and Philosophy*, pp. 507, 547. Also see Ricoeur's *Fallible Man*, trans. Charles Kelbley (1960; reprint, Chicago: Henry Regnery Co., 1965), pp. 161–91.

33. See Sartre, *Being and Nothingness*, pp. 340–400.

34. See Heidegger, *Being and Time*, pp. 91–107, 149–68.

35. Kierkegaard, *Concept of Dread*, p. 110. For an extended analysis of images of opening and closing in *The Portrait of a Lady*, see Charles R. An-

derson, *Person, Place, and Thing in Henry James's Novels* (Durham, N.C.: Duke University Press, 1977), pp. 80–123.

36. Ricoeur, *The Symbolism of Evil*, p. 156.

37. See Heidegger, *Being and Time*, p. 373.

38. Henry James, *The Art of the Novel*, p. 57.

39. See Merleau-Ponty, *Phenomenology of Perception*, pp. 3–63.

40. Henry James, *The Art of the Novel*, p. 57.

41. William James quotes this phrase of Kierkegaard's in *Essays in Radical Empiricism*, p. 70.

42. See Merleau-Ponty, *Phenomenology of Perception*, pp. vii–xxi, 23, 30, 250, 369–409, and *The Primacy of Perception*, pp. 12–27.

43. See G. W. F. Hegel, *The Phenomenology of Mind*, trans. J. B. Baillie (1807, 1910; reprint, New York: Harper and Row, 1967), pp. 229–40. See Spiegelberg, *The Phenomenological Movement*, 1:12–15, and 2:413–15, for a judicious examination of the relations between Hegelianism and modern phenomenology, particularly the French strain.

44. See William James, *The Will to Believe*, pp. 283–84.

45. Sartre, *Being and Nothingness*, pp. 702–3.

46. See Heidegger, *Being and Time*, pp. 340–48, 376, 385–89.

47. See Erikson, *Identity*, p. 139. Erikson regards the conflict between "integrity" and "despair" as the critical dilemma of old age. But he also argues, according to his "epigenetic" principle of psychosexual development, that this conflict is involved in every stage of life. For Erikson, "integrity" results from coming to terms with the prospect of death in much the same way that Heidegger describes the achievement of existential wholeness (or *Ganzsein*) as the consequence of "being-towards-death" (or *Sein-zum-Tode*) as one's "ownmost, non-relational possibility."

48. *A Doll's House* made its English debut on 7 June 1889. See Samuel Hynes, *The Edwardian Turn of Mind* (Princeton: Princeton University Press, 1968), p. 174.

49. William Veeder, *Henry James—the Lessons of the Master* (Chicago: University of Chicago Press, 1975), pp. 167, 182. Also see Annette Niemtzow, "Marriage and the New Woman in *The Portrait of a Lady*," *American Literature* 47, no. 3 (November 1975): 377–95.

50. Niemtzow cites a number of libidinally charged passages in the novel to refute the claim that Isabel lacks sexual desire. She argues that Isabel "possesses an almost obscene—certainly not frigid—imagination, filled with disturbing sexual fantasies" ("Marriage and the New Woman," p. 386). No less than "frigidity," however, an "obscene imagination" is a sign of an inadequate understanding and acceptance of one's sexuality.

51. William James, *The Will to Believe*, p. 202.

52. Henry James, *Notebooks*, p. 18.

53. Merleau-Ponty, *The Primacy of Perception*, p. 6.

54. The ending of *The Portrait* is an example of James's typical refusal to satisfy what Conrad calls "the desire for finality, for which our hearts yearn

with a longing greater than the longing for the loaves and fishes of this earth. . . . His books end as an episode in life ends. You remain with the sense of the life going on" ("An Appreciation," p. 17). The characteristic openness of the Jamesian ending has some other consequences beyond those that my analysis of the conclusion of *The Portrait* has specified. By frustrating the reader's desire for closure, James's inconclusive conclusions simultaneously stimulate and discourage our drive to fit all the elements of the work together into a coherent whole—promoting a reconsideration of patterns already constituted but preventing any finally definitive arrangement of the novel's parts into a complete, stable design. This blockage calls upon the reader to reflect about the processes of understanding that it has interrupted. These processes ordinarily go unnoticed because they do their work successfully. The reader's inability to discover finality and completeness at the conclusion of *The Portrait* draws attention to the ordinary workings of understanding by disrupting them—that is, by defying our effort to make aspects cohere in a uniform whole and by thwarting our tendency to fill in hidden sides that are not immediately given to consciousness (in this case, what Isabel is thinking as she leaves for Rome and what will happen there). Consistency-building and the projection of hidden sides are epistemological processes that James often takes as explicit dramatic themes in his novels; his open endings make them themes for the reader's reflection by foregrounding them in the experience of construing the text.

The blockage in the reader's quest for a final consistency also refutes what Iser calls "the classical norm of interpretation"—the notion that meaning is "a detachable message," a "thing" hidden in the text, rather than a process and an event (see *The Act of Reading*, pp. 3–19, where Iser introduces his argument through an analysis of James's "Figure in the Carpet"). The Jamesian open ending can have a moral function as well. It can encourage the meditation that James considers to be "the most the moralists can do for us." For example, by depriving the reader of any last word about Isabel Archer, James incites us to reflect about the reasons why her story is unfinished and her future indeterminate—reasons that, as I argued, have to do with the logic of the servile will. By not tying things up at the level of plot, James thus encourages the reader to reflect at more profound levels about existential issues that may seem all the more pressing because they are not yet fully resolved.

CHAPTER 5

1. Philip Rahv, "Attitudes toward Henry James," and André Gide, "Henry James," both essays in *The Question of Henry James*, ed. F. W. Dupee (New York: Henry Holt and Co., 1945), pp. 279, 251.

2. Henry James, *The Question of Our Speech*, p. 10.

3. Henry James, *The Art of the Novel*, p. 330.

4. See Husserl, *Cartesian Meditations*, pp. 108–20. Two particularly

helpful analyses of Husserl's response to the problem of solipsism are Ricoeur, *Husserl*, pp. 115–42, and Quentin Lauer, "The Other Explained Intentionally," in *Phenomenology: Its Genesis and Prospect* (1958; reprint, New York: Harper and Row, 1965), pp. 148–62. For an interesting, historically important study of empathy and intersubjectivity, see Max Scheler, *The Nature of Sympathy*, trans. Peter Heath (1913; reprint, London: Routledge and Kegan Paul, 1954).

5. See Merleau-Ponty, *Phenomenology of Perception*, p. 364.

6. See Sartre, *Being and Nothingness*, p. 105; *Saint Genet*, pp. 136, 337.

7. See Ricoeur, *Freud and Philosophy*, p. 545; Merleau-Ponty, *Phenomenology of Perception*, p. 354. Also see "Sartre at Seventy: An Interview," *New York Review of Books*, 7 August 1975, p. 12.

8. Krook, *The Ordeal of Consciousness*, p. 240. For supporting views, see Quentin Anderson, *The American Henry James*, pp. 281–346, and Manfred Mackenzie, *Communities of Honor and Love in Henry James* (Cambridge: Harvard University Press, 1976), pp. 169–81.

9. Firebaugh, "The Ververs," pp. 404, 401, 409. Also see Maxwell Geismar, *Henry James and the Jacobites* (Boston: Houghton Mifflin Co., 1963), p. 329; Matthiessen, *The Major Phase*, p. 100; F. R. Leavis, *The Great Tradition* (1948; reprint, London: Chatto and Windus, 1955), p. 159; Jean Kimball, "Henry James's Last Portrait of a Lady: Charlotte Stant in *The Golden Bowl*," *American Literature* 28, no. 4 (January 1957):449–68.

10. See Walter Wright, "Maggie Verver: Neither Saint nor Witch," in *Henry James*, ed. Tanner, pp. 316–26; Cargill, *The Novels of Henry James*, pp. 404–5; Sallie Sears, *The Negative Imagination: Form and Perspective in the Novels of Henry James* (Ithaca: Cornell University Press, 1968), pp. 168–87.

11. See Heidegger, *Being and Time*, pp. 153–63, 225–56, 312–48. Also see Schrag, *Existence and Freedom*, particularly pp. 40–49, 65–66; Richardson, *Heidegger*, pp. 40, 59, 68, 71–74.

12. See Sartre, *Being and Nothingness*, pp. 301–558; *Saint Genet*, pp. 17–48. For examples of the controversy that Sartre's negative picture of personal relations inspired, see Emmanuel Levinas, *Totality and Infinity*, trans. Alphonso Lingis (1961; reprint, Pittsburgh: Duquesne University Press, 1969); Jean Wahl, *Philosophies of Existence*, trans. F. M. Lory (1959; reprint, New York: Schocken Books, 1969), pp. 80–81, 101–2.

13. See Heidegger, *Being and Time*, pp. 153–68; Merleau-Ponty, *Phenomenology of Perception*, p. 361; "Sartre at Seventy," p. 12.

14. "Sartre at Seventy," p. 12. Also see Sartre, *Saint Genet*, pp. 281–82.

15. Sartre, *Saint Genet*, p. 518n.

16. See Henry James, *Notebooks*, pp. 194, 233.

17. Matthiessen, *The Major Phase*, p. 90.

18. Henry James, *The Golden Bowl*, in *The Novels and Tales of Henry James*, 23:10. All references in the text are from this edition and will cite the work's two volumes as "1" and "2."

19. See Heidegger, *Being and Time*, pp. 102–7.

20. Sartre, *Saint Genet*, p. 550.

21. Ibid., p. 578.

22. Merleau-Ponty, *Phenomenology of Perception*, p. 357.

23. Henry James, *The Art of the Novel*, p. 327.

24. My analysis here is indebted to Iser, *The Implied Reader*, pp. 291–94. *The Golden Bowl* is marked by much more technical and epistemological variety than James admits when he claims in his preface that the consciousness of the Prince controls the first volume, except for Fanny Assingham's interludes, and then yields to the consciousness of the Princess in the second (see *The Art of the Novel*, pp. 329–30). For some inexplicable reason, most critics have accepted James's claim without examination. Thus Segal—ordinarily a close and careful reader—argues that "James presents the first half of the international domestic drama exclusively from the Prince's point of view" (*The Lucid Reflector*, p. 191). Actually, different registers are announced in the opening words of each of the first volume's three books—Book First: "The Prince had always liked his London" (1:3); Book Second: "Adam Verver, at Fawns, . . ." (1:125); Book Third: "Charlotte, halfway up the 'monumental' staircase, . . ." (1:245). And within each book, sometimes within the space of a few pages, James varies his registers still further, with the result, as I have argued, of making his characters alternately transparent and opaque by making them alternately Self and Other (see 1:138–40, for example, during Adam's reflections after Mrs. Rance's intrusion, where Adam cedes to the Prince who cedes in turn to Adam).

25. For more extensive studies of Fanny in particular and the Jamesian confidante in general, see Segal, *The Lucid Reflector*, especially pp. 193–210, and Sister Corona Sharp, *The Confidante in Henry James* (Notre Dame, Ind.: University of Notre Dame Press, 1963).

26. Henry James, *Notebooks*, p. 131. The point that follows is based in part on Freud's essay, "The Dissolution of the Oedipus Complex" (1924), in *The Standard Edition of the Complete Psychological Works*, ed. James Strachey (London: Hogarth Press, 1955), 19:173–82.

27. See Heidegger, *Being and Time*, pp. 158–59.

28. For example, see Charlotte's and Fanny's conversation at the embassy ball (1:258–60). Charlotte says that Maggie "likes to arrange" and is "always arranging" to be alone with Adam to "make up" the "arrears" that have accumulated during his honeymoon with his new wife in America. "Tonight for instance has been practically an arrangement," Charlotte continues, because she and the Prince have been left alone at the party so that Maggie could join her father. This arrangement, she explains, is "what I mean therefore by being 'placed.'" To which Fanny responds:

"So placed that *you* have to arrange?"

"Certainly I have to arrange."

"And the Prince also—if the effect for him is the same?"

"Really I think not less."

"And does he arrange," Mrs. Assingham asked, "to make up *his* arrears?"

Maggie does not understand, of course, how Charlotte's and Amerigo's arrangements differ from hers because she does not yet know that they might have "arrears to make up" because of their earlier intimacy. We should also note that Charlotte and the Prince are reified once again by being "arranged" and "placed" and that they reassert their freedom and subjectivity by "arranging" on their own.

29. See Merleau-Ponty, *Phenomenology of Perception*, pp. 361, 364; Sartre, *Being and Nothingness*, pp. 340–400.

30. A relatively rare exception, John Carlos Rowe does examine *how* the bowl signifies in *Henry Adams and Henry James*, pp. 44–45. Although more semiotic than phenomenological, his analysis of the bowl's signifying ability is compatible with mine.

31. William James, *Essays in Radical Empiricism*, p. 43; Merleau-Ponty, *Phenomenology of Perception*, p. 348. On the importance of objects as intersubjective mediators in James, see particularly Anderson, *Person, Place, and Thing*, p. 4.

32. See Ingarden, *The Literary Work of Art*, pp. 331–55, where he argues that a literary work "lives" in its concretizations and can thus be said to change to the extent that they change.

33. See Ricoeur, *Freud and Philosophy*, p. 12.

34. Ricoeur, *The Conflict of Interpretations*, p. 17.

35. See Peirce, *Philosophical Writings*, p. 31.

36. As we have seen in our analysis of the opacity that Maggie must penetrate in her talks with Fanny and the Prince about the bowl, not all dialogue in the late James is the "peculiarly solipsistic communing of self with self" that Ruth B. Yeazell finds dominant—a kind of conversation, as she explains, in which the interlocutors "often talk in sentence fragments— extending and completing one another's thoughts as if they were not so much separate persons as parts of a single self." See her "Talking in James," in *Language and Knowledge in the Late Novels of Henry James* (Chicago: University of Chicago Press, 1976), pp. 71, 69. Yeazell rejects Beach's rough distinction between the dialogue of "confederates" and "antagonists" in James, the former relatively transparent to each other and the latter relatively opaque (see *Language and Knowledge*, p. 138). Rather than reject such a distinction completely, though, it might do more justice to the varieties of talk in James to chart them along a continuum from the mutual transparency of collaboration to the mutual opacity of misunderstanding and conflict. Somewhere between these two poles, most talk in James is a mixture of intimate comprehension and mutual mystification.

37. Richard E. Palmer, *Hermeneutics: Interpretation Theory in Schleiermacher, Dilthey, Heidegger, and Gadamer* (Evanston, Ill.: Northwestern University Press, 1969), p. 9; Peirce, *Philosophical Writings*, p. 305.

38. See Heidegger, *Being and Time*, pp. 188–95.

39. Merleau-Ponty, *Phenomenology of Perception*, p. 347. Also see Thomas Langan, *Merleau-Ponty's Critique of Reason* (New Haven: Yale University Press, 1966), pp. 72–88.

40. This is in line with the argument that Sears makes forcefully in *The Negative Imagination*, pp. 220–22.

41. See Binswanger, "The Case of Ilse," in *Existence*, ed. May, p. 220.

42. Frederick C. Crews, *The Tragedy of Manners: Moral Drama in the Later Novels of Henry James* (New Haven: Yale University Press, 1957), p. 109. He quotes *The Golden Bowl*, 2:367.

43. Sartre, *Being and Nothingness*, p. 131.

44. Philip M. Weinstein, *Henry James and the Requirements of the Imagination* (Cambridge: Harvard University Press, 1971), p. 185; Sears, *The Negative Imagination*, p. 219.

45. Dupee, *Henry James*, pp. 228–29.

46. See Heidegger, *Being and Time*, pp. 172–79, 225–35.

47. Sartre, *Saint Genet*, p. 54.

48. See Krook, *The Ordeal of Consciousness*, p. 266.

49. See Michel Foucault, *Madness and Civilization*, trans. Richard Howard (1961; reprint, New York: Vintage Books, 1973), particularly pp. ix–xii, 63–64, 82–84, 199–220, 259–60, 279–85. Although Foucault's work is a study of how madness was defined in a particular historical period, I give his theory of scapegoating in the present tense for rhetorical convenience and because the process he identifies has transhistorical relevance.

50. See Sartre, *Saint Genet*, pp. 17–48.

51. René Girard, *Violence and the Sacred*, trans. Patrick Gregory (1972; reprint, Baltimore: Johns Hopkins University Press, 1977), p. 8.

52. Weinstein, *The Requirements of the Imagination*, p. 184.

53. Henry James, *The Art of the Novel*, pp. 202–3.

54. William James, *Pragmatism*, p. 97.

CHAPTER 6

1. Henry James, *Partial Portraits*, pp. 379–80.

2. Ford Madox Hueffer (Ford), *Henry James: A Critical Study* (London: Martin Secker, 1913), p. 22.

3. Henry James, *Letters*, 1:138.

4. Geismar, *Henry James and the Jacobites*, p. 7.

5. Van Wyck Brooks, *The Pilgrimage of Henry James* (New York: E. P. Dutton and Co., 1925), pp. 106, 110.

6. Rahv, "Attitudes toward Henry James," p. 279.

7. Henry James, "The Great Good Place," in *The Novels and Tales of Henry James*, 16:251.

8. See Herbert Marcuse, "The Concept of Essence" (1936), in *Negations: Essays in Critical Theory*, trans. Jeremy J. Shapiro (Boston: Beacon Press, 1969), pp. 43–87. More recently, for a similar argument see Max W. Wartofsky, "Consciousness, Praxis, and Reality: Marxism vs. Phenomenology," in *Interdisciplinary Phenomenology*, ed. Don Ihde and Richard M. Zaner (The Hague: Martinus Nijhoff, 1977), pp. 133–51.

9. Mikel Dufrenne, *The Notion of the "A Priori,"* trans. Edward S. Casey (1959; reprint, Evanston, Ill.: Northwestern University Press, 1966), p. 168.

10. Paul Ricoeur, "The Political Paradox," in *Existential Phenomenology and Political Theory*, ed. Hwa Yol Jung (Chicago: Henry Regnery Co., 1972), p. 347.

11. Quoted in Jean-Paul Sartre, *Search for a Method*, p. xviii. For more on the relation between Marxism and phenomenology, see Sartre, *Search for a Method* and *What Is Literature?*; Merleau-Ponty, "Freedom," in *Phenomenology of Perception*, pp. 434–56, and *Sense and Non-Sense*, trans. Hubert L. and Patricia Allen Dreyfus (1948; reprint, Evanston, Ill.: Northwestern University Press, 1964); and Ricoeur, "Work and Word," in *Existential Phenomenology and Political Theory*, pp. 36–64. Also see Fredric Jameson, *Marxism and Form* (Princeton: Princeton University Press, 1971), and Mark Poster, *Existential Marxism in Postwar France* (Princeton: Princeton University Press, 1975).

12. Henry James, *The American Scene* (1907; reprint, Bloomington: Indiana University Press, 1969), pp. 232, 279, 23.

13. We cannot account for these contradictions by invoking James's awareness of the limits to transcendence. Elsewhere we have been concerned with necessary limits to perception, imagination, freedom, and intersubjectivity. In contrast, the limits that James's political views would impose on social relations and history seem relatively arbitrary because they owe more to personal preferences than to the inherent structure of our worlds.

Actually, James's political views do seek to serve transcendence in a certain sense. His nostalgia for a quasi-feudal social order, his Arnoldian reverence for tradition, his preference for the private over the public—all of these elements of his conservative social outlook are part of his desire to go beyond the ugly emptiness of commercial, industrial life. Like Carlyle and Henry Adams, James sees in the past richer, more ennobling meanings and values that go beyond the limits of the present. With its emphasis on the past, however, this kind of social transcendence is at odds with the essentially futural process of going beyond that is so important to such other aspects of James's world as the teleology of the impression or the imagination's wonders.

14. Divergences of this sort between the meanings of an author's works and his self-conscious convictions happen frequently and should remind us of the distinction I made earlier between "intention" and "intentionality." James's "intentions" (or deliberate purposes) as a social commentator do not coincide with the "intentionality" (or meaning) lodged in his art. Intention and intentionality diverge whenever we are self-deceived about our own motives or goals. If these two levels of consciousness did not differ, we could never be deluded about ourselves—as Marx and Freud have shown we so often are. In James's case, however, it is somewhat unusual that his political pronouncements should be at odds with his understanding of the politics of experience as evidenced in the intentionality of his works, since his self-understanding elsewhere can be so accurate.

15. See Lionel Trilling, *The Liberal Imagination* (1950; reprint, Garden City, N.Y.: Anchor Books, 1953), pp. 55–88; Irving Howe, *Politics and the Novel* (1957; reprint, New York: Avon Books, 1970), pp. 143–59, 186–203.

16. See Goldmann, *Towards a Sociology of the Novel*; Hans Robert Jauss, "Literary History as a Challenge to Literary Theory," and Robert Weimann, "Past Significance and Present Meaning in Literary History," both in *New Directions in Literary History*, ed. Ralph Cohen (Baltimore: Johns Hopkins University Press, 1974), pp. 11–42, 43–62. Also see Ian Watt, *The Rise of the Novel*.

17. For my purposes, the differences between Marx's generation and James's (and even ours) or between America and Europe (although *Poynton* is not an international novel) are not essential, however substantial they may be. The social and political understanding that concerns me has to do with patterns of personal relations that have prevailed, with little variation in structure, since the secure establishment of a free-market society based on industrial organization. The forms of alienation and reification have changed over the history of capitalism and may vary with national differences, but their essential structure remains the same.

18. Edmund Wilson, "The Ambiguity of Henry James," in *The Triple Thinkers* (1938; reprint, New York: Farrar, Straus and Giroux, 1976), p. 119.

19. Henry James, *The Art of the Novel*, pp. 126–27.

20. Stephen Spender, *The Destructive Element* (Boston: Houghton Mifflin Co., 1936), p. 62.

21. See Karl Marx on "commodity fetishism" in *Capital*, trans. Samuel Moore and Edward Aveling, 3 vols. (1867; reprint, New York: International Publishers, 1967), 1:71–83.

22. See Cargill, *The Novels of Henry James*, pp. 226–31, 240–41.

23. Henry James, *The American Scene*, p. 96.

24. Karl Marx and Friedrich Engels, *The German Ideology*, trans. C. J. Arthur (1845–46, 1965; reprint, New York: International Publishers, 1970), p. 53. For the sake of terminological clarity, I should point out that the process of "self-objectification" that Marx describes is not the same as the process by which, according to Sartre, the Other's gaze threatens our subjectivity with "objectification."

25. See Marx, *Capital*, 1:35–83, 167–98; Georg Lukács, *History and Class Consciousness*, trans. Rodney Livingstone (1922; reprint, Cambridge: MIT Press, 1971), pp. 83–110; Jameson, *Marxism and Form*, pp. 295–98.

26. Marx, *The German Ideology*, p. 83.

27. Henry James, *The Spoils of Poynton*, in *The Novels and Tales of Henry James*, 10:145. All references in the text are from this edition.

28. Marx, *Capital*, 1:72.

29. Ibid., 1:35–93.

30. "Sartre at Seventy," p. 12.

31. See Ricoeur, "The Political Paradox," and Sartre, *Critique de la raison dialectique* (Paris: Gallimard, 1960). See Jameson, *Marxism and Form*,

pp. 240–74, for a discussion of Sartre's anti-utopian views on the obstacles to community that must remain even after the eradication of economic inequities.

32. Of the many studies of "collectors" and "connoisseurs" in James, see particularly Viola Hopkins Winner, *Henry James and the Visual Arts* (Charlottesville: University of Virginia Press, 1970), pp. 127–69. She rightly argues that "the ultimate test of sensibility for James's characters is not whether they are correct in their aesthetic judgment but whether they also consider things as survivals or as expressions of a common humanity" (p. viii). Also see Anderson, *Person, Place, and Thing*, pp. 3–8.

33. Geismar, *Henry James and the Jacobites*, pp. 441–43.

34. I am referring particularly to Cleanth Brooks, *The Well Wrought Urn* (New York: Harcourt, Brace and World, 1947), and W. K. Wimsatt and Monroe C. Beardsley, *The Verbal Icon* (Lexington: University of Kentucky Press, 1954).

EPILOGUE

1. Henry James, *The Art of the Novel*, p. 3.

2. Ibid., p. 31.

3. Henry James, *The Golden Bowl*, 2:195.

4. Henry James, *Partial Portraits*, pp. 387–88.

5. Henry James, *The Golden Bowl*, 2:345, 243–44.

6. Henry James, *The Ambassadors*, 1:253.

7. Ford Madox Ford, *Joseph Conrad: A Personal Remembrance* (Boston: Little, Brown and Co., 1924), pp. 194–95.

8. Joseph Conrad, *Lord Jim* (1900; reprint, New York: W. W. Norton and Co., 1968), pp. 87, 27.

9. William James, *Pragmatism*, p. 169.

INDEX

Adams, Hazard, 38
Adams, Henry, 235 (n. 13)
Anderson, Quentin, 34–35
Angst, 25, 71, 111
Aristotle, 188
Auerbach, Erich, 60
Austen, Jane, 51

Bachelard, Gaston, xi, 76–78, 104
Balzac, Honoré de, 56, 60
Barthes, Roland, 108
Beach, J. W., 34
Beckett, Samuel, 206
Besant, Walter, 48, 66
Binswanger, Ludwig: "tomb-world," 23, 74, 78–81, 85–86; "ethe-real world," 23, 74–78, 85; on extravagance, 69–70, 73–74, 81–82, 85, 89; on grounded ac-tivity, 78, 81, 89, 93; on inter-subjectivity, 82, 90–91, 173
Blackmur, R. P., 45
Brontë, Charlotte, 51
Brooks, Van Wyck, 187

Care, 19–22, 65–66, 119, 136–86; and society, 20–21, 29–30, 182–83, 196–203; and free-dom, 22, 28–29, 134–35, 144–46, 154–57, 170–81; and extravagance, 90–93, 97
Cargill, Oscar, 9, 73, 101
Carlyle, Thomas, 235 (n. 13)
Coleridge, Samuel Taylor, 46
Conrad, Joseph, 3, 209–10, 229 (n. 54); *Heart of Darkness*, 210; *Lord Jim*, 210
Conventions, 29, 128, 132; and morality, 5–6, 212–13; and ex-pression, 108–9, 114
Crews, Frederick C., 173

Derrida, Jacques, 210–11
Dickens, Charles, 51; *Great Expec-tations*, 20
Dufrenne, Mikel, 188
Dupee, F. W., 17, 34, 73–74, 104, 181

Edel, Leon, 34, 73, 83
Edgar, Pelham, 9
Eliot, George, 53
Eliot, T. S., 210
Emerson, Ralph Waldo, 101–2, 115
Erikson, Erik H., 107, 228 (n. 20), 229 (n. 47)
Existentialism, 3–4, 7–8, 99, 217 (n. 10)
Extravagance (*Verstiegenheit*), 73–74, 81–82, 86, 89, 94–95, 97; and freedom, 78–81, 88–89, 105; and vanity, 83–85; and intersubjectivity, 90–93

Firebaugh, J. J., 138
Ford, Ford Madox, 187, 209–10; *The Good Soldier*, 209–10
Foucault, Michel, 182, 186, 234 (n. 49)
Freedom, 19, 23, 26–28, 32, 88, 99–135, 179; and "thrownness," 19, 22, 25, 100, 109–11, 119, 128–33, 143; and imagination, 22, 24, 71, 79, 97, 105; and consciousness, 54–56, 102, 116–17, 122–25; and care, 93, 118–19, 134–35, 144, 146, 154–55, 186; and society, 100, 132, 189, 193–96
Freud, Sigmund, 76, 83, 133, 148, 169, 210, 235 (n. 14)

Geismar, Maxwell, 204–5
Gide, André, 136
Girard, René, 83, 183
Goldmann, Lucien, 190
Goncourt, Edmond de: *Chérie*, 53

Hawthorne, Nathaniel: *The Marble Faun*, 72
Hegel, G. W. F., 125, 178
Heidegger, Martin, 7–8, 71, 111–12, 229 (n. 47); on Being, xi, xii; on "thrownness," 19, 51, 100, 109, 131; on transcendence, 32, 40; on understanding, 40, 43; on care, 65–66, 119, 138–39, 144, 154, 184; on freedom, 104, 107
Hobbes, Thomas, 173
Howe, Irving, 190
Husserl, Edmund, 3, 5, 188, 221 (n. 16); on intentionality, 7–8, 10, 12, 32, 47–48, 100; on intersubjectivity, 16, 137; on "aspects," 42–44, 166; reduction, 45–46, 60

Ibsen, Henrik: *A Doll's House*, 132, 229 (n. 48)
Imagination, 32, 69–98, 186; and consciousness, 11–14, 45–46, 48, 69–72; and freedom, 22, 24, 71–72, 75, 105
"Impression." *See* James, Henry: on consciousness; Ritchie, Anne Thackeray: her "impression"
Ingarden, Roman: on representation, 58–61; on reading, 62–63; quasi-judgments, 64–67
Intentionality, 7–8, 33, 47, 52, 122, 235 (n. 14); and temporality, 10, 32, 122; and hypotheses, 12, 41, 116; "aspects," 32, 42–44, 52; positionality, 49–50
Intersubjectivity, 16, 32, 90–92, 137, 140; and mediation, 29, 161, 197; validation through, 53, 55–56, 62, 165; and reading,

56, 61–63, 147–48, 222 (n. 35)
Iser, Wolfgang, x–xi, 61, 222 (n. 35); immersion and observation, 14–15; on realism, 15, 59, 63–64; indeterminacy, 15, 59, 96; consistency-building, 15, 230 (n. 54); anticipation and retrospection, 116

James, Henry, ix, xii, xiv, 8, 33, 73, 87, 110, 133, 187, 205, 219 (n. 46), 235 (nn. 13, 14); moral vision, ix, 3–10, 18, 23, 30–31, 65–67, 99, 101–2, 206, 211–13; on consciousness, ix, 3–19, 30–31, 37–57, 102, 116, 122, 166, 206–7, 209, 230 (n. 54); point of view, 14, 43, 47, 63–64, 109, 124, 146, 206; *The Golden Bowl*, xii, 31, 44, 48, 96, 136, 138–86, 198, 202–4, 207–9, 212, 232 (n. 24); *The Wings of the Dove*, xii, 48; *The Ambassadors*, xii–xiii, 40–41, 48, 54, 99, 124, 207–8; *The Sacred Fount*, xii–xiii, 54, 207; *The Portrait of a Lady*, 4, 31, 40–41, 44, 48–49, 101, 103–35, 141, 153, 160, 169, 204, 207, 212, 229–30 (n. 54); *What Maisie Knew*, 8–31, 40–41, 71, 100, 116, 123, 132, 166, 168, 209, 212–13; "The Art of Fiction," 31, 37–68, 70, 187, 207; *Roderick Hudson*, 31, 69, 72–97, 102, 105, 111, 129, 141, 204, 212; *The Spoils of Poynton*, 31, 190–204; *The Aspern Papers*, 54; *The Turn of the Screw*, 54, 96, 207; "The Figure in the Carpet," 63; "The Beast in the Jungle," 107; "The Jolly Corner," 107; "Madame de Mauves," 133; *Notebooks*, 133, 148; *The American Scene*, 189; *The Bostonians*, 190; *The Princess Casamassima*, 190

James, William, ix, xiv, 3, 58,
123, 185; on experience, 6, 47,
135, 211; on reality and truth,
12–13, 41, 46, 49; on pluralism, 50–51; on other minds, 53,
161; on freedom, 102–5, 125,
133; *The Principles of Psychology*, 3; *The Varieties of Religious
Experience*, 102
Jauss, Hans Robert, 190
Joyce, James, 206
Jung, C. G., 210

Kafka, Franz, 210
Kant, Immanuel, 41, 117
Kierkegaard, Søren, 123, 220
(n. 51); on freedom, 19, 70, 104,
111, 119; *Either/Or*, 94
Krook, Dorothea, 34–35, 138,
182

Lévi-Strauss, Claude, 210
Locke, John, 34
Lubbock, Percy, 34

Marcuse, Herbert, 188
Marx, Karl, 125, 188–89, 191,
199–200, 205, 210, 235 (n. 14);
on freedom, 189, 191, 193, 202;
on self-objectification, 192–93,
203, 236 (n. 24); commodity fetishism, 195, 198, 204
Matthiessen, F. O., 34, 72, 141
Merleau-Ponty, Maurice, 5, 33; on
unreflective experience, 10, 123,
168; on Self and Other, 16, 137,
146, 161; on perception, 42–43,
48–49, 52, 122, 134; on freedom, 100, 134

New Criticism, 204–5
Niemtzow, Annette, 229 (n. 50)
Nietzsche, Friedrich, 77, 210, 220
(n. 51)

Peirce, Charles Sanders, 4, 12, 41,
56, 64, 165

Phenomenology, ix–xi, xiii, 3–4,
215 (n. 1); literary theories, x–
xi; on consciousness, x–xi, 5, 7,
39, 41–42, 50–51, 58–60; and
existentialism, 3–4, 7–8, 217
(n. 10); on experience, 5, 31,
66, 205, 211; reduction, 45–
46; on intersubjectivity, 137–
38; politics, 188–90
Poe, Edgar Allan, 145
Poirier, Richard, 96, 101, 109,
115
Poulet, Georges, ix–x, 47

Rahv, Philip, 136, 187
Raleigh, J. H., 34–35
Reading, x–xi, 14–15, 116, 218
(n. 25), 230 (n. 54); and indeterminacy, 15, 29, 59–61, 96; and
intersubjectivity, 35, 62, 147–
48, 222 (n. 35); and representation, 59–64, 124
Representation, 37, 39, 51, 64–
68, 80; epistemology of, 51, 57–
60, 206–7, 209; reader's role in,
59–63; point of view, 63–64,
124, 146–47, 206
Ricoeur, Paul, xii; on symbols, 67–
68, 161–62; on suspicion and
faith, 95, 97, 102, 113; on freedom, 100–101, 103, 111–
12, 117, 120; on politics, 188,
190, 203
Ritchie, Anne Thackeray: her "impression," 38–49, 53, 70, 75,
109, 117, 122, 166, 194, 211
Rowe, John Carlos, 217 (n. 3), 233
(n. 30)

Sartre, Jean-Paul, x, 8, 112; on
freedom, 25, 71, 104, 125, 179–
80; on consciousness, 32, 71; on
imagination, 69, 71–72, 75; on
Self and Other, 118, 137–40,
144–46, 156, 170, 177, 181–
82, 186, 200, 202–3, 236
(n. 24)

Self-consciousness: and conscious-
ness, 44, 63–64; and represen-
tation, 67–68; and freedom, 88,
125, 169, 178; and intersubjec-
tivity, 125, 160, 162–63
"Servile will." *See* Ricoeur, Paul: on
freedom
Society, 20, 29, 132, 186–205
Spender, Stephen, 192
Spilka, Mark, 47
Stevenson, Robert Louis, 57–58,
62
Structuralism, 108, 210
Swedenborg, Emanuel, 34

Tolstoy, Leo: *Anna Karenina*, 20
Transcendence: and experience,
32–33, 40, 70–71, 135, 189,
235 (n. 13); and knowing,
40–42, 68, 70, 118, 145
Trilling, Lionel, 190
Trollope, Anthony: *Barchester
Towers*, 58

Troy, William, xiv

Unreflective experience, 10, 123,
125, 168–69, 209

Value, 64–68
Van Ghent, Dorothy, 101
Veeder, William, 132

Watt, Ian, 60, 190
Weimann, Robert, 190
Weinstein, Philip, 183
Wellek, René, 65
Wells, H. G., 67
Wilson, Edmund, 191
Winner, Viola Hopkins, 237 (n. 32)
Woolf, Virginia, 46, 206

Yeazell, Ruth B., 233 (n. 36)

Zabel, Morton Dauwen, 101